The Study of Religion in an Age of Global Dialogue

The Study
of Religion
in an Age of
Global
Dialogue

Leonard Swidler
and Paul Mojzes

Temple University Press
Philadelphia

Temple University Press, Philadelphia 19122

♾ The paper used in this publication meets the requirements of the
American National Standard for Information Sciences—Permanence
of Paper for Printed Library Materials, ANSI Z39.48-1984

Library of Congress Cataloging-in-Publication Data

Swidler, Leonard J.
    The study of religion in an age of global dialogue / Leonard
Swidler and Paul Mojzes.
        p.   cm.
    Includes bibliographical references and index.
    ISBN 1-56639-792-8 (cloth : alk. paper) — ISBN 1-56639-793-6
(pbk. : alk. paper)
        1. Religion—Study and teaching.   I. Mojzes, Paul.   II. Title.
    BL41 .S89   2000
    200'.7–dc21   00-034784

Contents

Introduction: The Study of Religion in an
Age of Global Dialogue. Toward a Global Ethic
in the Third Millennium   1

1   What Is Religion?   3

2   Philosophy of Religion   43

3   History of Religions   55

4   Scriptural Studies   61

5   Evolution in Religion   73

6   Anthropology and Sociology of Religion   91

7   The Psychological Study of Religion   110

8   The Relationship Between Religion and Economics   128

9   Comparative Religion   135

10 Phenomenology of Religion   140

11 From the Age of Monologue to the
    Age of Global Dialogue   145

12 Universal Declaration of a Global Ethic   179

13 A Proposed Draft: A Universal Declaration
    of a Global Ethic   188

    Conclusion   195

Appendix: Explanatory Remarks Concerning
the "Declaration Toward a Global Ethic"   197

Notes   213

Index   225

Contents

Introduction: The Study of Religion in an
Age of Global Dialogue. Toward a Global Ethic
in the Third Millennium   1

1   What Is Religion?   3

2   Philosophy of Religion   43

3   History of Religions   55

4   Scriptural Studies   61

5   Evolution in Religion   73

6   Anthropology and Sociology of Religion   91

7   The Psychological Study of Religion   110

8   The Relationship Between Religion and Economics   128

9   Comparative Religion   135

10   Phenomenology of Religion   140

11   From the Age of Monologue to the
Age of Global Dialogue   145

12   Universal Declaration of a Global Ethic   179

13   A Proposed Draft: A Universal Declaration
of a Global Ethic   188

Conclusion   195

Appendix: Explanatory Remarks Concerning
the "Declaration Toward a Global Ethic"   197

Notes   213

Index   225

The Study of Religion in an
Age of Global Dialogue

Introduction

The Study of Religion in an Age of Global Dialogue.
Toward a Global Ethic in the Third Millennium

AT THE CORE of every culture and every civilization lies its religion. Religion both reflects and shapes the cultures and civilizations in which it lives. One of the "fathers of sociology," Emile Durkheim, stated the matter clearly when he wrote:

> Religion has given birth to all that is essential in society. . . . We have established the fact that the fundamental categories of thought, and consequently of science, are of religious origin. . . . In summing up, then, it may be said that nearly all the great social institutions have been born in religion.[1]

Hence, if we wish to understand human life in general and our specific culture and history, it is vital to gain an understanding of religion and its role in general and specifically in our culture and history. That is why we need to study religion.

Studying something involves more than casually looking around in a subject. It is an investigation of the subject organized according to certain principles and following certain methods which arrives at particular conclusions. What the conclusions will be obviously depends on both the subject that is being studied and the principles and methods followed. The subject of this book is religion and, more specifically, the methods contemporary scholars use in the study of religion. Those methods are several, including the following: historical, scriptural, philosophical, anthropological, sociological, psychological, comparative, and dialogical.

The last, dialogue, is in fact much more than a "method." It is a whole new way of thinking, as will be spelled out in detail later. It radically shifts our entire view of reality and immensely expands and deepens our grasp of the meaning of life.

One way to describe the essential difference between humans and the other higher animals is to note not just that humans are aware of things

1

(my dog is aware of the presence of a prowler or a piece of meat), but that we are aware that we are aware of things. We are reflecting animals; we can look at ourselves looking at things.

Religion is the most fundamental and comprehensive of all human activities—that is, it tries to make sense not simply out of one or other aspect of human life but out of all aspects of human experience. Hence, the study of religion needs to start out in that most fundamentally human way of being: looking at how we are looking at things—in this case, looking at how we are looking at religion. But before we can look at our methods of studying religion, we first need to reflect on how we understand the object of our study: religion.

This volume, then, will look at the ways we humans have developed, especially in the past century and a half, to study religion. However, it will do more, for we are convinced that as helpful as the ways are that the nineteenth and twentieth centuries have devised to analyze religion, a new age in human consciousness is upon us: the "Age of Global Dialogue." It is that radically new consciousness that will fundamentally shift the ways we understand everything in life, including, of course, that most comprehensive approach to life, religion. This global dialogical way of understanding life will not lead to one global religion. It will lead to a consciously acknowledged common set of ethical principles, a "Global Ethic." It is this inbreaking "Age of Global Dialogue" and the inchoative "Global Ethic" that will be the subjects of the last chapters—to help readers understand what is going on around them so they can make informed, intelligent decisions about the meaning of life and how to live it.

1   What Is Religion?

A DEFINITION FOR RELIGION?

RELIGION: Few words in our vocabulary evoke more instanta-
neous recognition, yet so elude precise understanding and definition,
than the word *religion.* It is perhaps the word's very commonness that
makes it hard to define. Practitioners and admirers of religion, as well
as its critics and enemies, think they know clearly what it is that they
support or reject. Yet despite years of effort, no clear agreement has
emerged in the scholarly community on how to define the phenomenon of religion. It is worse still with the average person, who under the
term *religion* often understands very different, even contradictory
notions. Instances of agitated debate about religion often show that the
partners are talking about different forms of the phenomenon. Thus, it
is hardly surprising that their assessments diverge so completely. They
are, in fact, addressing different realities.

Some see religion as a way of life of a group of people. Others see it
as belief in something greater than the human being—a search for a
divine being or reality. Wilhelm Schmidt believed that the notion of a
"high God" was common to all religions.[1] Still others view religion as
a set of specific actions—perhaps worship, ritual, ethical behavior,
prayers, sacrifices. There are those who look for religion's origin in our
instinct for survival, our need to deal with the fear of death. Then there
are those who see in religion human efforts to find or create a meaning for this life. Have there not been humorous portrayals of the seeker
climbing to a mountaintop to consult the proverbial guru about what
it all means? For others, religion is to be located in the world of feelings—certain emotions, inspirations, longings, and enthusiasm; a sense
of awe, fear, and fascination, and the like. Friedrich Schleiermacher, a
nineteenth-century German Protestant theologian in that vein, wrote:
"The essence of religion consists in the feeling of absolute dependence."[2] Certain great thinkers noticed the close link of religion with
morality and ethics and focused on that aspect of religion. The German

3

philosopher Immanuel Kant said that "Religion is (considered subjectively) the recognition of all duties as divine commands."[3]

PARTIAL APPROACHES

Partly responsible for the discrepancies are the types of approaches used to define religion. Some focus on individual experience (William James); others focus on social aspects (Emile Durkheim). Some think that the best way to discover religion's essence is to look at its roots—namely, what caused religion. Sigmund Freud located the roots of religion in our inability to deal maturely with the threats to ourselves and our culture, in certain oedipal fixations projected into the larger scale of the universe, a sort of childhood neurosis. Karl Marx located religion's roots in alienation caused by class societies: Such societies bring about unmet needs for happiness and community that lead to illusory, opiate solutions, which hamper true, realistic solutions. The last four named will be treated at length below. Others trace the roots of religion to the inability to interpret the dream world, to explain death, or to face human mortality. Branko Bosnjak,[4] a Marxist philosopher from Yugoslavia, postulates that there will be traces of religion as long as there is existential dread of death. Edward Scribner Ames[5] considers religion to be the consciousness of the highest social values.

Still another problem lies in whether the definition is descriptive, normative, functional, or essential. A descriptive definition attempts to summarize concisely the most important features of a phenomenon. This approach is difficult even in the case of a single religion, much less in the case of a notion that has so many manifestations. Thus, the descriptive approach usually is nearly impossible to carry out. Others follow a normative approach—namely, defining religion by what it ought to be. Usually, they take their own or a highly idealized form of religion as the norm, with which they later compare specific religions. Such a comparison usually yields notions of inferior and superior religions, depending on how closely each coincides with the norm. Such definitions generally come at the expense of certain religions and, needless to say, are not appreciated. One might say that there is an imperialistic tendency in normative definitions.

Many observers prefer the functional definition because it looks at religion from the perspective of what it does or attempts to do. Many social scientists favor this approach because it does not involve a value judgment regarding whether a given religion is right or wrong; rather, the religion can be observed and measured according to whether or not it succeeds in satisfying certain of its adherents' needs. This last can explain why certain religions decline or die out or why people change religions. Such a definition would claim, for instance, that religion is the human adjustment to the realities of existence in life-enriching ways. Another functional definition of religion was offered by the American sociologist J. Milton Yinger: "Religion is a system of beliefs and practices by means of which a group of people struggles with these ultimate problems of human life. It is the refusal 1) to capitulate to death, 2) to give up in face of frustration, and 3) to allow hostility to tear apart one's human associations."[6]

Critics find fault with functionalism because, in its focus on human need, it tends to overlook what Mircea Eliade called "the element of the sacred"[7] and Rudolf Otto called "the idea of the holy,"[8] which is both irreducible and unique to religions. Thus, there are those who propose an essential definition—that is, they try to focus on an essence that is common to all religions or is at their collective root.

COMPREHENSIVE APPROACHES

Although many of these approaches are fruitful and contain more than a bit of truth, some definitions of religion strike us as attempts at a comprehensive definition. One can start with one of the briefest, provided by Paul Tillich: "Religion is the area of ultimate concern." Although this statement is too broad to be an adequate definition, it is a highly suggestive and seminal idea that has been employed usefully by others, including in the preceding definition by Yinger. One of its challenges is that it tends to include in the category of the religious even those who do not think of themselves as religious, who perhaps even claim to be atheists, provided that they have an ultimate concern in terms of seeking life's ultimate meaning or that they attempt to relate themselves to that which is ultimately real or feel the claim of ultimate obligations. Contrary to those who see religion as a very specific, separate sphere of life, Tillich locates religion "in the depth of all functions of man's spiritual life. Religion is the dimension of depth in all of them. Religion is the aspect of depth in the totality of the human spirit.... [This] means that the religious aspect points to that which is ultimate, infinite, unconditional in man's spiritual life. Religion, in the largest and most basic sense of the word, is ultimate concern."[9]

The great twentieth-century Jewish thinker Martin Buber also advocated that religion be understood as the way we live the everyday, a position he adopted after he observed the inadequacy of the notion that religion was a special sort of emotion or inspiration.[10] Edgar Shefield Brightman provided this helpful comprehensive definition: "Religion is concern about experiences which are regarded as of supreme value; devotion toward a power or powers believed to originate, increase, and conserve these values; and some suitable expression of this concern and devotion, whether through symbolic rites or through other individual and social conduct."[11] John Wilson concluded that "the search for joy, for meaning, for an escape from alienation and loneliness, for a relationship with the 'other' is a *religious* search."[12]

William C. Tremmel offered a very comprehensive functional–experiential definition:

a) Religion is a complex form of human behavior whereby a person (or community of persons) is prepared intellectually and emotionally to deal with those aspects of human existence that are horrendous and non-manipulable.

b) Doing so from the conviction that there is at the center of human experience, and even of all reality, a being, or beings, or process (a divine reality) in which and through which a person (or community of persons) can transcend the life-negating traumas of human existence, can overcome a sense of finitude.

c) And doing so by the employment of various religious techniques: (i) a belief system (myths, doctrines, and theologies); (ii) a ritual system (reverent behavior and dramatic performances; (iii) a moral system (ethical doctrines and rules).

d) With all of this (and especially in the conviction that there is a divine order basic to life) religion turns out to be for people not simply a method of dealing with religious problems (those horrendous, non-manipulable circumstances of life), but also is itself an experience of great satisfaction and immense personal worth. Religion is not only something people "do" and "use"; it is also something that happens to them. It is an experience, and even, at times, an experience of sheer ecstasy.[13]

Niels C. Nielsen, Jr., confronted the problem of a cross-cultural definition of religion that would be adequate to the variety of world religions and remarked that religion should be explained as a process, a relationship, and a symbol system: "Religion is human involvement with sacred sanction, vitality, significance, and value. This involvement is mediated through symbolic processes of transformation. Religion is expressed in and transmitted by cultural traditions that constitute systems of symbols."[14]

John Clark Archer wrote, upon examining terms for religion such as *chiao, tao, hsiao, dharma, madhab, iman, din, yirath, daath, hieros, religio,* and *mana,* offered this definition: "Religion is man's whole and developing reaction within and upon life, 'the expression of his summed-up meaning and the purport of his consciousness of things,' such reaction, meaning, and consciousness implying the recognition of things spiritual and superhuman."[15]

OUR DEFINITION OF RELIGION

We would like to offer a brief definition of religion that we are convinced is at once simple enough that everyone will immediately understand its meaning and broad enough to include all the essential aspects of religion:

> Religion is an explanation of the ultimate meaning of life, based on a notion of the transcendent, and how to live accordingly; it normally contains the four Cs: creed, code, cult, and community-structure.
>
> *Creed* refers to the cognitive aspect of a religion; it is everything that goes into the "explanation" of the ultimate meaning of life.
>
> *Code* of behavior or ethics includes all the rules and customs of action that somehow follow from one aspect or another of the Creed.
>
> *Cult* means all the ritual activities that relate the follower to one aspect or other of the transcendent, either directly or indirectly. Prayer is an example of the former, and certain formal behavior toward representatives of the transcendent, such as priests, is an example of the latter.

Community-structure refers to the relationships among the followers. This can vary widely, from a very egalitarian relationship,
as among Quakers, through a "republican" structure as Pres-
byterians have, to a monarchical structure, as with some Hasidic
Jews vis-à-vis their Rebbe.

The *transcendent,* as the roots of the word indicate, means "that
which goes beyond" the everyday, the ordinary, the surface experience of reality. It can mean spirits, gods, a personal God, an
impersonal God, Emptiness, and so on.

Especially in modern times, "explanations of the ultimate meaning
of life, and how to live accordingly" have been developed that are not
based on a notion of the transcendent—for example, atheistic Marxism
and secular humanism. Although in every respect these "explanations"
function as religions traditionally have in human life, the idea of the
transcendent, however it is understood, does not play a central role in
them. For the sake of accuracy, it is therefore best to give these "explanations" a separate name. The name often used is *ideology.* Much, though
not all, in this volume will, "changing what needs changing" (*mutatis
mutandis*), also apply to ideology, even when the term is not used.

The Way

Religion, then, is much more than just an intellectual explanation of the
ultimate meaning of life—as absolutely vital to religion as that theoretical dimension is. Religion is also "how to live according to" that explanation. It is a *way* of living, of life. This is reflected in the interesting fact
that many major religions of the world have the very term *the Way,* or
some variation of it, at the heart of their self-understanding.

For example, in the three Semitic, or "Abrahamic," religions—
Judaism, Christianity, and Islam—all of the following terms mean *the
Way:*

Central to Judaism, the Hebrew word *Halacha* (the Way) has come
to mean the rabbinic teachings, the "legal" decisions to be followed, in order to lead a life according to the Torah—that is, as
"instructed" by God (the Hebrew word *Torah* means "instruc-
tion").

At the beginning of Christianity, the followers of Jesus (*Yeshua* in Hebrew) were not called Christians but followers of *the Way* (*Hodos,* in the Greek of the New Testament, Acts 9:2; 19:9, 23; 22:4; 24:14, 22) that "Rabbi" Yeshua taught and exemplified.

In Islam, the traditional way to live a correct life is to follow the *Shari'a,* an Arabic term for the *Way*—specifically, the path to find water in the desert. Analogous to *Halacha* in Judaism, *Shari'a* has also come to mean the myriad "legal" decisions that should be followed by the devout Muslim.

Much the same is also true for the major religions coming out of India—Hinduism and Buddhism:

In Hinduism, there are three major *Ways* (*Margas* in Sanskrit) to attain the goal in life (*Moksha:* Sanskrit for "liberation")—namely, *Jnana* (the Way, or *Marga,* of knowledge); *Karma* (the *Marga* of works); and *Bhakti* (the *Marga* of devotion).

In Buddhism, the key term meaning *the Way* is *Magga* (in Pali); it refers to the Noble Eightfold *Path* (the fourth of Siddhartha Gautama's fundamental Four Noble Truths) to be followed in order to reach *Nirvana,* the goal of life. Moreover, Gautama in his first, fundamental sermon—and Buddhism after him—described his way as the Middle *Way* (*Majjhima Patipada* in Pali) between harsh asceticism and loose sensuality, which will lead to the goal of life.

For religions of the Far East, too, the term *the Way* was central. The very name of Chinese Taoism places *the Way,* or *Tao,* at the center, at the foundation of the entire religion, the goal of which was to discern the *Tao* of the universe and live in harmony with it.

This notion of *the Way,* the *Tao,* was also central to the doctrine of Confucius, who taught that *Ren-Tao* (the Way of Humanity) is to follow *T'ien-Tao* (the Way of Heaven). For Confucius, Heaven, or *T'ien,* was largely *Theos* (personal); eventually, and especially for the neo-Confucianists of the Song Dynasty (960–1279 C.E.) and afterward, *T'ien* became largely non-personal.

Japan's native religion, Shinto, likewise has embedded in its very name the term the *Way*—namely, *To* in *Shin-To* (the Way of the Gods). The term was taken from the Chinese with the same meaning, *Shen-Tao,* to distinguish the original Japanese religion (which in pure Japanese was called *Kami-no Michi* [the Way of the *Kami*, or Gods]) from the religion of India, Buddhism, which came to Japan by way of China through Korea and is also known in Chinese as *Butsu-Tao* (the Way of Buddha).

POPULAR RELIGION—REFLECTIVE RELIGION

The goal, or goals, of religion has been described in many different ways. At times, the goal seems to be quite crude, and at others it appears to be quite sublime. For example, on a rather primitive level, one goal might be to gain a self-benefiting power or to deflect an injurious power. Here religion tends to merge with magic or emerge from magic. On the other hand, on a higher level one goal of religion might be to engage in selfless praise of Beauty, Truth, and Goodness, or to pour one's self out for another. Thomas Aquinas's "Beatific Vision" of Christianity would be an example of the first, and the Bodhisattva of Mahayana Buddhism an example of the second.

This wide variation in goals underlines the importance of bearing in mind the distinction between popular-level religion and reflective-level religion. In popular religion, the degree of reflexive consciousness, or self-awareness, is quite low. It is rather like that of children experiencing something. Children are not very aware that they are experiencing something; rather, they tend to focus exclusively on the thing being experienced. We thus say that children are *naive*—that is, their mentality is still close to the way it was when they were born (*natus*). Children tend to understand things in a fashion that is rather literal, straightforward, immediate—that is, with no intermediate element, with no mental distance between the thing experienced and the one experiencing.

But as children grow through puberty into adulthood, they gain a certain distance on themselves and on the things that they learned when they were young. They become reflexive, reflective. They become aware not only of the things they encounter, that they experience; they also become increasingly aware of their *experiencing* of things. They often become critical of the things they have learned, at times rejecting them because they judge that they could not possibly be literally true, as they had earlier understood them to be.

If the process of maturation continues as it should, young adults will gradually move to the stage of a "second naivete," as Paul Ricoeur names it. Adults realize that, often, those things they understood when they were children as literally true, and rejected as not literally true when they were young adults, are in fact true—far *more* true than the children who took them literally, or the adolescents who rejected them in the same way, thought. Now they are seen for what they truly are— and they often are metaphors, symbols, images pointing to a much deeper reality than can be expressed in literal language.

Matters of deep human import are far too weighty for prose to carry them adequately; poetry, metaphor, symbol, and image must be brought into play to carry such a message even partly adequately. For example, a prose description of one's beloved (hair color, height, weight) is much too feeble to express the object of such an important human experience as being in love. Hence, the world is full not of love prose, or literal description, but of love poetry, which bursts with metaphors, symbols, images.

This is true of the development not only of individuals but also of whole communities, and indeed ultimately of the entire human race. We see the breakthrough to the level of "reflective religion" particularly in what Karl Jaspers called the "Axial Period," a period in human development in which the major world religions in several different cultures were born.[16] Humankind in general moved through a kind of "communal puberty."

Thus, there will be people, regardless of age, whose religious consciousness stays on a quite naive level, and those whose religious consciousness reaches a very reflective level—and people everywhere in between. There will also be whole communities of these different types—for example, certain Protestant Christian churches tend to be "fundamentalist" (naive), and others tend to be "liberal" (from the critical to the "second-naivete" level).

Some communities may even officially reach the "second-naivete" level while some of its leadership and membership remain largely, or at least to a significant extent, on the "pre-critical" level. Some would see this to be the case, for example, with the Catholic Church: Vatican II (1962–65) made official commitments to a historical, dynamic, dialogical, collegial, freedom-oriented, turned-toward-this-world self-understanding, yet a pre-Vatican II static, authoritarian, fortress mentality persists among some of the church's leaders and members.

It is also important to keep in mind that one can hardly expect the level of a person's religious consciousness to be higher than her or his general human consciousness. So a person who generally is rather naive would also tend religiously to be rather naive. However, perhaps because religious institutions frequently are so old and, hence, are often very traditional and conservative, it is often true that many people's level of religious consciousness is below that of their general consciousness. This is especially true in modern society, whose rapidly expanding educational system tends to raise the general level of consciousness of whole populations. James Fowler, for example, judges that American churches and synagogues tend to cultivate their congregants at a level significantly below that of their moral and faith ability.[17]

Different Terms for the Goals of Religion

Many different terms are used in the religions of the world to describe the goal of religion. These terms reveal an understanding of human nature, and of Ultimate Reality to which it is related, that is held by at least part of that religion's tradition. Hence, it will be revealing for us to analyze, however briefly, some of the most prominent of these terms—perhaps permitting us thereby to conclude with a consensus understanding of the goal of religion in general.

REDEMPTION.   *Redemption* is a term used in the Abrahamic and other religions—very prominently in Christianity—that etymologically means "buying back," or "ransom." At times in both the Hebrew Bible and the New Testament, however, it simply means the "liberation" of humans. Although it is not always clear in the Hebrew biblical texts what humans are liberated from, both there and in the New Testament the liberation usually is from "sin," meaning from the condition of being in thrall to the power of evil resulting from humans' having committed evil acts. Humans are prevented by sin from attaining their goal, which ultimately is living in harmony or union with Ultimate Reality—that is, for monotheists, with God.

LIBERATION.   *Liberation* (*Moksha* in Sanskrit) is a Hindu term that describes the goal of life in negative fashion—that is, the freeing of the individual human self or soul (*atman* [Sanskrit for "breath"], which is related linguistically to *atmo* [Greek for "breath," as in the English word *atmosphere*]) from a constant round of new physical lives (*samsara* [Sanskrit for "passing through" or "transmigration"]). Some (in fact, Buddhism also uses the term *samsara*) describe this samsaric ring as being within a single human lifetime, but traditionally it meant a series of lifetimes that a single *atman* passed through until it attained *Moksha* (liberation) so that it could accomplish its desired end—that is, union with Ultimate Reality, which in Hinduism is called *Brahman*.

It is clear that there is a close resemblance between the largely Hindu term *liberation* and the largely Judeo-Christian term *redemption*. Both are a freeing of the inner "spirit" (*spiritus*, which is simply a Latin-rooted word for "breath") from that which prevents the self, the soul, from reaching its goal. In both traditions, the goal is fundamentally the same: union with Ultimate Reality. How that Ultimate Reality is understood, and what "union" with it means, is variously explained—but more on that later.

ENLIGHTENMENT. *Enlightenment* is a term most often found in Buddhism to describe the goal of life. Indeed, the very name "Buddhism" contains the term *enlightenment*: *Bodhi* in Sanskrit means "enlightened," and Siddhartha Gautama (563–487 B.C.E.) was a *Buddha*, an "Enlightened One." At bottom, *enlightenment* means the perception of reality, including pre-eminently one's self, as it truly is. Hence, *enlightenment* is a human state of being that can be attained in this life.

Theravada Buddhism teaches that only a few can attain enlightenment (or *Nirvana*, to be discussed further later); hence it is called *Hinayana* ("Small Vehicle") by those who disagree with it. *Mahayana* ("Great Vehicle") Buddhism, on the other hand, claims that many, or even all, humans can attain *Nirvana*. Japanese Zen Buddhism refers to this kind of enlightenment as *Satori*, and according to one sect, Rinzai Zen, it comes suddenly, whereas according to another, Soto Zen, it comes gradually. It should also be noted that this "enlightenment" is not a theoretical kind of knowledge. It is an experiential one that utterly transforms all subsequent experience.

NIRVANA. *Nirvana* is another term that Buddhism uses to describe the ultimate goal of human life. (Hinduism and Jainism have also used the term from about the same time as the rise of Buddhism and Jainism in the fifth century B.C.E., though in somewhat different ways.) Literally, in Sanskrit *Nirvana* means "blown out." What is blown out is the *Tanha* (the distorting "craving") that causes the *Dukkha* ("suffering") that humans experience throughout life (because they unrealistically attempt to "cling to"—*Tanha*—things, even though all life is in reality "transient," *Anicca*). When that state of *Nirvana* is attained, a person is then in a condition of blissful calm. However, as has already been mentioned, *Nirvana* can be arrived at only by perceiving reality, and most of all one's self, as it truly is. To some extent, this is like the view of the slightly later Greek thinker Socrates (470–399 B.C.E.), who taught that "ignorance" is the source of human evil.

HEAVEN.   *Heaven* as the final goal of human life is a term that has been prominent in the Judeo-Christian-Islamic tradition. In fact, however, the term appears in many religions, coming from more primitive times, when the heavens above were seen as the source of light, heat, and life, and hence as the abode of the gods—whither humans then also wanted to migrate. In popular religions of all kinds—not just the three Abrahamic ones—heaven became a *place* of bliss where humans went after death. The same localizing misunderstanding of heaven also occurred in the Buddhist notion of *Nirvana*: in popular Buddhism, it, too, became a *place* of bliss where humans went after death. On the reflective level, however, as Jesus stated, "The kingdom of God [or "heaven"[18]] is not here or there; it is *within* you" (*entos hymon*; Luke 17:20). Clearly for Jesus, and for subsequent reflective Christianity (and the same is true for reflective Judaism and Islam), heaven as the ultimate goal of life is not a place to go to after death; rather, it is a "state of being" to be attained in this life that does not, however, cease at the grave. In fact, the customary English translation of the New Testament *Basileia tou Theou* as "Kingdom of God" is really a mistranslation, reflecting the localizing tendency of popular religion. *Basileia tou Theou* is more accurately translated as the *"Reign* of God"—that is, the state of being in which one lives entirely in harmony or union with God, a state of being that should exist now and continue after death.

Medieval Christianity combined this understanding with Aristotelian philosophy and described the ultimate goal of human life as holiness in this life and complete union with God after death. That is when humans will be "face to face" with God, using to the fullest their highest human capacities, the intellect and will, in knowing and loving Truth, Goodness, Beauty, Being—which are various aspects of the Infinite Ultimate Reality of God—in what Thomas Aquinas called the *Visio Beata*, or the "Beatific Vision."

COMMUNISM.   *Communism* is the "final" state humanity is expected to arrive at in the historical future, according to Karl Marx and his subsequent theorists. That situation will bring about the "withering away of the state" because the new "Soviet man" will have evolved, and the force of the state will no longer be necessary. At this time, the "communist" goal will be fulfilled in which everyone will "give according to his ability and take according to his needs." Before that time, the penultimate condition, Socialism, will have to be enforced through the "dictatorship of the proletariat."

Whether Marx himself held this position literally has been debated by subsequent Marxists, but clearly most of the "orthodox" variety (i.e., those who took power under Lenin and Stalin and maintained it in the Marxist world until recently) did hold such a position, despite obvious contradictory evidence in Marx's writings. Thus, it is evident, except to naive "orthodox" Marxists, that the condition of "communism" lies beyond human history as an always receding horizon.

"Non-orthodox" Marxist thinkers have argued this cogently from Marx's writings—for example, Roger Garaudy when he was a member of the Politburo of the Communist Party of France in the 1960s. Garaudy wrote: "Yes, man will always be capable of an always greater future. For us, Communism is not the end of history, but the end of pre-history, man's pre-history which is made up of the jungle-like encounters common to all class societies. 'This social formation,' Marx writes in his *Contribution to the Critique of Political Economy*, 'constitutes ... the closing chapter of the prehistoric stage of human society.'"[19]

SALVATION.   *Salvation* is a term that is widespread especially in the Abrahamic religions, but it is also one that can be used in regard to the final goal of humans in most, if not all, religions.

It should be noted, however, that *salvation* is used in both its primary and secondary senses in religions. Its primary meaning is, literally, living a "whole, healthy" life. The term comes from the Latin *Salus* ("health"), whence a number of English- and Romance-language cognates are derived, all of which refer fundamentally to health: salutary, salubrious, salute, salutation. The Germanic counterparts are *Heil* ("salvation") and *heilig* ("holy"), from which are derived the English cognates health, hale, heal, whole, holy. To be "holy" means to be "(w)hole."

The secondary meaning of *salvation* is "saving"—as when a "savior" rescues someone in danger of losing his or her "health" (e.g., when "saving" a person from drowning, whether in water or in "sin"). Thus, even in its secondary meaning, the term *salvation* ultimately means attaining, preserving, or restoring a healthy, holy, whole human life—however that is understood.

Some religions emphasize the secondary meaning in claiming that "wholeness" or "(w)holiness" can be attained only through the help of the "savior." For example, in traditional Protestant Christianity, a person can be saved only *sola fide* ("by faith alone"), *sola gratia* ("by grace alone"), or *solus Christus* (by "Christ alone"). In Pure Land Buddhism, calling on the name of Amida Buddha (*Namu Amida Butsu,* shortened to *Nembutsu* ["Praise to Amida Buddha"] in Japanese) is the only certain way for *anyone* to attain Nirvana. This way of being saved is described in Japanese as *Tariki* ("Other Power"), in contrast to *Jiriki* ("Self Power").

Faced with the generally human religious question of whether humans are "saved" by *Jiriki* or *Tariki,* it appears to us that the traditional Protestant principle of *sola* ("only") is not appropriate. Rather, the Catholic principle of *et ... et* ("both ... and") is. On the one hand, *we* can become as authentically and wholly human as is possible for *us* only if *we* persistently and wisely make the necessary effort. But on the other hand, we can, of course, attain success in this lifelong endeavor only to the extent that we have been given the wherewithal. If we had not been born, we could not become (w)holy human; if we die too young, if we do not have loving care in infancy, or if we do not have a good education and training, encouragement, love, moral example, inspiration, and on and on, we cannot become (w)holy human according to our inborn potential. So, we become (w)holy human by both *Jiriki* and *Tariki.* But we must remember that when we speak of these two "powers," we are speaking on two different levels of causality. As a consequence, there can be no clash—only complementarity.

What it means to be authentically and wholly human, and the best way to attain this state, however, is precisely where the greatest, most fundamental divergences among religions appear to be found. As a consequence, it is important to reflect, however briefly, on the major ways to understand what it means to be human. We will approach this question by looking at the fundamental ways to understand human nature—as fundamentally good, fundamentally corrupt, or fundamentally mixed. Then we will offer a resolution of our own, followed by an excursus on a contemporary understanding of human nature. Many examples could be proffered, but it will be sufficient to allude to only one or two representatives of each fundamental view of human nature.

DIFFERENT VIEWS OF HUMAN NATURE

Human Nature Is Fundamentally Good

In the ancient world of the East, one of the strongest proponents of the idea that humans by their nature are good was the great Confucian Mencius (*Meng Tzu* in Chinese; 371–289 B.C.E.). He argued that humans commit evil only because they forget their original good nature. The human who does evil is like a hillside that was once covered with trees (i.e., with virtue, with instinctive goodness) but has been deforested by sawtoothed vice. That is, that person has been so abused by vice that she or he can no longer even discern her or his own instinctual spontaneous tendency toward altruism and justice—as, for example, anyone seeing a child about to fall into a well would instinctively rush to prevent it.

In the modern, eighteenth-century West, Jean-Jacques Rousseau represented well the optimist tradition. For him, humans are born good but are corrupted by "civilization": "Man is born free, and everywhere he is in chains!"[20] According to Rousseau, humanity's problems would be solved if the education of the young were such as to "lead out" the goodness inherent in the child, as the very term education (*e-ducere*) suggests, and keep the corrupting influences of "civilization" at bay.

Human Nature Is Fundamentally Evil or Corrupt

In the ancient East a much younger contemporary of Mencius, the Confucian Hsün Tzu (c. 313–238 B.C.E.), took the exact opposite position of his elder and argued that "the original nature of humans is evil."[21]

He was very detailed in his description of the innate evil tendency of humans: "Man, by his nature, at birth lusts for profit . . . is envious and hateful . . . and because he follows these tendencies, impurity and disorder result."[22]

In the post-medieval West, the sixteenth-century Protestant Reformers stressed the fundamental corruption of human nature after its sinful "fall" in the "mythic" paradise of Eden. Fallen humanity's state is so dismal, according to Martin Luther and John Calvin, that it can do nothing at all to attain its true goal, union with God. It can be "saved" only by God's free gift, *sola gratia,* and that, as noted earlier, comes only through faith in Christ, *sola fide, solus Christus.* Humanity's inability to do anything for itself was so thoroughgoing for Luther that he taught that humans have no free will, and Calvin taught that each human's ultimate fate was predetermined, predestined, by God, regardless of what the individual allegedly freely chose to do.

Human Nature Is Fundamentally Both Good and Evil

For Catholic Christianity, humanity was created good (following the biblical Genesis story of creation, where the Hebrew original says that when God looked over his creative handiwork on the sixth day of creation he saw that it was all *mod tov,* or "very good"). But through humanity's disobedience in the Garden of Eden, it fell into a state of Original Sin—that is, its intellect was darkened; its will was weakened; and it developed an inclination toward evil.

Concerning the posing of the problem as Luther, and particularly Calvin, did—namely, asking about the relationship between God's omnipotence or complete foreknowledge (providence) and human free will—Thomas Aquinas, and Catholicism following him, steered thus between Scylla and Charybdis: "All things are subject to divine providence, but rational creatures are so in a superior way. For they are under divine providence by participating in it, since they are called to in some way *be* divine providence for themselves and for others."[23]

Thus, Catholicism taught that human nature was originally fundamentally good but had been so stricken that it needed a "savior"; at the same time, however, each person must also freely collaborate with God's freely offered help, or grace. Hence, humans attain the goal of life—union with God—not through faith alone, but through "faith *and* good works."

A Problem in the Posing of the Question

As "balanced" as the Catholic "both . . . and" position appears in comparison with the Protestant "only," the terms in which the question to be answered were posed caused Catholics endless logical problems (not to mention the immense intellectual antinomies—that is, contradictions—that Protestants ran into).

For example, how can one affirm both an absolute Ultimate Reality, an ultimate uncaused cause of everything, and, at the same time, a radically free human will (which, of course, must be the cause of its own decisions; otherwise it would not be free)? The difficulty, it seems to me, is the result of posing the question badly. If I ask, for example, How far is yellow? I will, of course, receive a non-sense response. So here, too, Christian thinkers in this matter were actually doing something even more irrational. They were dealing with two elements, both of which by definition cannot be "comprehended" rationally—namely, God (the infinite, which cannot be "comprehended" by the finite) and free human will (if it could be "rationally" understood, it would then be "determinable" by reason—and therefore not radically free). These thinkers then had the hubris to ask how they were to understand the relationship between these two elements, neither of which they could rationally understand. This is like trying to solve a mathematical equation with three unknowns—and no knowns.

Human Nature: Love of Self and Others Mutually

We would like to offer an alternative description of human nature as found in its beginning and development in each human being. We hope that it will be true to our universal human experience and, at the same time, avoid the antinomies that the traditional solutions inevitably run into as a result of how they pose the issue.

What differentiates humans from all other living beings is the fact that they are animals with the ability to think abstractly. They therefore can become reflexive, and, as a result of this capacity, possess the ability of free choice (also called "love"). All our faculties of knowing—our cognitive faculties, mainly our senses and abstract intellect—present reality to us under the aspect of "the true." All our faculties of desiring—that is, our appetitive faculties, mainly our physical and emotional "drives" and our will—relate us to reality under the aspect of "the good."

The cognitive faculty moves outwardly and then inwardly, reaching out and drawing the outside world to itself by *knowing* it, and thereby "becoming one" with it. The appetitive faculty also moves outwardly and then inwardly, reaching out and drawing the outside world to itself by *loving* it, and thereby "becoming one" with it. To restate the latter: The nature, the very structure, of the appetitive faculty is to reach out toward what the cognitive faculty presents as true and good and to draw it to itself, thereby becoming one with it. Thus, the fundamental meaning of the term *love* is, having perceived the good, to reach out and draw it to oneself.

When humans are born, they do not know even themselves as different from the rest of reality. They learn to know themselves only by coming to know the "other"—as, for example, infants come to know their own fingers as different from the flame when they learn to know the flame by touching it. Thus, as children develop, they gradually become aware of their own selves and of others.

A similar mode of mutuality operates in the appetitive, the love, area. Infants begin by perceiving the good—their mothers' breast, for example; they naturally draw it to themselves, and in that sense "become one" with it. When they perceive the good, they will identify with it in one way or another—the natural manner for the appetitive faculties to operate. If in the process of growing up they receive much love, children will necessarily perceive the ones loving them, their "lovers," as the source of pleasure, as good. They will therefore reach out to the "lover," identify with her or him, and the "lover" will also become the "beloved."

When the sense of identity with the beloved becomes strong enough, we speak of an "other self," an *alter ego*. In the natural process, when a person's appetitive faculties perceive the good and draw it to its self—to its ego—she or he will also tend to draw the good to his or her alter ego. If the love identification of the *primus ego* with the *alter ego* is strong enough, more and more of the perceived good will be drawn to the *alter ego* rather than to the *primus ego* (e.g., the father giving food to his child rather than keeping it for himself), possibly even to the extreme of "giving up one's life for one's friend." As Jesus said, "Greater love than this has no one" (John 15:13).

Thus, the very nature of humans is 1) to love the good as it is presented to them. 2) Humans' greatest good, however—because it is the most "human," most "humanizing"—is to have others act in a loving way toward them. 3) They would then naturally identify with these "others," making the others to a greater or lesser extent *alter egos*, "other selves," 4) thereby drawing the perceived good to them as well as— or even, instead of—themselves.

It should be noted that what is operating here is something like a psychical version of the physical law of inertia—that is, "a body at rest remains at rest, unless moved by another body already in motion." Humans would not perceive other loving humans as their "greatest good" were they not first loved by those other humans. In other words, they would "remain at rest" if they were not first "moved" by the "motion," the loving action, of the other, and hence in turn find them good—and therefore love them in return.

But how does all this get started? Ultimately, Ultimate Reality has to be ultimate not only as a goal, a final cause (a *telos*), but also as a beginning (a *protos*), an efficient cause (*causa efficiens*). Process philosophers speak of Ultimate Reality as this initial efficient cause by its acting as a lure, or a "divine lure." The New Testament says much the same when John remarks that "We love because God first loved us" (1 John 4:19).

It is doubtless the awareness of the humanly natural movement from the *primus ego* to the *alter ego* that has led the great religious traditions to phrase their fundamental principles accordingly. For example, for both Judaism and Christianity, the second of the two "great command-ments," and the main way the first one is *de facto* carried out, is "to love your neighbor *as* yourself" (Leviticus 19:18; Matthew 22:38). One begins with an authentic self-love, which then extends to the neighbor, the *alter ego*.

One must also remember that it is precisely through this mutual knowing and loving that humans develop their humanity ever more fully. It is the nature of humans potentially to be open to all being, cog-nitively and appetitively (i.e., humans always want to know more and always desire more), as far as their faculties can reach—and they can always reach farther. Humans are by nature "open-ended." In other words, humans fulfill their nature by a process of constant self-tran-scendence, a going beyond themselves, knowing and loving ever more "being"—and, a convinced theist would add, ultimately knowing and loving "Infinite Being," the "Ground of Being," "Being Itself," called God.

The same principle of mutuality that starts from the center and moves outward is phrased in another way in most of the world religions in the various forms of the Golden Rule: "Do unto others as you would have them do unto you." This principle appears in all major, and many not so major, religions—and will be discussed in more detail later.

Such an understanding of human nature avoids the "dead-end" categories of humans' being naturally good, evil, or mixed. Rather, it focuses on the process, the evolutionary character of humans, and is based largely on empirical data from observing how humans in fact are born and develop.

DIFFERENT UNDERSTANDINGS OF ULTIMATE REALITY

Because religion (and ideology) are concerned about providing an explanation of the ultimate meaning of life, two key elements in this explanation obviously are the understanding of human nature and the understanding of Ultimate Reality. Only after grasping these at least vaguely can one hope to explain something of the relationship of the two—being careful not to fall into the trap of trying to explain the two elements and their relationship in a rationalistic manner, which happened to so many Christian theologians of past centuries when they tried to explain the relationship of an omnipotent God and a radically free human will, referred to above.

Having looked at the various major understandings of human nature, it is necessary now to turn to an investigation of the major understandings of Ultimate Reality. Because the conceptions of Ultimate Reality in the three "Western," or Semitic, religions (Judaism, Christianity, and Islam) appear so strikingly different from those of the Eastern religions (Hinduism, Buddhism, Taoism, and Confucianism), it will be helpful to look at those understandings by comparing the Eastern and Western notions. This discussion will be followed by a comparative look at a Marxist (as a chief representative of an ideology) understanding of "ultimate reality."

Hindu and Semitic Understandings

There are, in fact, some extremely interesting disparities and similarities between the Judeo-Christian-Islamic and Hindu understandings of Ultimate Reality.

First, both traditions distinguish between Ultimate Reality, or "God," in self (*in se*) and God as related to or perceived by others (*ad extra*). God is said to be in-finite, so any perception of God by something other than God—that is, by something finite—is by the very nature of the knowing receptacle bound to be finite. ("Things known are known according to the mode of the knower," as Thomas Aquinas said.[24]) Hence, God, the in-finite, is not known directly. God is not known *in se* (in self) but only as God relates to non-God—that is, *ad extra* ("toward the outside").

This distinction was very clear in the Hebraic tradition as between God (Yahweh), whose "face no one can see and live"; the Spirit (*Ruach*) of God, who moves over the waters in creation; and Wisdom (*Hokmah*), through whom all things were created.[25] An interesting aspect of these depictions of the divine *ad extra* (which include *Shekhinah* and *Torah*) is that they are feminine—not only in grammatical gender, but also in general imagery. This is matched to some extent by the Hindu distinction between *Brahman*, analogous to God *in se,* and the feminine *Shakti,* which, like the Hebrew *Ruach* and *Hokmah,* is understood as "the Divine *Sakti* penetrating everything and manifesting God, disclosing him in his immanence and being present in all his manifestations—this Spirit of God."[26]

In the Christian tradition, the feminine figure of Wisdom (*Hokmah*) was in many instances assimilated in its traits into the Christ figure. *Christos* is simply the Greek form of the Hebrew *Meshiach,* the Anointed One, but in Christian tradition it quickly took on the much more far-reaching characteristics of *Hokmah.* This is seen perhaps most strikingly in the prologue of John's Gospel (John 1:1–4), where the talk is about the Word, the *Logos.* However, one must bear in mind that the Jewish scriptures had already identified God's Word (*Dabar* in Hebrew) with Wisdom (cf. Psalm 119; Ben Sira 24:1–3, 9, 23; also Wisdom 9:1–2), and many Christian scriptural scholars today suggest that in John's prologue, *Logos* was simply substituted for *Hokmah–Sophia* in a previously existing hymn to Wisdom.[27] Thus, in the Christian tradition *Christos* and *Logos* are very like the Hebraic figure *Hokmah*—that is, the creative aspect of God, God *ad extra* (facing outward)—and both are like the Hindu *Shakti* and, even more prominently (as will be discussed later), like the masculine Lord (*Ishvara*).

Ultimate Reality is not only variously named. It is also variously conceived, in both the West and the East. The proper Hebraic name for

Ultimate Reality or God is Yahweh, which was long understood to mean "I am who am," as the Latin Vulgate translates it, but now is usually thought to be more accurately understood as the more dynamic "I will be who I will be." This does seem largely to describe divinity *in se*. Nevertheless, the Bible and most subsequent Jewish and Christian writings speak almost exclusively of God *ad extra*. Not so in Hinduism.

The preferred term in Hinduism for Ultimate Reality is *Brahman* (occasionally referred to as *Atman*, written with a capital *A*). *Brahman* is not exactly divinity *in se*, but at times it is understood in a way that is close to that concept. In that case, it is *Brahman* without attributes (*Nirguna Brahman*), as opposed to *Brahman* with attributes (*Saguna Brahman*), the latter being largely identified with the Lord (*Ishvara*). In any case, *Brahman* usually is not thought of as personal but, rather, as the "Ground of Being"—or "Pure Potency" in Aristotelian terms (quite the opposite of God in the West, who would be thought of as "Pure Actuality"). This contrasts with the Judeo-Christian-Islamic understanding of divinity as personal—that is, God is person (capacity to know and love). Hence, the Greek term *Theos* (related to the Latin *Deus*; both are rendered in English as "God"), including as it does the notion of personal divinity, leads to the concept of "theism" as affirming a personal God. In brief, it can be said then that the notion of "God" is personal, theistic, whereas the notion of *Brahman* usually is non-personal, non-theistic.

A related teaching in Hinduism is that the authentic self, or *atman*, lies at the absolute inner foundation of the human person. This individual self was seen by the Hindu tradition following the *advaita* (non-dualistic) teaching of Shankara to be identified with *Brahman* (sometimes this is expressed as *"atman is Atman"*). Because *Brahman* is the innermost "breath" of everything (as noted earlier, *atman* fundamentally means "breath"), the Hindu *Brahman* is best understood in terms of immanence, the "within" of things, and the Semitic "God" is best understood in terms of transcendence, the "beyond" all things. The former stresses unity; the latter, otherness.

> Indian speculation for the most part is inclined to search for identity; Semitic speculation, on the other hand, characteristically emphasizes the uniqueness of each being and differences among beings. The first kind of mind, typically Indian, probes the depths of being to find the truth; the second kind of mind is directed upward, looking for the truth in the most

sublime heights. The conception of *Brahman* scarcely coincides at all with the conception of God; the two conceptions are almost as opposed as is pure potentiality to pure actuality.[28]

However, neither religious tradition was content with affirming its "traditional" conception of Ultimate Reality. The West did try to speak of God *in se*, as, for example, in the Jewish Kabbalah's term *En Sof* (Infinite), from which come Ten Lights, the last of which is the *Shekhinah* (i.e., the manifestation of God to humanity). Of course, in Christianity there is the development of the doctrine of the Trinity, which is an attempt to describe God *in se*. In the 13th–14th century, the Christian mystic theologian Meister Eckhart distinguished between the Godhead, which he called *Deitas* (God *in se*), and God, which he called *Deus* (God *ad extra*). In modern times, Paul Tillich has spoken of "the God above the God of theism."[29] Alfred North Whitehead and subsequent process theologians have distinguished between the primordial nature of God (*in se*) and the consequent nature of God (*ad extra*). It should be added that the Muslim Sufi term *Al Haqq* as the underlying "abyss" below the personal Allah and the Taoist *Tao Te Ching*'s comment that "the Tao that can be expressed is not the eternal Tao"[30] are both references to similar distinctions in other major religious traditions.

Although relatively less stress has been laid on God *in se*, on divinity in itself, in the Judeo-Christian-Islamic traditions than in the Hindu, every major religious tradition eventually must deal with, or reflect, both dimensions—that is, Ultimate Reality *in se* and *ad extra*. How this is done is a question of emphasis.

Though the emphasis in Hinduism has been on Ultimate Reality *in se*, on *Nirguna Brahman*, the notion of God as perceived by humanity, God for us (*ad nos*), did develop and took a form that has some extraordinary parallels to the Jewish and, even more, the Christian tradition. In Hinduism, *Brahman* acting *ad extra* is referred to as Lord, as *Ishvara*:

> Brahman is absolutely transcendent and in a sense beyond being and non-being. It is pure silence and utter nothingness, truly absolute, i.e., unrelated. It can thus perform no external function, and it is for this that the figure of Ishvara appears.... In other words Brahman is devoid of relations, and it is precisely Ishvara who provides for them.... He is, properly speaking, the revelation of Brahman, the first issue, so to speak, of the unfathomable womb of Brahman. Ishvara is God. Brahman cannot be a person, for if it were it would have to relate to others (things or persons),

which would compromise its absoluteness. Ishvara is the personal aspect of Brahman.... Brahman *as such* cannot be creator of the World, again because of its absolute transcendence. Ishvara, therefore, is that "aspect" of Brahman responsible for the creation of the World.... Brahman is so immutable and unmanifest, beyond every capacity for action, that Ishvara has to take over its functions in relation to the universe and to souls.[31]

Despite the differences, the similarities of *Ishvara* to *Ruach, Hokmah,* and *Shekhinah* in the Hebraic–Jewish tradition and to the Spirit, *Logos,* and *Christos* in the Christian tradition are striking. Important differences also exist, to be sure: *Hokmah* in the Hebraic tradition is not associated with a historical person, whereas *Christos* is associated with Yeshua of Nazareth. There are "incarnations," or "*Avatars,*" of *Ishvara* (Vishnu) in Hinduism—for example, Rama and Krishna—but these are not true historical figures. However, according to the *Bhagavata Purana,* another *Avatar* is Buddha, who was a historical figure.

Buddhist and Semitic Understandings

The fundamental difference in approach to the basic question of the meaning of life between the rabbis, Yeshua (as Jesus was called in his native Semitic tongue), and the Muslim ulama on the one hand and Siddhartha Gautama on the other—and, consequently, between Judaism–Christianity–Islam and Buddhism—can be summed up in one word: God. In the theistic tradition, God is understood in a most positive sense, whereas in Buddhism, some of the basic terms—for example, *Nirvana* and *Sunyata* ("emptiness")—are understood in a totally negative manner, or at least are misunderstood thus by many. Because there has been a growing tendency among both Buddhist and Western scholars to claim that Gautama's original meaning was ultimately positive, and therefore to give a positive meaning to terms such as *Sunyata,* the question arises as to whether there might be common ground for fruitful dialogue even in this bedrock difference. The Catholic theologian Hans Küng thus writes:

It has already been indicated how the concept of emptiness in Mahayana has increasingly turned into something positive.... For on the highest level of mystical experience the human person recognizes that "emptiness"—beyond all concepts and words—is the expression of the deepest reality, of the Absolute, of that which Christian theology calls "God" ... as an expression of the "*ineffabilitas*" of the Godhead.... Nirvana is understood positively as a happy final goal of unshakable calm, of definitive peace and inexpressible blessedness (instead of *dukkha, sukkha* [happiness]) . . . the presentation of *nirvana* then is very like the Christian presentation of "eternal life."[32]

For Christians, this starts not after death, but "now,"—as it also does in the teaching of Gautama. Küng then asks the following pointed question: "Would the conclusion be disallowed that that which Christians call 'God' is likewise present under very different names in Buddhism insofar as it does not in principle completely disallow all positive statements? . . . Against the background of what has been developed here, I would like to attempt the answer in a single sentence," which Küng then encapsulates as follows:

If God truly is the Absolute, then he is *all these in one:*

> *Nirvana,* insofar as he is the goal of the path of liberation;
> *Dharma,* insofar as he is described as the law of the cosmos and humanity;
> *Emptiness,* insofar as he constantly escapes all affirmative specifications;
> *Primordial Buddha,* insofar as he is the origin of all that is.

Could one not, after all the explanations of emptiness, *nirvana* and *dharmakaya* in comparison with the Christian understanding of the Absolute, despite all the divergences, also speak of *convergence between Christianity and Buddhism?*

Küng then points to the writings of the Japanese Mahayana Kyoto school and the Theravada Thai monk Buddhadasa for contemporary Buddhist substantiation of his position.[33]

It is not only Christian or Western thinkers who have been concerned with trying to express the understanding of Ultimate Reality in ways that will take into account both the various theistic affirmations and the non-theistic affirmation of much of Buddhism. For example, Masao Abe, the Zen Buddhist of the Kyoto school, most recently attempted to build such a bridge between the theistic notion of "God" and Buddhist "emptiness," or *Sunyata.*[34] To do so, he makes use of the Mahayana doctrine of the *Trikaya* (the threefold body) of the Buddha—that is, of Ultimate Reality. In this "trinitarian" doctrine, the three bodies are named, in ascending order: *Nirmana-kaya* (the manifestation body); *Sambhoga-kaya* (the heavenly body), and *Dharma-kaya* (Ultimate Reality itself). The

Nirmana-kaya is like the various human manifestations of Ultimate Reality—for example, Moses, Yeshua, Buddha, Muhammad. The *Sambhoga-kaya* is like the several personal Gods affirmed by the various traditions—for example, Yahweh, the Holy Trinity, Allah, *Ishvara,* Amida (of Pure Land Buddhism)—who have various virtues, characteristics, names, and so on. At the highest point is Ultimate Reality itself, *Dharma-kaya,* which Abe describes as "Formless Emptiness or Boundless Openness."

In many ways, this suggestion is reminiscent of the earlier discussion comparing the Semitic and Hindu notions of the ultimate. On the Hindu side, the distinction was made between *Brahman* without attributes (*Nirguna Brahman*) and *Brahman* with attributes (*Saguna Brahman,* later identified with *Ishvara*); on the Semitic side, various expressions were made of the distinction between God *in se* and *ad extra.* It seems that the Semitic, Hindu, and Buddhist notions of Ultimate Reality are similar in that they all affirm that the Ultimate is boundless, infinite, and unutterable in itself, and that various aspects of it are encountered, or perceived, by humans. John Hick, in commenting favorably on Abe's suggestion, likens this distinction to Kant's distinction between the *noumenon* (the "thing in itself"), which we do not perceive, and the *phenomena,* which we do.[35]

It is not difficult for thinkers of the Semitic religious traditions and the theistic strand of the Hindu traditions to accept a *theologia negativa,* an apophatic (from the Greek *apo-phanai,* "not speaking") theology, that acknowledges that the grandest proclamations about God are like whispers in the face of the Infinite Hurricane. It is true that the theistic traditions would tend to speak of God more in terms of Pure Act (*Pleroma,* Fullness) rather than Pure Potency (*Sunyata,* Emptiness). However, the contradiction that appears on the surface here might not exist, for just as the theistic notion of God as Pure Being is conceived as the very opposite of the static (*Stasis*)—namely, as the dynamic (*Dynamis*)—so also the non-theistic notion of the Ultimate (Nothingness; *das Nichts,* an alternative term for Meister Eckhart's term for *Deitas;* Emptiness, *Sunyata*) is also thought of not in static but in dynamic terms:

> This Emptiness is not a static state of emptiness, but rather a dynamic activity constantly emptying everything, including itself. It is formless formlessness, takes various forms deeply by negating its own formlessness. This is the reason that "Formless Emptiness" or "Boundless Openness" is here regarded as the ultimate ground which dynamically reveals

itself both in terms of personal "Gods" and in terms of "Lords" that are historical religious figures.[36]

A more serious difficulty does come in, however, in that the theist tradition is reluctant to give up the affirmation that Ultimate Reality is ultimately personal and accept that it is "Formless Emptiness" in the sense that negates, or even "goes beyond," the personal in a way that obviates it. The Hindu Santosh Sengupta probably speaks for the theistic tradition in general when he writes: "In the upanishadic view there is no negation of the personality of the ultimate. There is no need for the transcendence of personality, for the personality, which the ultimate is, is free from the limitations of human personality."[37]

Perhaps a resolution of the apparent contradiction lies in an analysis of how the human mind and language work. When theists state that the Ultimate is personal, they mean to affirm something positive about it. But by the very fact of making an affirmation, the theist necessarily asserts certain limitations, even when she or he immediately rushes in with a "not this, not that" (*neti, neti*) disclaimer, asserting that all limitations are automatically to be rejected.

For example, when asserting the positive characteristic of personality, the theist will necessarily, if not reject, at least temporarily ignore the possible characteristics of the Ultimate as Energy, Force, and so on. The theist might then hurry to assert: Of course, all the positive characteristics of Energy, Force, and so on are also to be attributed to God. But this job goes on endlessly—or, as Abe might say, with "Boundless Openness." This the theist would gladly grant, but would want to add that, far from eliminating or negating the positive affirmations of personality, Energy, and so on, this "Boundless Openness" in fact gives them a boundless depth, dynamism, openness. With this, perhaps Abe and much of Buddhism might also agree, as perhaps would Taoism, with its notion of "Dynamic Vacuity" (*Kung Ling*).[38]

Exactly what is understood by *Sunyata* ("Emptiness") warrants a little more probing. It can be said that "Emptiness" is another name for the Buddhist doctrine of *Pratitya samutpada* ("Dependent Co-origination"), which in short means that nothing exists as a self-subsisting isolated thing. Rather, everything is ultimately a net of relationships and, consequently, is always in flux, is "becoming." This, of course, is not a new thought to the West; it was expounded by the ancient Greek Heraclitus (536–470 B.C.E.), a near-contemporary of Gautama.

However, this relational understanding has received greater prominence in the West in recent times. It is largely from the second-century C.E. Nagarjuna, the second patriarch of Mahayana Buddhism, that the doctrine of *Sunyata* comes. He clearly denied that there are any self-subsisting substances, insisting that whatever "is" at any moment of space and time consists of conditions or relationships, and that these, too, are dependently co-originated: "The 'originating dependently' we call 'emptiness.'" "Emptiness *is* dependent co-origination."[39]

It should also be noted that how one describes Ultimate Reality depends, among other things, on one's culture. What is thought to be of greatest value in a culture will be attributed to Ultimate Reality. The fact that Ultimate Reality is so described will, of course, in turn dialectically reinforce that value in the culture.

For example, when women were thought to be the sole source of life and, hence, power, divinities were described in female terms—which in fact is how divinities first turn up in human cultures, as we know from archeological excavations at the most primitive layers. However, when it was discovered that men also played a role in producing new life, male divinities slowly began to appear and develop. As cultures became patriarchal—and practically all cultures did by the time humankind arrived at the historical period of development (around 3000 B.C.E., when writing was first invented in Sumer)—it became less and less acceptable to refer to the divinity as female. Hence, for example, God became almost exclusively a male, father God in the Semitic traditions. It would have been denigrating and blasphemous to refer to God in female terms, because woman was of lesser value in the culture.

So it was also for a long time in Western culture concerning the notions of "being," "substance," "stability," and the like. These were high values in the culture, so naturally they were attributed to the Ultimate Reality. But now in the West, immutability, substance, status quo, and so on, are increasingly less valued than change, relationality, evolution. Hence, it would have been difficult to speak of Ultimate Reality as being in constant change, in complete relationship, in the earlier West, because one would have seemed to be saying that Ultimate Reality was less than ultimate. With the recent cultural shift, however, speaking thus seems to be more and more appropriate. Consequently, a Methodist theologian, for example, could now publish an article titled, "Can God Be Change Itself?" and conclude in the affirmative by insisting that this is more in keeping with the original genius of the Hebrew God, whose very name, Yahweh, means "I will be who I will be"—always changing.[40]

But what about the apparently opposite trend in the modern Judeo-Christian tradition—namely, the emphasis not on the Emptiness of Ultimate Reality, of God, but on God's passion, commitment, and involvement in history, and particularly on the side of the oppressed? That is, the talk of God as the "God of the Oppressed." This tradition grew out of the line of the Hebrew prophets, continued in Judeo-Christian history, and was expanded in the nineteenth century as Western awareness of the influence in human life of social structures grew and the idea took hold that religion had to be concerned about changing these structures for the better if individuals are to be changed for the better. This has led in the past one hundred years to the Jewish passion for social justice, the *Jüdischer Bund*, Christian Socialism, the Social Gospel, and the several contemporary "liberation" theologies. One Christian answer has been that

> liberation theologies can themselves learn from Buddhism that the "God of the Oppressed" to whom they point is also a "God who is empty." . . . in a Buddhist sense, referring to that absence of self-subsistence and, hence, that radical relationality of which all beings are exemplifications. To say that God is "empty" is to say that God, too, is relational. It is to affirm (1) that the efficacy of God's action in the world depends partly on worldly response, and (2) that the world's sufferings are God's own.[41]

Confucian and Semitic Understandings

There was, of course, religion in China before Confucius (c. 552–479 B.C.E.) and Lao-tzu (perhaps fifth century B.C.E.), the legendary founder of Taoism. But they gave religion a classical, highly developed form—or, rather, forms—for although they influenced each other considerably, Confucianism and Taoism are very different from each other.

Julia Ching notes that "[f]rom his own account of spiritual evolution, it might also be inferred that Confucius was a religious man, a believer in Heaven as personal God, who sought to understand and follow Heaven's Will."[42] Ching says that her understanding of religion includes a consciousness of a dimension of transcendence that she "perceive[s] as present in Confucianism from the very beginning, even though this has not always referred to a belief in a personal deity. . . .

The very insistence upon the priority of the 'way of Heaven,' and the quest itself for the discovery and fulfillment of such within the way of man, point to a movement toward self-transcendence." Consequently, she says, Confucianism "remains religious at its core, on account of its spiritual teachings of sagehood or self-transcendence."[43]

Closely connected to this question is the understanding and even the name of the transcendent in Confucianism. Careful research has shown that by the Shang period (1766–1123 B.C.E.), the term *Shang-Ti* (Lord on High) or *Ti* (Lord) was already in use to refer to the highest of the gods and eventually to a transcendent being, perhaps even a creator god. In the Chou period (1122–249 B.C.E.), the term most often used for God was *T'ien* (Heaven), symbolized by a large human head. After the Chou conquered the Shang, both *Ti* and *T'ien* were used to refer to God, which was understood as a personal God.

James Legge, the nineteenth-century English Protestant missionary and translator of many of the Chinese religious classics, found in his research the name for the highest God, *Shang-Ti*. "There was, then, before Confucius and many of the sage kings, a monotheistic religion: '*the* Confucian religion.'"[44] Of course, even earlier, in the sixteenth century, Matteo Ricci, the great Catholic scholar, scientist, and missionary to China, had learned much the same about Chinese, and especially Confucian, religion and wrote accordingly.

Though many traditions see the transcendent and the immanent as opposites, the contemporary Confucian Mou Tsung-san "sees the Confucian as joining the ethical and religious dimensions in an effective unity of lived experience. . . . There is no ultimate separation of the subjective and objective, the inner and outer, the immanent and the transcendent."[45]

In the writings of Mencius (371–289 B.C.E.), we find the tendency to speak less in terms of a personal God—or in terms of the transcendent as *ganz anders*, or "completely other," but more in terms of the transcendent, Heaven, being reflected in the human heart: Who knows his or her own heart and nature also knows Heaven.[46] Hence, instead of being "out there," the transcendent was increasingly found within, immanent. Such an understanding is, of course, congenial to a very important strand in the Judeo-Christian tradition that starts with the creation story, where it is said that humanity is made in God's image.

It is in this relationship between the transcendent and the immanent, between Heaven and Humanity, that Confucianism's special characteristic comes to the fore. The core of Confucianism is humanism, but it is a humanism that, as the contemporary Confucian Tu Wei-ming has put it, includes "a faithful dialogical response to the transcendent." He goes on to say that "the mutuality of Heaven and man (in the gender-neutral sense of humanity) makes it possible to perceive the transcendent as immanent." In other words, "the Confucians advocate a humanism which neither denies nor slights the transcendent. . . . Humanity is Heaven's form of self-disclosure, self-expression, and self-realization."[47] By 1958, a number of Chinese scholars in Taiwan had issued a "Manifesto for the Reappraisal of Sinology and Reconstruction of Chinese Culture," in which "the harmony of the 'way of Heaven' (*T'ien-tao*) and the 'way of man' (*Ren-tao*) is extolled by those who signed it as the central legacy of Confucianism."[48]

Again, this conceptualization contains certain parallels to a Christian theology of the *Imago Dei,* or of an incarnational theology. Perhaps most of all, it is like Hegel's notion of the World Spirit, *Welt Geist*—this latter parallel offers especially to Western, including Christian, thinkers many possibilities, as well as problems. But Hegel's thought—and all modern historical, dynamic, processive, immanentist thought—stands in severe tension with much of traditional Christian philosophy and theology: As noted earlier, the older tradition gave being, stasis, and nonchange the pride of place, whereas much of contemporary thought holds up becoming, the dynamic, and change as the highest values, seeing the static as the mode of death.

Nevertheless, as was argued earlier in these pages, the stress on the dynamic is clearly the mode of thought of more and more critical-thinking persons, including Christian theologians—witness Vatican II and subsequent Catholic and Protestant theology, despite various inevitable, temporary backlash movements. Hence, here is a very promising contemporary basis for Christian, and other, dialogue with Confucianism: Because "being religious, in the Confucian perspective . . . means being engaged in the *process* of learning to be fully human,"[49] and learning to become "human is the real informing characteristic of all authentic Confucian religious sentiment. This *process* of 'humanization' has no limits and is therefore called a transcendent reference. . . . [T]he *process* is unending in its scope and completely moral in its intention, while transcendent in ultimate reference."[50]

If becoming human for Confucianism, and Christianity, is an unending process that aims at an ever-receding horizon of heaven, God, the transcendent ("Our inborn ability to respond to the bidding of Heaven impels us to extend our human horizon continuously so that the immanent in our nature assumes a transcendent dimension"[51]), Confucians make clear that it is a process that is engaged in by self-transcendence, self-effort: "The Confucian faith in the perfectibility of human nature through self-effort is, strictly speaking, a faith in self-transcendence."[52] Mou Tsung-san speaks in similar terms, stressing the centrality of creativity in being human: "For him the heart of being human is creative reason, the capacity to transform self and relate in a meaningful and humane way to others. The essence of being human is hence the creation of new values."[53]

Taoist and Semitic Understandings

Tao, of course, means "Way," though it also has the meaning of "Word" or "Saying." It implies that humans are to follow *the Way,* but it is quite the opposite of the Jewish and Muslim analogues *Halacha* and *Shari'a,* respectively. *Halacha* and *Shari'a,* as seen earlier, came to have a specialized meaning concerning the legal decisions governing the proper way to live. For Taoism, following the Tao essentially means "doing nothing" (*wu wei*) in the sense of being unattached to any particular thing, and thereby living in harmony with Ultimate Reality, which is also named *Tao.*

Tao as Ultimate Reality, however, is the all-embracing first and last principle, indefinable, unutterable, and indescribable, the "Ground of all worlds before all worlds," which existed even before heaven and earth. It is the mother of everything, and it calls all things into being, without action, in stillness. It is the "power" (*Te*) of Tao that is working in all creation, all unfolding, and all preservation of the world. It is the *Te* of Tao in all appearances that makes them what they are, but the Tao with its power is nowhere tangible or available. Tao is a "not-being" in the sense of "not-being-thus." It is "empty," without any characteristics that are perceptible to the senses. If, however, everything that exists is the Tao, then it would seem that the Tao is identical with *Being*— that is, not "Being" as understood in a static Greek sense but, rather, as understood in the dynamic modern sense. In this sense, "Being" is understood as "Being in Becoming," or quite literally, as our dynamic English term names it, Be-*ing*.

However, if Tao can be understood as "Being," as "Being in Becoming," then is it not ultimately identical with God? Of course, this can be meant not in a primitive, anthropomorphic or in an ontological, pantheistic sense but, rather, in the differentiated way of the Western philosophical and theological tradition from St. Augustine through St. Thomas Aquinas to Nicholas of Cusa—that is, as "Being Itself" (*Ipsum Esse Subsistens*, according to Thomas), to which the being of all contingently existing beings refers.

Küng asks, "If *nothingness* is the *veil of being* through which being reveals itself, then could the *being* in which humanity participates not also be understood as the *veil of God*?" His response is that "the being of what exists in becoming covers over the 'Being Itself' that can rightly be called God." Conversely, "the Tao can be identified with the original and final reality."[54] Or "It can be identified with ultimate transcendent reality ([Henri] Maspero)."[55] Hence, there is a possible parallel in structure in the concepts of Tao, Being, and God that could be of great importance to the understanding of Ultimate Reality that would bridge cultures and religions.

One more important point needs to be looked at here. During the Han dynasty (206 B.C.E.–220 C.E.), *yin-yang* thinking began to be absorbed into both Confucianism and Taoism. Although a reading of the Taoist material might give one the impression that it claims that Ultimate Reality is somehow a combination of opposites, *yin* and *yang*, dark and light, good and evil, such a reading would indeed be superficial, for in the *Tao Te Ching* itself, the Tao is *prior* to heaven and earth—that is, before duality.

Küng notes: "Indeed, the Tao is before the one and the two, is the origin of the world before all worlds, and is thus the origin of the polarity, not the polarity itself." He adds: "No, an ultimate reality that is both double-sided and contradictory is part of neither the great Chinese nor the great Western tradition. Only penultimate reality is double-sided and contradictory."[56]

Thus, one can say that *Tao* is unchanging "Being" behind all reality—like the early Chinese understanding of *Shang-ti* (the "Lord on High;" God *in se*)—but it later also takes over the active aspect of *T'ien*

("Heaven"; God *ad extra, ad nos*). For it is then also understood as a "divine" pattern for humans to follow, not unlike the Jewish *Torah*.

In the end, Christians can, on the basis of their tradition of mystical and negative theologies, appreciate completely why Taoists refuse all definitions of the *Tao*, whether positive or negative. Even that giant of Christian speculative theology, St. Thomas Aquinas, insisted that God's proper essence remains inaccessible to human reason. He concurs with the mystic Pseudo-Dionysus when he writes: "Wherefore man reaches the highest point of his knowledge about God when he knows that he knows him not, inasmuch as he knows that which is God transcends whatever he conceives of him."[57]

Marxist and Christian Understandings

From the beginning, the history of the Christian–Marxist encounter was characterized by pervasive hostility and conflict. In the 1960s, however, several exceptions to this prevailing pattern occurred, which led to a sporadic Christian–Marxist dialogue. This nevertheless remained an exception to the general pattern, although in many ways it represented the best in both movements. Almost simultaneously, Marxist intellectuals and Christian thinkers in Poland, Italy, France, Czechoslovakia, Germany, and Austria began to reach out toward one another. Under the auspices of the Austrian–German *Paulus-gesellschaft,* and subsequently in Yugoslavia, then through international agencies, several international meetings took place in which creative analyses of important social, and even spiritual, issues were pursued. What follows is a small sample of such novel approaches; they should not, however, be regarded as a full picture of this dialogue.

At first blush, one might assume that Marxists would have no notion of *Ultimate Reality,* but if the term is not filled ahead of time with theistic content, the matter is not so simple. For example, Roger Garaudy, as a representative of Marxist thinkers who have in the past several decades been in serious dialogue with Christians,[58] sees in the positive attitude toward matter and evolution—that is, the immanent force within matter rising unendingly up to the level of consciousness and beyond, as expressed pre-eminently in the thought and writings of the Jesuit scientist and theologian Pierre Teilhard de Chardin—a Copernican turn in Christian thought that enables Marxists not only to join with Christians in "building the earth," as Teilhard put it, but also to learn something from them in their efforts to relate the immanent and transcendent in the universe. As Garaudy cited Teilhard: "The synthesis of the [Christian] God of the Above and the [Marxist] God of the Ahead: this is the only God whom we shall in the future be able to adore in spirit and in truth."[59]

This Teilhardian idea is also much like Karl Rahner's notion that the ultimate of humankind is the Absolute Future, the ever-receding, ever-beckoning horizon within which humankind lives and moves forward. Garaudy, as noted earlier, understood Marxism to see the future of humankind similarly: "Yes, man will always be capable of an always greater future."

Writing in 1965, Garaudy argued that for a quarter of a century there had been an "intellectual hardening of the arteries within Marxism," but that this was followed by a "vigorous reappearance of the problems of subjectivity, choice and spiritual responsibility." Garaudy insisted that "this development ... occurred because of the inescapable abandonment of old values and the birth-pangs which accompany the creation of new ones," but granted that "to the extent that Marxism has failed to answer these questions adequately, youth has turned elsewhere to seek the answer which it is our job today to seek, though we may not yet fully discover it." He emphasized that in seeking answers to these critical human questions, Marxism, at least in part, could not evade the quest for what it "owes to Christianity as a religion of the absolute future and as a contributing factor in the exploration of the two essential dimensions of man: subjectivity and transcendence. We cannot, without impoverishing ourselves, forget Christianity's basic contribution: the change in man's attitude toward the world, preparing a place for subjectivity."

Moreover, he claimed that he was not alone in "this realization of the Christian contribution to civilization and culture, and of the revolutionary potential of the faith," which he said had been "operative not only within the French Communist Party since the great step forward in 1937 but also within all ... those countries where progressive movements were taking shape within the Catholic Church,"—meaning, especially, Italy and Spain.

Garaudy claimed that Marxism has an interest in the questions that women and men raise "about the meaning of their life and their death, about the problem of their origin and their end, about the demands of their thought and their heart." He also granted that there is much that "Marxists must assimilate from the rich Christian heritage." However, he went on to claim that, although the greatness of religion is displayed by its awareness and concern for these fundamental human questions, its weakness is in its fixing of its once-given answers as always-given answers, despite humanity's advances in thought and ways of understanding. Both Marxism and Christianity, he stated, live under the same exigencies, or needs, but they differ in their answers.

He began by saying that, "If we reject the very name of God, it is because the name implies a presence, a reality, whereas it is only an exigency which we live, a never-satisfied exigency of totality and absoluteness, of omnipotence as to nature and of perfect loving reciprocity of consciousness." But then he added that "[w]e can live this exigency, and we can act it out, but we cannot conceive it, name it or expect it. Even less can we hypostatize it under the name of transcendence. Regarding this totality, this absolute, I can say everything except: It is. For what it is is always deferred, and always growing."

Garaudy then wanted to stake out a claim for Marxism of being a doctrine of subjectivity and of transcendence, an unendingly self-transcending future for humanity: "I think that Marxist atheism deprives man only of the illusion of certainty, and that the Marxist dialectic, when lived in its fullness, is ultimately richer in the infinite and more demanding still than the Christian transcendence." But "it is undoubtedly such only because it bears within itself the extraordinary Christian heritage, which it must investigate still more," and in the end it "owes it to itself in philosophy to work out a more profound theory of subjectivity, one which is not subjectivist, and a more profound theory of transcendence, one which is not alienated."

Most Christian theologians will today admit that the old arguments for the existence of God do not have the rational force of a demonstration that they were once thought to have had. Many will, with Küng, claim that in the end it is reasonable to affirm the existence of God, not ineluctably so, but in fundamental trust, although in the very affirmation one is confirmed in the reasonableness of one's affirmation.[60] The transcendental theologians and philosophers, such as Karl Rahner and Joseph Marechal, however, have argued that the very presence of the open-ended thirst for knowledge, for being, found in the inner nature of humankind demands that there be an open-ended source and goal of that spiritual drive. Garaudy took that idea up when he said, "My thirst does not prove the existence of the spring." But ultimately, does-n't it? Is it conceivable in this world as we know it that there could develop a being that has a need for something—say, water—if there were no such thing as water? No. It would die aborning. But humankind has not died aborning. Therefore....[61]

In any case, Garaudy took seriously the Teilhardian–Rahnerian notion of God as no-*thing*, as the unendingly, infinitely creative absolute future (again reminding one of Buddhism's *Sunyata*, or "Boundless Openness"): "In such a perspective God is no longer a being or even the totality of being, since such a totality does not exist. Being is totally open to the future to be created. Faith is not the possession of an object by cognition." Garaudy then added that "the transcendence of God implies its constant negation since God is constant creation beyond any essence and any existence. A faith which is only assertion would be credulity. Doubt is part and parcel of living faith. The depth of faith in a believer depends upon the force of the atheist he bears in himself and defends against all idolatry."

For his part, of course, Garaudy did not find what theists call a divine presence, only its absence. Still, he was aware that his affirma-tion of absence also was not an ineluctable rational affirmation but a choice of his whole being and, in that sense, a "faith." "We thus reach the highest level of the dialogue, that of the integration in each of us of that which the other bears in himself, as other," he wrote. "I said ear-lier that the depth of a believer's faith depends upon the strength of the atheism that he bears in himself. I can now add: the depth of an atheist's humanism depends on the strength of the faith he bears in himself."

More than twenty years later, the Hungarian Marxist Pal Horvath made a similar point when he said that "the existence of God cannot be theoretically proved or denied.... Whoever sees the essence of Marx's atheism in this is mistaken." He then quoted another Hungar-ian Marxist, Tamas Nyiri, as saying: "Until a communist society with-out religion has developed, the Marxist theory pretending that religion is essentially a false form of consciousness cannot be considered as proved. It is just one of several potential theories to be verified or refuted by historical–social practice." After all, Horvath said, "When we turn to the question of whose ultimate hypotheses of a cosmic nature will prove true, I am convinced that an answer can only be expected in a perspective of world history."[62]

Garaudy in the end pleaded—to both sides, obviously—for both the ideological and the practical dialogue to continue and deepen. He said that it would be one of the tragedies of history "if the dialogue between Christians and Marxists and their cooperation for mutual enrichment and for the common building of the future, the city of man, the total man, were still longer to be spoiled, perhaps even prevented, by the weight of the past." He was not asking for "conversion" of one side to the other; rather, he said, "[W]e offer a dialogue without prejudice or hindrance. We do not ask anyone to stop being what he is. What we ask is, on the contrary, that he be it more and that he be it better." He then added, "We hope that those who engage in dialogue with us will demand the same of us."

All this is rather stunning stuff, coming as it did from a Marxist philosopher and French Politburo member of such prominence and profundity. Garaudy admonished, however: "Let us be clearly aware of the fact that we are still only at the start of a great turning point in the epic of man. The turning point itself will not be reached until we have graduated from the meetings of a few lonely scouts, possibly even suspect in their own communities, to the authentic dialogue of the communities themselves." Then, in words that were far too painfully prophetic, he continued: "The road is heavily ambushed and ... we must confess that present political conditions do not make any easier the requisite clarification of the problems." That was in 1965. Then came the 1968 Soviet crushing of the Prague Spring (against which Garaudy spoke out vigorously) and Garaudy's expulsion from the Communist Party in 1970. These events and similar retrenchments elsewhere just about destroyed the dialogue between Christians and Marxists for a number of years.

The dialogue did revive slowly in the late 1970s and into the 1980s, but then it became largely moot with the sudden "Great Transformation" in Eastern Europe in 1989–90, which left very few reputable thinkers overtly espousing Marxist ideology. (In China, the one remaining major Marxist stronghold, there do not seem to be any Marxist thinkers; there are only political ideologues.) Still, the serious Marxist thinking by reflective philosophers such as Garaudy in the 1960s, Zagorka Golubovic in the 1980s, and others[63] offer an approach to the questions of Ultimate Reality by a very important and influential ideology in human history.

CONCLUSION

If these reflections are at all close to the mark in trying to discern the meaning of *religion* (and *ideology*), then we would like to draw them together in kind of summary of what religion means and what its purpose is. The definition of religion we began with was, in fact, our conclusion after much study and reflection. Hence, we would simply paraphrase it here, stressing its various elements with the help of the four Cs (creed, code, cult, and community structure) and the *T* (transcendent):

> Religion is an explanation (creed) of the ultimate meaning of life and how to live (code and community structure) accordingly, which is based on the notion of the transcendent with whom the believers have a relationship (cult). Because religion is an explanation of the ultimate meaning of life, it provides a code of behavior in the fullest possible sense, including all the psychological, social, and cultural dimensions of human life, and is hence a way of life—for *humans*. The way of life that religion tries to provide is not, however, just a more or less acceptable way of life. It is an attempt, on the basis of its "explanation" and experience, to put forth the best possible way of life.

As has been seen, there are many different ways to describe the best possible "way of life" that will lead humans most effectively to the goal of life, which is also variously described according to the different religious "explanations" of the ultimate meaning of life. What they all surely have in common, however, is that they aim to provide *humans* with the best possible way to live to attain the goal of their lives. Hence, it can be concluded that all religions aim ultimately at making humans as authentically and wholly human as possible—that is, they aim to provide *salvation*, however it is described, for humans, however they understand themselves.

A variety of ways also exist for understanding Ultimate Reality, with a major distinction between the theist, personal understanding on the one hand, and the non-theist, non-personal understanding on the other.

Still, the theistic understandings of Ultimate Reality also make room for non-personal understandings—without forfeiting their personal understanding. Also, some versions of the non-personal understanding, especially in dialogue, also stretch to make room for a "personal" understanding of God—as, for example, in the writings of the Zen Buddhist Masao Abe, who has been deeply involved in dialogue with Christians. There is promise of a deeper, richer understanding of Ultimate Reality by both theists and non-theists in the pursuing of dialogue. The dialogue between adherents of religion and of ideology, which is temporarily largely in abeyance, also promises to lead to a further understanding of what it means to be human.

2 Philosophy of Religion

The Relationship Between Philosophy and Religion

One of the most abiding relationships between religion and another discipline is that between religion and philosophy (from the Greek, *love of wisdom*). The origins of philosophy can be found in early musings about religious insights.[1] From time immemorial, a facet of religion has expressed itself in the "love of wisdom." Wisdom was cherished and passed down from generation to generation in oral or written form, beginning with the most ancient religions and continuing to the present. In the Orient, the link between philosophy and religion remained much closer than it did in the Near Eastern and Western traditions. For instance, in Hinduism, it is believed that the proper aim of philosophy is human liberation or salvation, and that philosophical speculation often leads to ecstatic mystical experience.

Much of that wisdom was proverbial and practical. Religious communities were the repositories and transmitters of the accumulated experience of the community, usually voiced by individuals who were the sages, the wise men and women of the community. The sages were both the collectors and the creators of insights helpful for living. Such wisdom was cherished in ancient Egypt, in Mesopotamia, in China, and in India, as well as in both traditional and historical religions of the past and present. The Semitic and Oriental cultures preferred this form of wisdom and wove it into the fabric of their religion.

The second type of wisdom was speculative in nature, where the great thinkers of a civilization explored questions of the ultimate significance of life. This form of philosophy is also very ancient. The Greek and Hindu thinkers were among the foremost ancients to engage in this type of thinking. The Upanishads (800–300 B.C.E.) of India are evidence of the sophisticated and complex speculative philosophy of the Indian Subcontinent, while Plato (428–348 B.C.E.) and Aristotle (384–322 B.C.E.) represent the pinnacle of Greek thinking. In speculative philosophy, one can distinguish a rational and a mystical orientation. The former affirms the possibility of using reason to penetrate the problems of life and the universe, and the latter prefers a more intuitive grappling with what are believed to be the impenetrable dark secrets of the universe.

Both philosophy and religion are interested in the whole. They often ask the same questions and deal with the same issues. The relationship between religion and philosophy is one of mutual interaction. Religion often provided philosophy with the experiences and raw insights that philosophers systematized, shaped, critiqued, and developed. Some of the philosophers' insights were in turn appropriated by religionists as ways to understand what transpired in their community. Also, various philosophical approaches were used as the means of interpreting and organizing religious experiences and ideas. One might say that practically every philosophical approach ever invented has been used by some religious group as a basis for organizing and expressing its ideas. The basic difference between religion and philosophy is in their ultimate goal: While philosophy seeks understanding, religion seeks deliverance, salvation, or liberation.

The religious person's insights lead to a commitment, to action, very often in more or less organized communal fashion. This is not usually the case with philosophy (the exception being Marxism, which for that very reason often assumed quasi-religious dimensions). Winston L. King has suggested that the interaction between the two is especially fertile because philosophy can remind religion to differentiate between notions in order to avoid superstition and credulity, while religion can remind philosophy to speculate not merely for speculation's sake but to achieve a higher quality living and being.[2]

Initially, no discrepancy or tension was experienced between religion and philosophy, though from the outset some philosophers scoffed at this or that religious expression, and some religious people suspected that philosophy was a danger that might undermine faith. Indeed, an implicit conflict exists even in the basic approaches of religion and philosophy. In religion, affirmation of the faith experience and its consequence is expected. In philosophy, generally, questioning of various affirmations is expected, and a skeptical attitude is deliberately nurtured. Some see in this a basic incompatibility between religion and philosophy, and thinkers in both camps have at times expressed the conviction that religion should dismiss philosophy, or the other way around.

William J. Abraham pointed out that there are five possible relationships between philosophy and religion:

1) Philosophy can complement religion, providing to religion a conceptual, intellectual framework;
2) Philosophy can make room for religion by pointing out the limits of reason and the possible place for religious faith and commitment;
3) Philosophy can provide the underpinning of religion by assuring that religious statements are not self-contradictory and that their formulations are intellectually respectable. Here religion and philosophy act in accord, in a synthesis;
4) Philosophy can be an analytic tool for clarification of the language of religion; and, finally,
5) Philosophy can be seen as a substitute for religion, a pseudo-religious approach to life.[3]

What is surely the case is that philosophers of nearly all orientations have raised important questions about religion.

THE DISCIPLINE OF THE PHILOSOPHY OF RELIGION

The discipline of the philosophy of religion is of a more recent origin. Abraham again specifies five tasks for this discipline:

1) Clarify the central concepts of religion;
2) Examine the internal consistency of religious concepts;
3) Scrutinize the philosophical presupposition of faith statements;
4) Explore the relationship between religion and other areas of life; and
5) Examine the philosophical presuppositions and consistencies of statements made by apologists or assailants of religion.[4]

Edgar S. Brightman provided one of the most succinct and adequate definitions: "Philosophy of religion is an attempt to discover by rational interpretation of religion and its relations to other types of experience, the truth of religious beliefs and the value of religious attitudes and practice."[5]

The methods used in philosophy of religion are identical to those used in other branches of philosophy. The branches of philosophy most interested in religion were metaphysics (the exploration of that which is beyond the physical) and axiology (the investigation of values and their relationship to existence—that is, ethics). Philosophy of religion takes for its data any and all religious experiences and scrutinizes them in accordance with the accepted canons of philosophical inquiry.

Although philosophy has dealt with religious issues from its inception, philosophy of religion as a separate discipline seems to have begun in the eighteenth century. Among the first explicit works in philosophy of religion were David Hume's *The Natural History of Religion* and *Dialogues Concerning Natural Religion;* Immanuel Kant's *The Critique of Pure Reason, The Critique of Practical Reason,* and *Religion Within the Limits of Reason Alone;* and Friedrich Hegel's *Lectures on the Philosophy of Religion.* These giants of Western classical philosophical thought were followed by many outstanding philosophers of religion, of whom the best known are Andrew Seth Pringle-Pattison, F. H. Bradley, Henri Bergson, Rudolf H. Lotze, Josiah Royce, William Hocking, and Alfred N. Whitehead.[6]

A number of philosophers of religion also took for their departure point the truth of the divine revelation as claimed by their own religious tradition. These philosophers sometimes claimed that such revelation was superior to the rational inquiry into religious experience.

Thus, it is evident that one of the key questions raised in philosophy of religion is the way of knowing—that is, epistemology—and specifically, the role of reason in religion. Not all philosophies follow the strict dictates of reason. For example, existentialists such as Sören Kierkegaard sharply questioned the usefulness of reason in the religious domain. Kant raised that question pointedly when he concluded that pure reason is not able to lead to reliable religious knowledge, but contended that practical reason is.

Reason is the means whereby people become self-aware and make judgments regarding conflicting truth claims. Religious experience has always been formulated and passed down in concepts understandable to other members of the community. When such formulations lose power over a period time, the faith is often refreshed by reinterpreting the old formulations or creating new formulations at a deeper level. Humanity grows by rejecting outworn, inadequate concepts that do not stand the scrutiny of reason and replacing them with more reasonable notions.

In the past two hundred years, the Western understanding of truth—that is, statements about reality—has been undergoing a radical shift, now often called a "paradigm shift." A paradigm is the model or set of assumptions that provide the mental context within which information is received and interpreted. For example, all the information about the movement of the planets used to be received in the context of the assumption that the Earth was the center of the solar system (a geocentric paradigm), whereas now the assumption is that the sun is the center (heliocentric paradigm).

A DE-ABSOLUTIZED VIEW OF TRUTH

Up to the past century, our Western notion of truth was largely absolute, static, and monologic, or exclusive. It has since become de-absolutized, dynamic, and dialogic—in a word, *relational*. This "new" view of truth came about in at least six different, but closely related, ways. In brief they are:

1) *Historicism:* Truth is de-absolutized by the perception that reality is always described in terms of the circumstances of the time in which it is expressed.
2) *Intentionality:* Seeking the truth with the intention of acting accordingly de-absolutizes the statement.
3) *Sociology of knowledge:* Truth is de-absolutized in terms of geography, culture, and social standing.
4) *Limits of language:* Truth as the meaning of something, and especially as talk about the transcendent, is de-absolutized by the limited nature of human language.
5) *Hermeneutics:* All truth, all knowledge is seen as interpreted truth, knowledge, and hence is de-absolutized by the observer, who is always also the interpreter.
6) *Dialogue:* The knower engages reality in a dialogue in a language that the knower provides, thereby de-absolutizing all statements about reality.

In short, our understanding of truth and reality has been undergoing a radical shift. The new paradigm that is being born understands all statements about reality, especially about the meaning of things, to be historical, intentional, perspectival, partial, interpretive, and dialogic. What is common to all these qualities is the notion of *relation-ality*—that is, that all expressions or understandings of reality are in some fundamental way related to the speaker or knower. It is while bearing this paradigm shift in mind that we must now proceed with our analysis.

ABSOLUTISM.   Before the nineteenth century in Europe, *truth*—that is, a statement about reality—was conceived in quite an absolute, static, exclusive either–or manner. If something was true at one time, it was always true. Not only empirical facts, but also the meaning of things or the "oughtness" that was said to flow from them, were thought of in this way. For example, if it was true for the Pauline writer to say in the first century that women should keep silence in the church, then it was always true that women should keep silence in the church; or if it was true for Pope Boniface VIII to state in 1302, "We declare, state, and define that it is absolutely necessary for the salvation of all human beings that they submit to the Roman Pontiff,"[7] then it was always true that they needed to do so. At bottom, the notion of truth was based exclusively on the Aristotelian principle of contradiction: A thing could not be true and not true in the same way at the same time. Truth was defined by way of exclusion: *A* was *A* because it could be shown not to be not-*A*. Truth was thus understood to be absolute, static, exclusively either–or. This is a *classicist* or *absolutist* view of truth.

HISTORICISM.   In the nineteenth century, many scholars came to perceive all statements about the truth of the meaning of something as partially the product of their historical circumstances. Those concrete circumstances helped determine the fact that the statement under study was even called forth, that it was couched in particular intellectual categories (for example, abstract Platonic or concrete legal language), particular literary forms (for example, mythic or metaphysical language), and particular psychological settings (such as a polemical response to a specific attack). These scholars argued that the truth statements could be properly understood only if they were placed in their historical situation, their historical "setting in life" (*Sitz im Leben*). The understanding of the text could be found only in con-text. To express that same original meaning in a later *Sitz im Leben*, one would require a proportionately different statement. Thus, all statements about the meaning of things were now seen to be de-absolutized in terms of time.

This is a *historical* view of truth. Clearly at its heart is a notion of *relationality*. Any statement about the truth of the meaning of something has to be understood in relationship to its historical context.

INTENTIONALITY.   Later thinkers such as Max Scheler added a corollary to this historicizing of knowledge: It concerned not the past but the future. Such scholars also saw truth as having an element of *intentionality* at its base, as being oriented ultimately toward action, or *praxis*. They argued that we perceive certain things as questions to be answered and set goals to pursue specific knowledge because we wish to do something about those matters. We intend to live according to the truth and meaning that we hope to discern in the answers to the questions we pose, in the knowledge we decide to seek. The truth of the meaning of things was thus seen as de-absolutized by the action-oriented *intentionality* of the thinker–speaker.

This is an *intentional* or *praxis* view of truth, and it, too, is basically *relational:* A statement has to be understood in relationship to the action-oriented intention of the speaker.

THE SOCIOLOGY OF KNOWLEDGE.   Just as some thinkers saw statements of truth about the meaning of things as historically de-absolutized in time, so, starting in this century with scholars such as Karl Mannheim, did such statements begin to be seen as de-absolutized by such things as the culture, class, and gender of the thinker–speaker. All reality was said to be perceived from the perspective of the perceiver's own worldview. Any statement of the truth of the meaning of something was seen to be perspectival—or *standortgebunden* ("standpoint-bound"), as Mannheim put it—and thus de-absolutized.

This is a *perspectival* view of truth and is likewise *relational:* All statements are fundamentally related to the standpoint, or the perspective, of the speaker.

THE LIMITATIONS OF LANGUAGE.   Following Ludwig Wittgenstein and others, many thinkers have come to see that any statement about the truth of things can be at most a partial description of the reality that it is trying to describe. Although reality can be seen from an almost limitless number of perspectives, human language can express things from only one, or perhaps a very few, perspectives at once. This is now seen to be true of what we call "scientific truths"; it is so much the more true of statements about the meaning of things. The very fact of dealing with the truth of the "meaning" of something indicates that the knower is essentially involved and hence reflects the perspectival character of all such statements. A statement may be true, of course—it may accurately describe the extra-mental reality it refers to—but it will always be cast in particular categories, language, concerns, and so on, of a particular "standpoint." In that sense, it will be limited, or de-absolutized.

This also is a *perspectival* view of truth, and therefore also *relational.* This limited and limiting, as well as liberating, quality of language is especially clear in talk of the transcendent. The transcendent is by definition that which goes beyond our experience. Any statements about the transcendent must thus be de-absolutized and limited far beyond the perspectival character seen in ordinary statements.

HERMENEUTICS. Hans-Georg Gadamer and Paul Riceour more recently led the way in developing the science of hermeneutics, which, by arguing that all knowledge of a text is at the same time an *interpretation* of the text, further de-absolutizes claims about the "true" meaning of the text. But this basic insight goes beyond knowledge of texts and applies to all knowledge.

Some of the key notions here can be compressed in the following mantra (a mantra traditionally is a seven-syllable phrase that encapsulates an insight): "Subject, object, two is one." The whole of hermeneutics is here *in nuce:* All knowledge is interpreted knowledge; the perceiver is part of the perceived; the subject is part of the object. When the object of study is some aspect of humanity, the obvious fact that the observer is also the observed "de-objectivizes," or de-absolutizes, the resultant knowledge, truth. But the same thing is also fundamentally true of all knowledge, of all truth, even of the natural sciences. The various aspects of nature are observed only through the categories we provide, within the horizons we establish, under the paradigms we use, in response to the questions we raise, and in relationship to the connections we make. This is a further de-absolutizing of truth, even of the "hard" sciences.

"Subject, object, two is one." Knowledge comes from the subject perceiving the object, but because the subject is also part of its object, as described earlier, the two are in that sense one. Likewise, in knowing, the object in some form is taken up into the subject, and again the two are one. And yet, there is also a radical twoness there, for it is the very process of the two *becoming* one—or the two being perceived as one, or, even better, the becoming aware that the two, which are very really two, are also in fact on another level very really one—that we call *knowing.*

This is an *interpretive* view of truth. It is clear that *relationality* pervades this hermeneutical, interpretive view of truth. (It is interesting that one dimension of this interpretive understanding of truth can be found in the thirteenth century, in St. Thomas Aquinas, who states that "things known are in the knower according to the mode of the knower— *cognita sunt in cognoscente secundum modum cognoscentis.*"[8])

DIALOGUE.   A further development of this basic insight is that I learn not by being merely passively open or receptive to, but by being in dialogue with, extra-mental reality. I not only "hear" or receive reality; I also—and, I think, first of all—"speak" to reality. I ask it questions, and I stimulate it to speak back to me, to answer my questions. In the process, I give reality the specific categories and language with which to respond to me. The "answers" that I receive from reality will always be in the language, the thought categories, of the questions I put to it. It can "speak" to me, can really communicate with my mind, only in a language and in categories that I understand.

When the speaking, the responding, grows less understandable to me, if the answers I receive are sometimes confusing and unsatisfying, then I probably need to learn to speak a more appropriate language when I put questions to reality. If, as mentioned earlier, I ask the question, "How far is yellow?" I will, of course, receive a nonsensical answer. Or if I ask questions about living things in mechanical categories, I will receive confusing and unsatisfying answers. Thus, I will receive confusing and unsatisfying answers to questions about human sexuality if I use categories that are solely physical–biological. Witness the absurdity of the answer that birth control is forbidden by the natural law: The question falsely assumes that the nature of humanity is merely physical–biological.

This is a *dialogic* view of truth, whose very name reflects its *relationality.*

IMPLICATIONS OF A DE-ABSOLUTIZED VIEW OF TRUTH

With this new and irreversible understanding of the meaning of truth, the critical thinker has undergone a radical Copernican turn. Just as the vigorously resisted shift in astronomy from geocentrism to heliocentrism revolutionized that science, the paradigm or model shift in the understanding of truth statements has revolutionized all the humanities, including theology and ideology. The macro-paradigm or macro-model with which critical thinkers operate today (or the "horizon" within which they operate, to use Bernard Lonergan's term) is characterized by historical, social, linguistic, hermeneutical, *praxis*, and dialogic—*relational*—consciousness. This paradigm or model shift is far advanced among thinkers and doers. But as in the case of Copernicus, and even more dramatically that of Galileo, there are still many resisters in positions of great institutional power.

It is difficult to overestimate the importance that the conceptual paradigm or model one has of reality plays in the "understanding of reality and how to live accordingly." The paradigm or model within which we perceive reality not only profoundly affects our theoretical understanding of reality; it also has immense practical consequences. For example, in Western medicine, the body is usually conceived of as a highly nuanced, living machine; therefore, if one part wears out, the obvious thing to do is to replace it. Hence, organ transplants originated in Western, not in Oriental, medicine.

However, in Chinese (Oriental) medicine, the body is conceived of as a finely balanced harmony. Pressure exerted on one part of the body is assumed to have an opposite effect in another part of the body. Hence, acupuncture originated in Oriental, not Western, medicine.[9]

Further, some particular paradigms or models for perceiving reality obviously will fit the data better than others, and they will be preferred—for example, the shift from the geocentric to the heliocentric model in astronomy. But sometimes differing models will each in its own way "fit" the data more or less adequately, as in the example of Western and Oriental medicine. The differing models are then viewed as complementary. Clearly, it would be foolish to limit one's perception of reality to only one of the complementary paradigms or models. Perhaps a more comprehensive model, a mega-model, can at times be conceived to subsume two or more complementary models, but surely it will never be possible to perceive reality except through paradigms or models. Hence, *meta*-model thinking is not possible, except in the more limited sense of meta-*mono*-model thinking—that is, perceiving reality through multiple, differing models that cannot be subsumed under one mega-model, but must stand in creative, polar tension in relationship to each other, or what might be called "multi-model thinking." This pattern has been characteristic of nuclear physics for decades, as it uses both particle and wave descriptions of subatomic matter.

RELATIONALITY VERSUS RELATIVISM

With the de-absolutized view of the truth of the meaning of things, we come face to face with the specter of relativism, the opposite pole of absolutism. Unlike *relationality,* a neutral term that merely denotes the quality of being in relationship, *relativism,* like so many "-isms," is a basically negative term. If it can no longer be claimed that any statement of the truth of the meaning of things is absolute, totally objective, because that claim does not square with our experience of reality, it is equally impossible to claim that every statement of the truth of the meaning of things is completely relative or totally subjective, for that also does not square with our experience of reality, and, of course, would also lead logically to an atomizing isolation that would stop all discourse, all statements to others.

Our perception, and hence description, of reality is like our view of an object in the center of a circle of viewers. My view and description of the object, or reality, will be true, but it will not include what someone on the other side of the circle perceives and describes, which will also be true. So neither of our perceptions and descriptions of reality is total, complete—"absolute" in that sense—or "objective" in the sense of not in any way being dependent on a "subject" or viewer. At the same time, however, it is also obvious that there is an objective, doubtless "true," aspect to each perception and description, even though each is relational to the perceiver–"subject."

At the same time that the always partial, perspectival, de-absolutized view of all truth statements is recognized, the common human basis for perceptions and descriptions of reality and values must also be kept in mind. All human beings experience certain things in common. We all experience our bodies—pain, pleasure, hunger, satiation. Our cognitive faculties perceive such structures in reality as variation and symmetry in pitch, color, and form. All humans experience affection and dislike. Here, and in other commonalities, we find the bases for building a universal, fundamental epistemology, esthetics, value system. Although it will be vital to distinguish carefully between those human experiences and perceptions that come from nature and those that come from nurture, it will also, at times, be difficult to discern precisely where the distinctions lie. In fact, all of our "natural" experiences are more or less shaped by our "nurturing," because all of our experiences and knowledge are interpreted through the lens of our "nurturing" structures.

Although we can no longer hold to an absolutist view of the truth of the meaning of things, we must take certain steps to prevent being forced logically into the silence of total relativism. First, in addition to striving to be as accurate and fair as possible in gathering and assessing information and submitting it to the critiques of our peers and other thinkers and scholars, we also need to dredge out, state clearly, and analyze our own presuppositions—a constant, ongoing task. Even in this, we will, of course, be operating from a particular "standpoint."

Therefore, we need, secondly, to complement our constantly critiqued statements with statements from different "standpoints." That is, we need to engage in *dialogue* with those who have differing cultural, philosophical, social, and religious viewpoints to strive toward an ever more complete perception of the truth of the meaning of things. If we do not engage in such dialogue, we will not only be trapped within the perspective of our own "standpoint." We will also be aware of our lack. We will no longer with integrity be able to remain deliberately turned in on ourselves. Our search for the truth of the meaning of things makes it necessary for us as human beings to engage in dialogue. Knowingly refusing dialogue today could be an act of fundamental human irresponsibility—in Judeo-Christian terms, a sin.

Paul Knitter noted much the same thing concerning the shift from the former exclusively either–or model of truth to the dialogic or relational model: "In the new model, truth will no longer be identified by its ability to exclude or absorb others. Rather, what is true will reveal itself mainly by its ability to *relate* to other expressions of truth and to grow through these relationships: truth defined not by exclusion but by relation. The new model reflects what our pluralistic world is discovering: no truth can stand alone; no truth can be totally unchangeable. Truth, by its very nature, needs other truth. If it cannot relate, its quality of truth must be open to question."[10]

Let this suffice for the moment regarding this radical shift in our understanding of our human way of understanding, which will be discussed later in the section on dialogue.

3   History of Religions

ONE FUNCTION of the *Religionswissenschaften* ("sciences of religion"—that is, history, psychology, anthropology, and sociology)—is to provide the raw material for philosophy of religion so it can attempt to relate the data to one another and explore their meaning and significance. However, each of these sciences of religion itself provides important knowledge of various aspects of religion and of humanity, the creator of religion. Hence, having analyzed the philosophy of religion somewhat, it is important that we likewise explore these "sciences of religion."

A HISTORICAL APPROACH TO THE STUDY OF RELIGION

The term *history of religions* can be understood in two distinct ways. The first involves simply looking at any religion or religious institution, occurrence, writing, teaching, or person from a historical perspective. The second involves the scientific or scholarly study of religion.

In the first sense, *history of religions* means applying the historical method to religious topics in the same way that one would apply it to non-religious phenomena. Seen in this way, history of religion or religions is one of the oldest scholarly disciplines in the field of the study of religion and one of the most ancient ways of presenting religious material. The reasons for the early interest in the history of religions are obvious. Many societies took an interest in their past. They remembered their great leaders, decisive battles, traumatic or joyous events, beginnings and transitional periods, and challenges to their communities. They tried to reconstruct and thereby understand the past, although they did not always aim to recount these events accurately; rather, they aimed to remember, perhaps selectively, those events that seemed to be formative in the life of the community. Such memory was usually extended by word of mouth. In many societies even today, these means are still used.

With the introduction of writing, other societies began writing such stories down. These accounts were usually called *chronicles* because they recounted times past, but they were not yet histories in the modern sense of the word. In the Hebrew Bible, there is even a book called Chronicles (it is one of several "books" in that collection of documents, which is of the nature of chronicles). In Japan, many of the Shinto traditions, myths, and legends were recorded in the ninth century C.E.. in the *Kojiki* and *Nihongi* chronicles.[1] In Russia in the eleventh century C.E., "The Chronicle of Ancient Events" was written, recounting some Hebrew and Christian memories.

For some religions, history was of crucial importance because their adherents believed that God (or the gods) was manifested primarily in historical events. This is true, for instance, for Judaism, Christianity, and Islam, among the major religions. Jews believed that Yahweh (God) entered into a covenant or contract with them that entailed their living according to God's commandments in their communal and individual lives. God's will was seen in historical events. In a similar manner, Christians believed that God was present in the events of the life and death of Jesus of Nazareth and that his followers likewise were to follow God's will thus shown forth. Islam accepted the previous salvation history of Jews and Christians, corrected and extended it, and believed that God's will was being played out in the daily events of each person and the community. Other religions—that of the Sikhs and the Baha'is, to name two—also affirm God's presence in historical events.[2]

The historical study of religions essentially follows the methodology of modern historiography that developed in the nineteenth century. History is a scholarly discipline that examines the past critically, attempts to ascertain the facts of past events as accurately as possible, and, most important, interpret the causes, meanings, and implications of those facts. That religion—that is, all religions—is a historical phenomenon is obvious. But it is equally obvious that reducing religion to only the product of the historical development of certain social forces—as, for example, Marx would have it—does not do justice to a much more complex human reality. A more holistic understanding of religion is needed.

A discussion is now under way among historians about whether they are social scientists, humanities scholars, or both. The issue in question concerns the degree of objectivity that historians are capable of bringing to their task. It is easy to see the dangers when one reads histories of a certain time period written, say, by historians representing groups that were hostile to each other. Often, the interpretations of the events are at serious odds with one another: Many such historians simply justify their group's behavior. It was not at all uncommon for rival religious institutions to write their histories, extolling the behavior of their founders or major figures while maligning those of their enemies. Such histories also tend to emphasize exclusively the differences between the groups, rarely focusing on common features or similarities.

But truly scholarly historians try to guard against biases. Recognizing that no one can ever view reality except from a particular perspective, the serious historian nevertheless strives constantly to surface and neutralize his or her limitations. One of the benefits of such a competent examination, or reexamination, of the past is the possibility of avoiding destructive actions in the future. Carrying this concern further, it has not been uncommon in recent years for scholars from two or more religious traditions to attempt to work jointly on an inclusive common history.

So the tools of the historians were brought to bear upon the investigation of religions. Among the earliest results were Christian church histories and histories of Judaism. A large number of books, many of them comprising multiple volumes, were written that cover the entire history of the Christian church; others comprehensively cover some specific time period, institution, or life of an important person, or they record the history of one of the many branches of Christianity.

HISTORY OF RELIGIONS AS A TERM FOR THE SCHOLARLY STUDY OF RELIGION

The second use of the term *history of religions* came to be applied in the nineteenth century when scholars started to investigate religion in a "scientific"—that is, an "objective,"—manner. In German, that discipline was called *Religionswissenschaft*. Some English-speaking scholars used the term *science of religion,* but soon came to realize that the term had a narrower implication than the German word *Wissenschaft*. Eventually, they resorted to the term *history of religions,* with which they wanted to connote the intensive investigation of the many aspects of both ancient and contemporary religions, some of which were being discovered by Westerners at the time of this exploration. Today, a more inclusive term that may be preferable is the *scholarly study of religion.* It is more accurate than its predecessors, because it does not investigate religion using merely historical methods.

What was specific about the history of religions in this second meaning is that scholars became interested in exploring not merely their own or similar religious groups. Instead, they extended their research to all the religions they could find, and they tried to do so without viewing these religions explicitly from the perspective of their own religious convictions. To do this, they were forced into a dialectical engagement with the field that they studied and with the research methods they used. Their method led them to discover an increasing number of religious phenomena, some of which had not fit tidily into their previous notions of what religion is and is not. That, in turn, led them to broader and more inclusive ways to define religion, which influenced them to broaden the ways in which they studied these phenomena.

When the German Protestant theologian Friedrich Schleiermacher (1768–1834) explored religion as a "feeling of absolute dependence" in order to gain a better understanding of the Judeo-Christian heritage, he opened the door to a more universal study of religion than had been practiced in Europe. An even greater step forward was taken by another German scholar, Max Müller, who had collected a stupendous number of wisdom books, called *The Sacred Books of the East* (1879–1910), mostly from India and Japan. In focusing on the literary evidence left by the ancient East, he opened the way to the discovery of the enormous wealth of philosophical, theological, and spiritual concepts of non-Western religions. Some of those concepts were analogous to those known in Europe, but others were not. This led to a broadening of the concept of religion well beyond what had been recognized as religious. However, Müller neglected non-literary evidence. Other scholars, such as the Englishman James G. Frazer, followed an anthropological approach. Described in his multivolume *Sacred Bough,* this approach enormously expanded the understanding of the non-literary aspects of religious phenomena.

The scholars of the nineteenth and early twentieth centuries were curious particularly about the lives and teachings of the founders of religions (if a religion did have a founder)—or, at least, about the early stages of a religion. They were interested in whether the religion had holy scriptures, in who its major leaders were, in what developments took place and why, in whether the religion remained in one locality or spread to other countries, and in the changes that took place if the religion did spread and was acculturated elsewhere. They wanted to know about reforms, schisms, religious wars, reconciliations, interactions with other religions, and the present status of the religions in question.

In some instances, these early histories were biased or tendentious. Sometimes the historian used her or his own religion as a measuring stick, usually at the expense of the other religion. At other times, the historian put the emphasis only on those elements that were "exotic" or different. But increasingly, historians became aware of these unfortunate tendencies and attempted to correct them by consulting a larger number of experts from within the religious tradition and by trying to be more sympathetic to the authentic aims of the religion studied.

Of course, these historians needed to protect themselves against another common pitfall—namely, the temptation to write the kind of book that uncritically glorifies everything that the religion being studied has done. That is not history; it is propaganda, as is the writing of a mostly hostile account of a religion. A good historian of religion selects material so that the religion being studied is not unwarrantedly criticized, but, at the same time, unpleasant facts are not hidden or dressed up. This often dismays traditional followers of a religion, who would greatly prefer a book of praise, but the historical investigator must not succumb to the temptation to distort in either direction.

Soon, scholars became interested in distinguishing religions by type. They distinguished between living religions and extinct ones; between great historical religions, ancient and contemporary, and folk religions (sometimes classifying the latter as "primitive" or "primal" and the former as "high"); between religions that had founders and those that did not; between theistic and non-theistic religions and between polytheistic and monotheistic ones; between scriptural and non-scriptural religions; and so forth. The scholars themselves were often influenced by the intellectual tenor of the times and the prevalent interpretive views of the world. Thus, some of them espoused a theory that religions evolve from the simplest forms of animism to highly developed ethical monotheism. Others countered that there was an original monotheism, perhaps a universally held perennial wisdom, a pristine spirituality to be found best among the unspoiled natives of isolated lands, which gradually became debased and largely lost through cultural and historical developments. Some argued that the similarities in religious manifestations could be explained primarily through diffusion—namely, migrations of people and ideas.

The scholars of the first half of the twentieth century tended to produce comprehensive interpretive accounts of religions. This was followed, in the second half of the century by monographs that go into great detail about specific religious phenomena and often correct some of the unwarranted generalizations of the previous generation. One wonders whether the time has come to make new attempts to synthesize the enormous amount of discovered data into a more comprehensive magnum opus.

By now, a vast number of histories of religions (according to both the first and second meaning of the term) have been written and are studied on many levels in schools and universities. Sometimes, these histories include a very large number of religions. They are usually called "religions of the world," "religions of humankind," "surveys of religions," or some such title. An increasing number of institutions have added survey or general introductory courses on the history of religions to their curriculum.

Some scholars distinguish *history of religions* from *history of religion*. By the latter, they usually mean the history of the early stages of religion, usually prior to the development of the historical religions (e.g., animism, spiritism, mana). No single theory or interpretation of how religions came into existence and changed holds a monopoly in these studies.

And, of course, a large number of books provide more focused histories: of only a single religion (e.g., of Buddhism, Hinduism, Confucianism); of a shorter time period (e.g., the history of Islam during the Abbasid period or the history of Ryobu Shinto); of a branch of a religion (e.g., the history of Zen Buddhism); or of a person (e.g., Chuang Tzu, Guru Nanak, or Moses). The history of religions is one of the most extensive scholarly fields, and the material that has been collected is incredibly vast.

4   Scriptural Studies

NOT ALL RELIGIONS have sacred scriptures, but many do. Some of them have a large number of documents considered sacred by the adherents. In most instances, these scriptures originally took oral form and were transmitted by word of mouth, sometimes for generations. Only later were they committed to writing. Then they were meticulously copied by scribes and other learned members of the religion and often memorized by various adherents. Since it is believed that such holy writings have insights of enormous or even decisive significance for the life of the followers, they had to be applied to concrete situations. This required interpretations as to the meaning of the text. The study of the text and its meaning belong to the oldest known form of religious scholarship.

For instance, young Hindu students would be taught by their guru (teacher) to memorize the *Rig Veda*, the Sanskrit text of one of Hinduism's earliest holy scripture, with all the proper inflections and tones used to recite or chant the various passages; they were then taught the meaning of the text, on what occasions it was to be used, and so forth. A similar procedure was used in Judaism with the transmission of the text by scribes, priests, or rabbis; the latter, especially, created traditions of interpretations of the text as it was to be applied to concrete situations.

TRADITIONAL METHODS OF INTERPRETATION

There were basically two ancient methods of interpretation, which are still widely used by many religious people and leaders: the *literal* and the *allegorical*.

Following the *literal* method meant that the reader or listener would simply take the meaning of the words as commonly understood at the time that the interpretation was done. No attempt was made to discover either the real meaning as intended by the author or some metaphorical use of language; generally, the interpreter was satisfied that what met the eye was the real meaning of the text.

Despite its prevalence in at least some religious traditions, a literal interpretation can cause grave difficulties for religious communities. It is weak in interpreting poetry and mythology or any kind of parabolic or metaphorical use of language. Too frequently, the result is that the interpreter reads into the text a meaning that is desired, particularly through a method such as cross-referencing—that is, interpreting the meaning of one text by using another that might well be historically much later in origin. It is also evident that scriptural literalists tend to be very much at odds with one another, depending on how much weight they give to one segment or another of the scripture, which, they maintain is an unchanging, divine text, the divine word. Generally, literal interpretation has also tended to result in a very harshly opinionated hardening of lines, resulting in mutual condemnations and excommunications.

The *allegorical* interpretation method proceeded from the assumption that in addition to the surface, evident meaning of the text there is also a deeper, often hidden meaning, or even several layers of meaning, of the text—that is, people, things, and events in the text stand in symbolic fashion for something else. Sometimes very sophisticated approaches were developed in order to get at the deeper meaning, which, it was said, eluded the casual reader. Mystics of nearly all religious traditions have relished this allegorical approach. For instance, various Islamic Sufi orders have the tradition by which the shaykh, or teacher of the order, teaches the followers increasingly deeper meanings of the text, which are believed to be inaccessible to the uninitiated.

A number of very influential groups and individuals of the various traditions were quite fond of the allegorical method (e.g., the Jewish *Kabbalah,* the Gnostics, and St. Augustine). For example, both the Rabbis and the Christian Fathers interpreted the Hebrew scriptural text of the Song of Songs not as a sensuous wedding poem (which it was), but as an allegory of the love of God (the bridegroom) for God's people (identified as Israel or the Christian Church, depending on whether the allegorist was Jewish or Christian).

The allegorical method is helpful when dealing with an intended allegory as, for example, when Jesus said, "If your eye offends you, pluck it out!" But it distorts the meaning of those texts meant to be taken in a straightforward fashion. Then the allegorical method can result in a radical departure from the intended meaning of the text.

The Christian Middle Ages specified and gave names to two further ways to understand a sacred text, though Christians were surely not the first or only ones to use them: the *anagogical* and the *tropological* understanding of a text. Both understandings had more to do with the contemporary reader of the sacred text than with the author's intended meaning in the text's original context.

The *anagogical* (from the Greek, *to lead up*) meaning is the higher spiritual meaning of the text as understood and applied by the contemporary reader. The *tropological* (from the Greek, *the transferred meaning*) meaning is the moral meaning of the text as understood and applied by the contemporary reader. Obviously, if a sacred text is to have any influence on later people's lives, its significance will have to be applied to the contemporary situation, and that is what these two methods of interpretation attempted to do. The danger involved in them is that the original text can be gravely distorted in meaning. Instead of being an *exegesis* (from the Greek, *to lead out*), such a method of interpretation can very easily become an *eisegesis* (from the Greek, *to lead in*)—in other words, instead of being a drawing out of the meaning in the text it can easily become a reading in of an extraneous meaning that is not at all present.

MODERN SCHOLARLY METHODS OF INTERPRETATION

During the time of the Renaissance in Europe (from the fourteenth century onward), interest in the classical Roman and Greek heritage emerged. This interest was later enlarged to include the heritage of Egypt and Mesopotamia, and was further expanded after the sixteenth-century Age of Discovery to take in the heritage of India and China, and so on. The study of the ancient languages, especially Greek and Hebrew, was reinvigorated. The study of great epics such as the *Iliad* and *Odyssey* were undertaken, and questions were raised, such as whether the reputed author of these great legendary epics, Homer, was the real author or was the only author of these works.

In the study of the great ancient Near Eastern and Mediterranean classics, scholars developed both literary and philosophical methods to help resolve the puzzles attending the origin and meaning of these texts.

These secular methods were tested and found reliable, and were later, with initial reluctance or even serious opposition, applied to the holy scriptures of Judaism and Christianity.

The opposition was due to a twofold fear: first, that the "ecclesiastical" monopoly (of bishops, priests, ministers, and rabbis) would be eroded, leading to the weakening of their prerogatives, and second, applying a secular methodology to such lofty, divinely inspired writings would diminish the holy quality of the text. Hence, the opposition to the use of such critical methods by the early interpreters (starting in the seventeenth century) was enormous, leading to occasional excommunication of those who espoused such methods (some of whom were clergy themselves), suppression of their writings, and, consequently, fear on part of the researchers.

Textual Criticism

The method that was most quickly accepted by a very wide spectrum of people, called *textual criticism,* is an attempt to discover and make use of the earliest possible manuscripts of an ancient text as the basis for translations into the modern idiom. It provides the best readings of all available manuscripts in different languages and dating from different time periods, showing that sometimes a number of versions of the ancient text were in circulation at the same time, and that in some instances significant differences, such as additions, new endings, deletions, and variant segments, existed among them. What textual critics endeavor to do is ascertain which text is closest to the original, because in most instances, the original is no longer available. (If the original version had been preserved or found, after all, there would be no need for textual criticism.) Using these methods, it is possible today to detect both accidental mistakes as well as deliberate, intentional additions by later generations of transmitters of the text.

The time of discovery of ancient manuscripts is far from over: Every so often, ancient manuscripts of previously known texts, or even unknown ancient texts, are discovered. Relatively recent examples would include the Dead Sea Scrolls, the Nag Hammadi Library, and the Gnostic Gospels, all of which date from the first and second centuries of the Common Era. Because of the benefit gained by new studies in comparative linguistics and the grammar and rules of the ancient languages, the availability of more accurate texts, and, as a result, a better understanding of what the text actually says, most of the present texts of holy scriptures are actually more reliable than those used centuries or even decades ago. Further, today's scholars often provide very helpful textual notes that inform the reader about the background of sacred texts, variant meanings of words, and the likely meaning of difficult passages.

Historical Criticism

Textual criticism does not, however, venture into the interpretation of the meaning of the text. For this, other critical methods were developed. The overall name for the various critical[1] methods is *historical–literary criticism*. As the name suggest, this critical method consists of two components that are most effectively used in conjunction.

Historical criticism studies the historical circumstances that surrounded the writing of the text, but also places under historical scrutiny the claims of the content of the text. This means that a careful study is undertaken of the conditions existing at the time that the text was written, which helps provide a more accurate sense of why and when the author was writing. Many references in the text—to wars, historical figures, celebrations, tensions, and so forth—become much clearer when one knows the circumstances surrounding the text's writing. Likewise, the text itself starts making much more sense when additional, extra-textual information is brought to bear that can elucidate more oblique references in the text itself. Thus, while the text itself can often be the source of information about the history of a period, other information gained through archeology and history of the period to which the text refers can clarify the meaning of the text.

Of course, historical data will at times confirm the information of the text, but sometimes it will not. Thus, it has been discovered that some sacred texts were written long after the events that they describe took place, by which time the actual events had become blurred or confused. Occasionally, such errors were committed deliberately by the author, who may have wanted to convey to the readers that the actual focus of the writing is not on a distant past but on a more recent past. Or, in some instances, a great figure of the past may have been romanticized in retrospect and described only heroically, while earlier narratives about the same person also reflect the weakness of the hero—a tendency known in nearly all romanticized recollections of the past. So it is the task of history to describe the events as nearly accurately as possible, avoiding the embellishments added by the author.

It should be noted that there is a great difference between how ancient historians recorded the past and modern scholarly historians practice their craft. Lawrence Boadt provided the following comparison chart:

A COMPARISON OF ANCIENT AND MODERN METHODS
OF RECORDING HISTORICAL EVENTS

Ancient Israelite Historian

1) Records the traditions of the tribe or nation as they interpret them.
2) Uses oral sources, with few written records or lists.
3) Often includes several parallel versions of the same story.
4) Does not have much exact information of dates and places, and so gives rough approximations.
5) Relies strongly on fixed types of literary descriptions or motifs that can be applied to all similar situations.
6) Uses a common-sense approach to describing human behavior and does not guarantee every fact.
7) Uses past history to explain convictions for the present time or for a particular point of view.

Modern Scientific Historian

1) Attempts to reconstruct past events objectively and accurately.
2) Relies on documents and written records almost exclusively.
3) Sorts out the conflicting accounts in order to find the single original one.
4) Carefully searches out the correct chronology of events.
5) Seeks to get behind literary genres and narrative modes to find out what really happened.
6) Uses all the critical tools and means of information to check sources and their claims.
7) Writes history without special bias or undue emphasis towards only one side of the picture.[2]

Literary Criticism

Literary criticism consist of a series of methods that help determine the origin (author, date, place), purpose, composition, style, plan of writing, and content of a specific text. These methods include source, form, redaction, sociological, audience, hermeneutical, and rhetorical criticism.

SOURCE CRITICISM.   Source criticism is one of the oldest critical approaches. It is a tool by which scholars are able to decipher whether there are earlier written documents upon which the present text was based and how and when a text was composed. It has been discovered that in many instances, the version of a text that survived was composed from several earlier sources, which the last author or editor wove together. In the ancient past, it was not customary to acknowledge the existence of previous sources or their authorship. Source criticism makes it possible to reconstruct hypothetically the process of composition, separate the different sources, and date them (though authorship usually remains anonymous). The need for source criticism arose when it became evident that given texts contained contradictory styles of writing and data or repetitions appearing side by side.

Source criticism of the Torah (or Pentateuch) of the Bible can be used as an example. According to tradition, all five of the Torah's books were written by Moses. But a number of problems cast doubt on the accuracy of that claim. There were inconsistencies in the narratives, chronological problems, and repetitions (the so-called doublets and triplets) in which the same story recurred but in modified versions, as well as alternate uses of the divine name and changes in the vocabulary and theological conceptions. These had to be accounted for. In the nineteenth century, Karl Graf and Julius Wellhausen forwarded a hypothesis that the Torah consisted of the editions of four major sources—the Yahwist, Elohist, Deuteronomist, and Priestly—committed to writing over a span of about five hundred years. This hypothesis has been refined and modified by numerous later scholars, but it has stood the test of time through repeated investigation.

A similar investigation has been done of the New Testament, particularly the synoptic gospels of Mark, Luke, and Matthew. A hypothesis positing four different sources accounts for both the similarities and differences among the synoptic gospels and has been found helpful in explaining this phenomenon.

FORM CRITICISM.   As scholarly investigations continued, it became obvious that the nature of ancient textual transmission differed from the contemporary and that much more attention needed to be paid to the process of oral transmission. It became obvious that for much recorded ancient literature, an entire community, rather than a very gifted single author, created a form of literature typical to a given setting in life. This has led to the creation of *form criticism.*

Form critics study the customary forms in which content is packaged. Messages come in distinct forms—for example, a business letter differs from a love letter, which, in turn, differs from a vacation greeting sent to friends. Although oral tradition does not change rapidly, scholars have discerned some rules of transmitting messages on the oral stage—namely, what kinds of deletions and accretions or expansions of the original text were likely to take place over a period of time. Thus, they have been able to separate the core of the message closest to the original pronouncement from later elaborations. Form critics therefore have been able to distinguish among miracle stories, parables, pronouncements, speeches, laws, short stories, myths, legends, and so forth. It is essential that one distinguish the form in which a message is cast in order to understand the message accurately.

Form critics have pointed out that the ancients used mythological forms to convey profound truths and values, and that consequently those ancient texts will be completely misunderstood if they are interpreted in a literal manner. By de-mythologizing the content, form critics have led the attempt to figure out for contemporaries the profound messages cast in ancient mythological language. Such processes have helped us understand that myths are not lies or simply a primitive understanding of phenomena by people who had no scientific knowledge, as customarily has been believed since the eighteenth-century European Enlightenment. Instead, we have become aware that mythological language is sometimes the most appropriate vehicle for transmitting profound insights that may be as true today as they were at the time that the myth was created.

Appreciation of mythology has grown so substantially that many scholars even describe humanity as a myth-making species. This insight has been so valuable that many scholars maintain that one cannot merely de-mythologize, but must, of necessity, re-mythologize an ancient myth into contemporary idiom. It is obvious, though, that myths should not be interpreted literally if one does not want to destroy their message. Rather, myths need to be "broken"—that is, the symbolic nature of the myth must be recognized, and symbol must not be made identical with the reality that it represents and to which it points. As noted earlier, using Ricoeur's analysis and terminology, the reader must mature from the level of first naivete, wherein the symbol may be misunderstood literally, to the level of second naivete, wherein the symbol is affirmed as symbolic.

Form critics usually follow four steps, according to Boadt:

1) Define the unit that forms a piece of literature.
2) Name the form of the unit.
3) Describe the original context in which the literary unit is created, and
4) Identify its function and purpose, both in its original context as well as within the present larger document.[3]

Although form criticism is interested in tracing the entire development of a text, most scholars were preoccupied with the earliest oral stages and tended to neglect the development of the material into a written form.

REDACTION CRITICISM.   Out of the recognition that the surviving form of a text was not composed by the original author but someone who played mostly an editorial role emerged *redaction criticism,* or transmission or tradition history. (The term *redactor* simply means editor.) Redaction criticism points out that the editors were not merely collectors of more ancient sources; rather, they were selectors and arrangers of the material according to some consistent internal principle that they promoted in their final work. Such editors had a distinct purpose and audience in mind. When one becomes aware of the editor's key motif, it is easier to interpret the different segments of the text, because they tend to make sense as part of the whole. Hence, one sees the different segments of the text not in isolation, but as part of an organic whole intended by the editor.

Redaction criticism was very helpful, for example, in the study of the Gospels in the New Testament as scholars pondered the specific nature of the narrative used by each of the Gospel writers, who, indeed, were editors of materials preserved for a generation or two by the early Christian community. When one understands which key insights, for instance, the author–editor of the *Gospel According to Matthew* tried to communicate to the distinctly Jewish–Christian community he was addressing, it becomes much easier to understand the nature and function of the various parts of the narrative, as well as the organizing principle he used to present the material. For example, redaction criticism helps shed light on why in Matthew's Gospel Jesus delivers "The Sermon on the Mount," whereas Luke's Gospel has it as "The Sermon on the Plain." For Matthew's very Jewish readership, Jesus should appear as the new Moses delivering the new "law" as from *Mount* Sinai. For Luke's more Hellenized readership, this was apparently not an important parallel to draw.

SOCIOLOGICAL CRITICISM.   *Sociological criticism* attempts to discern the social position and striving of the writer and the community for whom he is writing. It makes a difference in understanding a document if one discovers that the author represented a people who were oppressed and exploited rather than a people who lived in comfort and control of their destiny. Questions such as these are raised: Does the writing attempt to soothe the wounds of a community, or is it trying to stir them to attempt to change their situation? Has the writing been used to condone and justify a specific social system and guide a community to passive acceptance of injustices, or does the writing express radical rejection of patterns of injustice and oppression? Thus, the notion of the "hermeneutics of suspicion" was introduced (*hermeneutics* is from the Greek, *interpretation*)—that is, an unwillingness to accept automatically the surface meaning and motivation; rather, one looks for the underlying, "real" meaning and interpretation. For example, that the Gospel writers, doing their work shortly after the Roman destruction of Jerusalem, were trying to "get along" with the Romans clarifies why the Roman authority in Jerusalem, Pontius Pilate, is described in the Gospels so much more benignly than in non-Christian documents.

AUDIENCE CRITICISM.   *Audience criticism* asks the question: What did the terms, images, and other elements used in a document mean to the "audience" for whom the document was intended? The answer to that question can make a huge difference in understanding the text. For example, Jesus is referred to as the "son of God" in the Gospels. Audience criticism asks whether the term *son of God* was intended the way Hellenistic Gentiles would have understood it—that is, as a supernatural being. Or was it intended as Jews and those under Jewish influence would have understood it—that is, as someone who lived according to God's will, as the Jew Jesus said: "That you may become sons of your Father in heaven" (Mt 5:45).

Because the Gospels were written almost entirely for Jews or those attracted to Judaism (for everywhere Paul, Barnabas, and other missionaries went to preach the "Good News of Jesus," as the term *gospel* means, they always went to the synagogues of the Jews), the correct answer here obviously is that the reference to Jesus as the "son of God" was understood (by the Jewish audience) in the Jewish manner, as someone who lived according to God's will, and not in the Hellenistic manner, as a supernatural being.

HERMENEUTICS.   *Hermeneutics* is the science of interpreting a text so it can be applied to the contemporary situation. Thus, it raises the issue of the relevance of a text for a contemporary religious community or individual. Or, as Roger Schmidt put it: "Hermeneutics is the science of interpretation that is concerned not only with drawing out the meaning of a text (exegesis) but also with the formulation and criticism of the methodologies operative in the interpretative process."[4] Hermeneutics, then, are the rules guiding the interpretation of a received message, applying it to the contemporary reader. The question is not whether interpretation is needed. Human beings constantly interpret everything they are exposed to in order to make sense of the received communication. Thus, there is only a choice between better or worse and appropriate or inappropriate interpretations, because there is no such thing as an uninterpreted communication or knowledge.

RHETORICAL CRITICISM.   In *rhetorical criticism,* the emphasis is on the impact that the rhetorical and artistic elements of the entire writing makes on the reader. The emphasis is also on appreciating the imagination of the author and the value and harmony displayed by the entire work.

Since the late 1980s, under the influence of contemporary literary–scholarly hypotheses (deconstructionism), a new trend has emerged that, unlike the previous literary hypotheses, shows little or no interest in the intentions of the original author or authors. Rather, it places the entire stress on how the reader receives the work. The question is posed: What kind of reactions does the work evoke in the specific reader? In some ways, this method is related to hermeneutics, but perhaps even more so it harks back to the medieval anagogical and tropological methods, and hence runs the same risk that they did of becoming eisegesis. For should rhetorical criticism be used without the other, earlier literary and historical scholarly methods, there is the possibility, even the grave danger, that entirely arbitrary meanings will be read into a text.

Although all of these critical methods of trying to understand the meaning of the scriptures of a religion for the most part have been worked out on biblical material, both Jewish and Christian, they are largely applicable to Muslim, Hindu, Buddhist, and other scriptures, as well. They will help both the follower of a religion and an outsider understand the scripture of a religion better. Exactly how that scripture will then be made to come alive in the life of a believer depends on the use of the liturgical, spiritual, pastoral, and other resources of the believer and the believer's tradition and community.

5   Evolution in Religion

THE EVOLUTION OF RELIGION

IN 1964, Robert Bellah published a germinal essay entitled "Religious Evolution."[1] In it, he noted that although sociology in general, and the sociology of religion in particular, began with a strong evolutionary approach, first under the impetus of the grandfathers of sociology Auguste Comte and Herbert Spencer and continuing through Emil Durkheim and Max Weber, by the 1920s the evolutionary wave "was in full retreat both in the general field of the science of religion [*Religionswissenschaft*] and in the sociology of religion in particular." In fact, Bellah's own teacher, Talcott Parsons, declared in 1937: Spencer is dead![2] A quarter-century later, Bellah returned to the earlier evolutionary understanding of religion, though with the valid criticisms raised against that approach taken into account.

Bellah defines evolution as a process of increasing differentiation and complexification of organization that provides a social system—or whatever is in question—with a greater capacity to adapt to its environment, thereby making it more autonomous in relation to that environment. In this, he is like many other thinkers, such as the contemporary anthropologist Mary Douglas, who wrote that we must "recognize the nature of historical progress and the nature of primitive and of modern society. Progress means differentiation. Thus primitive means undifferentiated; modern means differentiated."[3] For Bellah, however, evolution is not inevitable or irreversible. Nor does it have to follow a single particular course; nor does he assume that simple forms cannot prosper and survive alongside more complex forms. For him, evolution implies nothing metaphysical. It is "the simple empirical generalization that more complex forms develop from less complex forms."[4]

Bellah outlines five major stages in the evolution of religion: 1) Primitive Religion, 2) Archaic Religion, 3) Historic Religion, 4) Early Modern Religion, and 5) Modern Religion. He is careful to point out that this schema is that of a typology "of the most generally observable historical regularities," whereas in historical fact, there will be many overlaps, foreshadowing of later developments, and even regressions. "And of course," he wrote, "no stage is ever completely abandoned; all earlier stages continue to coexist with and often within later ones."

Briefly, the characteristics of Bellah's stages are as follows:

Primitive Religion

As Bellah and other scholars note, religion even of the simplest sort is an evolutionary advance. Animals and pre-religious men and women could only passively endure suffering or other limitations. "But religious man can to some extent 'transcend and dominate' them through his capacity for symbolization and thus attain a degree of freedom."

Primitive religion has three major features. First, the mythical world is very closely related to the specifics of the actual world; the sacred and the profane are largely one.[5] There is no separate religious organization; rather, "Church and society are one."

The second feature, related to the extreme specificity of the mythical material, is the fluidity of its organization. Precisely the fluidity and flexibility of primitive religion, however, is a barrier to radical innovation. Primitive religion gives little leverage from which to change the world, for any evidence that is apparently contrary to the myth is simply worked into the adjusted myth—that is, "Particular myths and ceremonies are in a process of constant revision and alteration."

Third, primitive religious action is characterized not by worship of a transcendent or sacrifice to a divinity, but "by identification, 'participation', acting-out." Just as the symbol system of primitive religion is myth par excellence, so also primitive religious action is ritual par excellence. "In the ritual the participants become identified with the mythical beings they represent."

Archaic Religion

What Bellah terms *archaic religion* (encompassing much that other scholars often classify as primitive religion—for example, the earliest religious systems of the ancient Middle East, India, and China, and many of the religions of Africa and Polynesia) is, in most categories, simply a further development and complexification of primitive religion. The ritual and myth of the latter is continued in the former, but it is far more systematized and developed. There is still only one world, one reality with gods dominating. That single world, however, is far more differentiated in archaic religion than in primitive religion, especially in archaic religions's hierarchies of huge arrays of gods and goddesses.

In archaic religion, religious action is reflected in cult "in which the distinction between men as subjects and gods as objects is much more definite than in primitive religion." As this distinction grows, the possibility for the individual to shape her or his own religious purpose increases, but, at the same time, so does the uncertainty of the divine response. Hence, through the more differentiated form of religious action in archaic religion, "a new degree of freedom as well as an increased burden of anxiety enters the relations between man and the ultimate conditions of his existence."

Even so, Bellah notes that the most significant limitation on archaic religious organizations was "the failure to develop differentiated religious collectivities including adherents as well as priests." The individual and society were still understood as united in a natural–divine cosmos, and traditional social structures and practices were thought to be grounded in a divinely established cosmic order. Social conformity was reinforced by religious sanction: Do this or avoid that because the gods say so.

Historic Religion

What Bellah refers to as *historic religion* are the great world religions that arose in the first millennium B.C.E.: Confucianism, Taoism, Hinduism, Buddhism, Zoroastrianism, Judaism, Christianity, Greek philosophy. This is the same period that the German psychologist and philosopher Karl Jaspers (1883–1969) refers to as the "Axial Period." (More on that later.)

Bellah notes a major shift in the attitude toward the world exhibited by the historic religions. Whereas in primitive religion there is practically no distance between human beings and the community and the world around them—men and women understand themselves solely as part of the community, of nature—in historic religion a transcendent world beyond this one is discerned. The transcendent world is seen as so vastly superior to this world that one learns to disdain this world, to distance oneself from it, in order to attain the transcendent world. This breaking with the cosmological unity of the primitive and archaic stages, and the holding of a common transcendentalism, makes all of the historic religions dualistic in the sense that there are two overarching realities: the this-worldly and the otherworldly, or transcendental.

Further, this superior transcendent world is essentially spiritual, and hence must be sought spiritually, which means interiorly. Thus, what is sought is not so much to be in harmony with the society and world about oneself, as in primitive religion, or to placate the gods through sacrifice, as in archaic religion. Rather, what is sought is "salvation" from "a basic flaw far more serious than those conceived of by earlier religions," whether "clinging" (*tanha*) to what is essentially fleeting (*anicca*)—namely, this world, in Buddhism; "ignorance" of ultimate reality in Hinduism (*avidya*) and Socratic religion (*agnoia*); or a turning away from God (*hamartia*, sin) in Judaism.

For the first time it is possible to conceive of humanity as such. The great historic religions promise humans that they can understand the fundamental structure of reality and, through salvation, participate actively in it. Of course, while the opportunity is far greater than before, so is the risk of failure. For the masses, the new dualism is "expressed in the difference between this world and the life after death. Religious concern, focused on this life in primitive and archaic religions, now tends to focus on life in the other realm," the otherworldly reality. Thus "the religious goal of salvation (or enlightenment, release and so forth) is for the first time the central religious preoccupation."

The historic religions all engage in a great "de-mythologization" vis-à-vis the archaic religions—that is, recognizing that the great religious myths are just that, symbolic stories rather than historical descriptions. Think of Socrates and his fate for challenging the ancient gods and assumptions (death by poison), or the priests of Baal when faced with the prophet of Yahweh Elijah (death by fire). At the same time, of course, all of the historic religions are weighted with the mortgages of their past in archaic religion, as Erich Voegelin puts it. Elements of that earlier cosmology are mixed in with the transcendental claims of the historic religions: for example, the "heavenly court" rather than the monotheistic single God reflected in the fifth-century priestly story of creation in Genesis 1:26, "Let *us* make humanity in *our* image."

With historic religion a religious leadership class also develops that is separate from the political leadership class. Thus, although a major function of religion has been, and continues in historic religion to be, the legitimation and reinforcement of the existing social order, the rise of the separate religious elite now offers the possibility of conflict with the political leadership and of social change. One thinks of the confrontations between the Hebrew prophet and the king, the Islamic ulama and the sultan, the pope and the emperor, the Confucian scholar–official and the emperor. There were now "higher" standards by which the political leaders were to be judged. "Religion, then, provided the ideology and social cohesion for many rebellions and reform movements in the historic civilizations. and consequently played a more dynamic . . . role in social change than had previously been possible."

Early Modern Religion

When speaking of *early modern religion,* Bellah refers to developments within Christendom, and the sixteenth-century Protestant Reformation in particular. The dualism of the historic religions remains part of early modern religion, but this duality takes on a new meaning as a result of the direct confrontation of the two realms: secular and spiritual. "Under the new circumstances salvation is not to be found in any kind of withdrawal from the world but in the midst of worldly activities." (One can likewise find similar developments in other religions, as for example in the Zen Buddhist notion that "Nirvana is in samsara"—salvation is found in the everyday.)

In the early modern state, religious action came to be understood as identical with the whole of life. The rejection of this world for the sake of the superior world in the next, as in the historic religions, was no longer felt to be necessary. Human life was seen as indeed ethically ambiguous, but salvation, based on faith, was worked through in the everyday of this world.

In fact, Bellah notes, the other historic religions—notably, Islam, Buddhism, Taoism, and Confucianism—developed similar reform movements of the early-modern-religion sort. However, he rightly observes that "the Protestant Reformation is the only attempt that was successfully institutionalized," and then comments that "religious movements of early modern type may be emerging in a number of the great traditions today." (More about that later, as Bellah was writing in 1968.)

Early modern religion in the form of the Protestant Reformation, especially the Calvinist version, also broke with the hierarchical structure of religion. The historic religions had established a two-class leadership system, a religious class differentiated from the secular. Salvation was attainable mainly through the religious-leader class (priests, monks, nuns). In the Protestant Reformation, this system in which salvation was mediated through the religious leader was broken through with the notion of the "priesthood of all believers." This provided a further increase in individual freedom.

Virtually all of the early Protestant experiments in self-governance tended to be restrictive, even dictatorial. Nevertheless, the direction was set toward a "self-revising social order expressed in a voluntaristic and democratic society." As the late-eighteenth-century Enlightenment drew near, an ever-increasing democratization manifested itself in religion and society. The Christian religion—in many instances, the Catholic as well as the Protestant form—fostered and participated in the embrace of this world, freedom and democracy, of especially the German version of the Enlightenment, the *Aufklärung*.[6]

Modern Religion

Bellah speaks of *modern religion* as flowing from the Enlightenment, when "the entire modern analysis of religion, including much of the most important recent theology ... has been forced to ground religion in the structure of the human situation itself." He stresses that the classic dualism—the sacred and the secular, with the former preferred—of the historic religions is definitely rejected. However, the dual structure is not rejected in favor of a return to a primitive monism. "It is not that a single world has replaced a double one but that infinitely multiplex one has replaced the simple duplex structure."

Humanity—or, at least, a significant portion of intellectuals since the nineteenth century—has come to learn more and more about why we think the way we do. Along with the advances in the philosophy of how we come to know things, the birth of the social sciences in the broad sense—history, sociology, anthropology, psychology, economics—has led humanity to a new stage of consciousness.

The historic religions discovered the self—as differentiated from nature. Early modern religion discovered a doctrinal ground on which to base the acceptance of the self in all its concrete moral ambiguity—have faith and work through salvation in the everyday. "Modern religion is beginning to understand the laws of the self's own existence and so to help man take responsibility for his own fate."

The religious symbols in modern religion are not being simply jetti-soned. Rather, they will increasingly be kept and understood as sym-bols. This is what Riceour has called the "second naivete." For exam-ple, the young child believes empirically that Santa Claus exists; this is the stage of naivete (to be as one is when born, *natus*). Then, at a cer-tain age, the child discovers that Santa does not really exist; this is the stage of rejection. When the child later has her or his own child, she or he may decide that the real meaning of Santa Claus is the spirit of gra-tuitous giving for the sake of others, and that this is a good thing to pass on to the next generation. Therefore, for the new parent, Santa Claus exists again, but this time as symbol whose existence is much more important than the earlier presumed empirical one. This is the stage of second naivete.

Religious action in modern religion is really a furtherance of what started in early modern religion—namely, an ethics that increasingly is based on our human reality rather than on a religious orthodoxy. In short, reason and human experience become increasingly important ethical guides. However, as the nineteenth and twentieth centuries wore on, that "human reason" became ever more complex, absorbing what has come to be known as the "hermeneutics of suspicion." These intel-lectual tools helped us to see the forces at play under the surface expla-nations of things—such as economics, gender, social position, psycho-logical needs, use and misuse of language, and other forces.

INTERIM CONCLUSION

Primitive and archaic religions' "naive" acceptance of the world can largely be explained as the only possible response to a reality that so invaded the self that men and women at that stage of development of consciousness could think of themselves and nature only as one reality. The wave of rejection by the historic religions of this world in favor of a transcendent one was a necessary move for humanity to become aware of its own self as distinct from the world around it. Early modern reli-gion then made it possible to maintain the centered self "without deny-ing the multifold empirical reality and so made world rejection in the classical sense unnecessary." In modern religion, increasing knowledge of why humans and the world exist the way they do "has opened up almost unlimited new directions of exploration and development."

Here Bellah rejects—rightly, we believe—a pessimistic characterization of modernity: "The analysis of modern man as secular, materialistic, dehumanized and in the deepest sense areligious seems to me fundamentally misguided." Rather, Bellah, and we, see the present situation as one of great opportunity: "The very situation that has been characterized as one of the collapse of meaning and the failure of moral standards can also, and I would argue more fruitfully, be viewed as one offering unprecedented opportunities for creative innovation in every sphere of human action."

In conclusion, human freedom is at the heart of the evolution of religion and human consciousness. At each stage, "the freedom of personality and society has increased relative to the environing conditions." Bellah clearly sees that the fundamental change leading to the increase of human freedom is that "at each successive stage the relation of man to the conditions of his existence has been *conceived* as more complex, more open and more subject to change and development" (italics added). It is the change in *consciousness,* the way humans see and understand themselves and everything around them, that is the locomotive that draws the train of history.

Marx had it backward. It is not the external economic realities that determine human history, but the consciousness of men and women that determine economics, and everything else. One must ask why, for example, West Germany vastly outproduced East Germany during the Cold War, or why South Korea outproduce North Korea during the same period, or why the mountainous islands called Japan outproduced resource-rich China. The answer lies not in the physical or economic external realities, but in the minds of the people. In the first cases in each of these pairs, the people "conceived [their existence] as more complex, more open and more subject to change and development." Fundamentally, it is minds, not strong backs, that create wealth.

THE FURTHER DEVELOPMENT OF EVOLUTIONARY THOUGHT

The Axial Period

A half-century ago, the German psychologist and philosopher Karl Jaspers pointed out the significance of this phenomenon in his book *The Origin and Goal of History.*[7] He called the period from 800–200 B.C.E. the "Axial Period"[8] because "it gave birth to everything which, since then, man has been able to be." It is in this period "that we meet with the most deepcut dividing line in history. Man, as we know him today, came into being. For short, we may style this the 'Axial Period.'" Although the leaders who effected this change were philosophers and religious teachers, the change was so radical that it affected all aspects of culture, for it transformed consciousness itself. It was within the horizons of this form of consciousness that the great civilizations of Asia, the Middle East, and Europe developed. Although many developments occurred within these horizons through the subsequent centuries, the horizons themselves did not change. It was this form of consciousness that spread to other regions through migration and exploration, thus becoming the dominant, though not exclusive, form of consciousness in the world. To this day, whether we are born and raised in the culture of China, India, Europe, or the Americas, we bear the structure of consciousness that was shaped in this Axial Period.

What is this structure of consciousness and how does it differ from pre-Axial consciousness? Much as Bellah pointed out a score of years later, Jaspers noted that prior to the Axial Period, the dominant form of consciousness was cosmic, collective, tribal, mythic, and ritualistic. This is the characteristic form of consciousness of primal peoples. It is true that between these traditional cultures and the Axial Period great empires emerged in Egypt, China, and Mesopotamia, but they did not yet produce the full consciousness of the Axial Period.

The consciousness of the tribal cultures was intimately related to the cosmos and to the fertility cycles of nature. Thus, a rich and creative harmony was established between primal peoples and the world of nature, a harmony that was explored, expressed, and celebrated in myth and ritual. Just as primal peoples felt themselves part of nature, so they experienced themselves as part of the tribe. It was precisely the web of interrelationships within the tribe that sustained them psychologically, energizing all aspects of their lives. Separation from the tribe threatened them with death—not only physical, but also psychological. However, their relation to the collectivity often did not extend beyond their own tribe, for they often looked on other tribes as hostile. Yet within their own tribe they felt organically related to the group as a whole, to the lifecycles of birth and death and to nature and the cosmos.

The Axial Period ushered in a radically new form of consciousness. Whereas primal consciousness was tribal, Axial consciousness was individual. "Know thyself" became the watchwords of Greece; the Hindu Upanishads identified the *atman,* the transcendent center of the self. The Buddha charted the way of individual enlightenment; the Jewish prophets awakened individual moral responsibility. This sense of individual identity, as distinct from the tribe and from nature, is the most characteristic mark of Axial consciousness. From this characteristic flow other characteristics: consciousness that is self-reflective and analytic and that can be applied to nature in the form of scientific theories; to society in the form of social critique; to knowledge in the form of philosophy; and to religion in the form of mapping an individual spiritual journey. This self-reflective, analytic, critical consciousness stood in sharp contrast to primal mythic and ritualistic consciousness. When self-reflective *logos* emerged in the Axial Period, it tended to oppose the traditional *mythos.* Of course, mythic and ritualistic forms of consciousness survive in the post-Axial Period even to this day, but they are often submerged, surfacing chiefly in dreams, literature, and art.

A Radically New Age

Let us fast-forward our reflections to the more recent past. Earlier in the twentieth century, a number of thinkers, with a great display of scholarship and historical–sociological analysis, predicted the impending demise of Western civilization. After World War I, in 1922, Oswald Spengler wrote his widely acclaimed book, *The Decline of the West.*[9] After the beginning of World War II, in 1941, Pitirim A. Sorokin published his likewise popular book, *The Crisis of Our Age.*[10] Following the Second World War, the world immediately slid into the world-dividing Cold War, which lasted until 1989—during which period many "Dr. Strangelove" doomsday scenarios were written.

Given the massive, worldwide scale of the unprecedented destruction and horror of the world's first global war, from 1914–18; the vastly greater destruction and horror of the second global conflict, from 1939–45; and the very real threat of a nuclear holocaust during the Cold War, the pessimistic predictions of these scholars and the great following they found are understandable.

Then, Samuel Huntington, a professor at Harvard University, named a central reality when he argued that, with the fading of the Cold War, a "Clash of Civilizations" is rising in its place.[11] Fundamentalism of all sorts—Christian, Muslim, Hindu, nationalist, ethnic, tribal—are tearing at the fabric of the New World Order even as it is being woven. We at least thought we understood the other side in the Cold War, whether we admired, respected, tolerated, or despised it. But today we have entered into a state of cacophonous confusion and are consequently floundering, or even foundering—take, for example, Rwanda, Bosnia, Northern Ireland, Sri Lanka, and the Middle East. Outbreaks of violence in these places are only the most visible flashpoints of the contemporary malaise. The problems run much deeper. They are cultural, ethical, religious, and spiritual.

In fact, however, the twentieth century's vast world conflagrations and division into First, Second, and Third Worlds were manifestations of the dark side of the unique breakthrough in the history of humankind in the modern development of Christendom–becomes–Western Civilization, now becoming Global Civilization. Never before had there been world wars; likewise, never before had there been world political organizations (e.g., the League of Nations, United Nations). Never before did humanity possess the real possibility of destroying all human life— whether through nuclear or ecological catastrophe. These unique negative realities and potentialities were possible, however, only because of the correspondingly unique accomplishments of Christendom–Western Civilization–Global Civilization—the like of which the world has never before seen. On the negative side, it will always be true from now on that humankind could self-destruct. Still, there are solid empirical grounds for reasonable hope that the inherent, infinity-directed life force of humankind will nevertheless prevail over the parallel death force.

The prophets of doom were correct, however, in their understanding that humanity is entering a radically new age. Earlier in the twentieth century the naysayers (e.g., Spengler, Sorokin) usually spoke of the doom of only Western Civilization, but after the advent of nuclear power and the Cold War, the new generation of pessimists—as said, not without warrant: *corruptio optimae pessima*—warned of *global* disaster. This emerging awareness of global disaster is a clear, albeit negative, sign that something profoundly, radically new is entering onto the stage of human history.

There have, of course, also been a number of more positive signs recently that we humans are entering a radically new age. In the 1960s, there was much talk of the "Age of Aquarius," and today, the fad of "New Age" consciousness continues. Some may be put off by the idea of an emerging radically new age because they perceive such talk to be simply that of fringe groups. We would argue, however, that the presence of the "crazies" around the edge of any idea or movement is far from being a sign of the invalidity of that idea or movement; on the contrary, it is a confirmation precisely of its validity, at least in its core concern. We would further argue that if people are involved with a movement that does not eventually develop its "crazies," its extremists, the movement is not touching the core of humankind's concerns. They should get out of the movement—they are wasting their time.

Moreover, there have likewise recently been a number of very serious scholarly analyses pointing to the emergence of a radically new age in human history. We will deal in some detail with two of them later. The first is the concept of the "Paradigm Shift," particularly as expounded by Hans Küng.[12] The second is the notion of the "Second Axial Period," as articulated by Ewert Cousins.[13] Then, including these two, but setting them in a still larger context, we shall lay out our own analysis, which we see as the movement of humankind out of a multimillennial-long "Age of Monologue" into the newly inbreaking "Age of Dialogue"—indeed, an inbreaking "Age of Global Dialogue."

Of course, there is a great deal of continuity in human life throughout the shift from one major "paradigm" to another, from one "period" to another, from one "age" to another. Nevertheless, even more striking than this continuity is the ensuing break, albeit largely on a different level from the continuity. This relationship of continuity and break in human history is analogous to the transition of water from solid to fluid to gas with increases in temperature. Throughout these processes, water remains H_2O on the chemical level. However, for those who have to deal with the water, it makes a fantastic difference whether the H_2O is ice, liquid, or steam. In the case of the major changes in humankind, the physical base remains the same, but the change on the level of consciousness is massive. And here, too, it makes a fantastic difference whether we are dealing with humans whose consciousness is formed within one paradigm or within another, whose consciousness is pre-Axial, First Axial, or Second Axial, whose consciousness is monologic or dialogic.

Excursus: Post-Modernism

Perhaps a word about the term *post-modernism* is in order, not because we think it is an important new concept, but because it is a term that rather confusedly tries to point to an extremely important contemporary reality. Further, it is found scattered about many writings in the 1980s and 1990s. We believe, however, that the term will not be used much in the future because 1) etymologically, it tells the reader nothing positive about its meaning ("modern" means "contemporary"; what can "post-contemporary" mean?); 2) it has almost as many meanings as users; 3) the meanings that seem to appear more frequently are in fact nothing new, nothing that had not long since been at the heart of modernity.

Concerning the third point, the term *post-modernism* seems to include the notion of a kind of pluralist, as opposed to an integrated, understanding of a subject, and a challenge to a "rational" or "reasonable" explanation of human affairs. Thus, the Enlightenment—as the alleged acme of modernity—notion of reason as the final arbiter of human knowledge is said to be too shallow. This would be true if one restricted the Enlightenment to the eighteenth century. However, the Enlightenment—that is, the probing of all questions with the best-developed tools of reason—was not restricted to the eighteenth century, but continues to this very day. Supposed post-modernists speak about the various "hermeneutics of suspicion," such as subconscious motivations; economic motivations; class, gender, and racial factors in decisions; and the like. But these dimensions of an ever-deepening understanding of human "reason"—that is, the process of thinking—were already being developed in the first half of the nineteenth century and have continued to the present.

The Second Axial Period

Following the lead of Cousins, then, when we shift our gaze from the first millennium B.C.E. to the eve of the twenty-first century, we discern another transformation of consciousness that is so profound and far-reaching that he calls it the Second Axial Period.[14] Like the First Axial Period, the Second Axial Period is happening simultaneously around the Earth, and like the first it will shape the horizon of consciousness for future centuries. Not surprisingly, too, it will have great significance for world religions, which were constituted in the First Axial Period. However, the new form of consciousness is different from that of the First Axial Period. Then it was *individual* consciousness; now it is *global* consciousness.

In order to understand better the forces at work in the Second Axial Period, Cousins draws from the thought of the paleontologist Pierre Teilhard de Chardin.[15] In light of his research on evolution, Teilhard charted the development of consciousness from its roots in the geosphere and biosphere and into the future. In a process that he calls "planetization," he observed that a shift in the forces of evolution, from divergence to convergence, had occurred over the past one hundred years. When human beings first appeared on this planet, they clustered together in family and tribal units, forming their own group identity and separating themselves from other tribes. In this way, humans diverged, creating separate nations and a rich variety of cultures. However, the spherical shape of the Earth prevented unlimited divergence. With the increase in population and the rapid development of communication, groups could no longer remain apart. After dominating the process for millennia, the forces of divergence have been superseded by those of convergence. This shift to convergence is drawing the various cultures into a single planetized community. Although we have been conditioned by thousands of years of divergence, we now have no other course open but to cooperate creatively with the forces of convergence as they draw us toward global consciousness.[16]

According to Teilhard, this new global consciousness will not level all differences among peoples; rather, it will generate what he calls "creative unions" in which diversity is not erased but intensified. His understanding of creative unions is based on his general theory of evolution and the dynamic that he observes throughout the universe. From the geosphere to the biosphere to the realm of consciousness, a single process is at work, which he articulates as the law of "complexity-consciousness" and "union differentiates." "In any domain," he says, "whether it be the cells of a body, the members of a society or the elements of a spiritual synthesis—*union differentiates.*"[17] From subatomic particles to global consciousness, individual elements unite in what Teilhard calls "center to center unions." By touching each other at the creative core of their being, entities release new energy, which leads to more complex units. Greater complexity leads to greater interiority, which, in turn, leads to more creative unions. Throughout the process, the individual elements do not lose their identity but, rather, deepen and fulfill it through union. "Following the confluent orbits of their center," he says, "the grains of consciousness do not tend to lose their outlines and blend, but, on the contrary, to accentuate the depth and incommunicability of their *egos*. The more 'other' they become in conjunction, the more they find themselves as 'self.'" At this point of history, because of the shift from divergence to convergence, the forces of planetization are bringing about an unprecedented complexification of consciousness through the convergence of cultures and religions.

In light of Teilhard's thought, then, we can better understand the meeting of religions at the beginning of the twenty-first century. The world religions are the product of the First Axial Period and the forces of divergence. Although in the first millennium B.C.E., there was a common transformation of consciousness, it occurred in diverse geographical regions within already differentiated cultures. In each case, the religion was shaped by this differentiation in its origin, and developed along differentiated lines. This produced a remarkable richness of spiritual wisdom, of spiritual energies and of religious-cultural forms to express, preserve, and transmit this heritage. However, now that the forces of divergence have shifted to convergence, the religions must meet each other in center-to-center unions, discovering what is most authentic in each other, thereby releasing creative energy toward a more complexified form of religious consciousness.

Such a creative encounter has been called the "dialogic dialogue," to distinguish it from the dialectic dialogue in which one tries to refute the claims of the other.[18] This dialogic dialogue has three phases:

1) The partners meet each other in an atmosphere of mutual understanding, ready to alter misconceptions about each other and eager to appreciate the values of the other.

2) The partners are mutually enriched by passing over into the consciousness of the other, so that each can experience the other's values from within the other's perspective. This can be enormously enriching, for often the partners discover in another tradition values that are submerged or only inchoate in their own. It is important at this point to respect the autonomy of the other tradition—in Teilhard's terms, to achieve union in which differences are valued as a basis of creativity.

3) If such a creative union is achieved, then the religions will have moved into the complexified form of consciousness that will be characteristic of the twenty-first century. This will be complexified

global consciousness, not a mere universal, undifferentiated, abstract consciousness. It will be global through the global convergence of cultures and religions and complexified by the dynamics of dialogic dialogue.

This global consciousness, complexified through the meeting of cultures and religions, is only one characteristic of the Second Axial Period. The consciousness of this period is global in another sense—namely, in rediscovering its roots in the earth. At the very moment that the various cultures and religions are meeting one another and creating a new global community, our life on the planet is being threatened. The very tools that we have used to bring about this convergence—industrialization and technology—are undercutting the biological support system that sustains life on our planet. The future of consciousness, even life on Earth, is shrouded in uncertainty.

Cousins is not suggesting a romantic attempt to live in the past; rather, like Teilhard and Hegel before him, he argues that the evolution of consciousness proceeds by way of recapitulation, or *Aufhebung*. Having developed self-reflective, analytic, critical consciousness in the First Axial Period, we must now, while retaining these values, reappropriate and integrate into that consciousness the collective and cosmic dimensions of the pre-Axial consciousness. We must recapture the unity of tribal consciousness by seeing humanity as a single tribe. And we must see this single tribe as related organically to the total cosmos.

This means that the consciousness of the twenty-first century will be global from two perspectives:

1) From a horizontal perspective, cultures and religions must meet each other on the surface of the globe, entering into creative encounters that will produce a complexified collective consciousness; and

2) From a vertical perspective, they must plunge their roots deep into the Earth to provide a stable and secure base for future development. This new global consciousness must be organically ecological, supported by structures that will insure justice and peace. The voices of the oppressed—of the poor, women, and racial and ethnic minorities—must be heard and heeded. These groups, along with the Earth itself, can be looked on as the prophets and teachers of the Second Axial Period. This emerging twofold global

consciousness is not only a creative possibility to enhance the twenty-first century; it is an absolute necessity if we are to survive.

The Age of Global Dialogue

Cousins has basically affirmed everything Küng described as the newly emerging contemporary paradigm shift, but he sees the present shift as much more profound than simply another in a series of major paradigm shifts of human history. He sees the current transformation as a shift of the magnitude of the First Axial Period, which will similarly reshape human consciousness. We, too, want basically to affirm what Küng sees as the emerging contemporary major paradigm Shift, as well as agree with Cousins that this shift is so profound that it matches in magnitude the transformation of human consciousness of the Axial Period. Thus, it should be referred to as a Second Axial Period.

More than that, however, we are persuaded that what humankind is entering into is not just the latest in a long series of major paradigm shifts, as Küng so carefully and clearly analyzed. We are also persuaded that it is even more than the massive move into the consciousness-transforming Second Axial Period, as Cousins has so thoroughly demonstrated. Beyond these two radical shifts—though, of course, including them—humankind is emerging out of the millennia-long "Age of Monologue" into the newly dawning "Age of Dialogue."[19]

The turn toward dialogue is, in our judgment, the most fundamental, the most radical and utterly transformative of the key elements of the newly emerging paradigm that Küng outlined and that Cousins discerns as one of the central constituents of the Second Axial Period. However, that shift from monologue to dialogue constitutes such a radical reversal in human consciousness, is so utterly new in the history of humankind from the beginning, that it must be designated as literally "revolutionary," that is, it turns everything absolutely around.

CONCLUSION

To sum up and reiterate: In the latter part of the twentieth century humankind is undergoing a Macro-Paradigm-Shift (Hans Küng). More than that, at this time humankind is moving into a transformative shift in consciousness of the magnitude of the Axial Period (800–200 B.C.E.), so that we must speak of the emerging of the Second Axial Period (Ewert Cousins). Even more profound, however, is that humankind, which is now at the beginning of the Third Millennium, is slipping out of the shadowy *Age of Monologue,* where it has been since its beginning, into the dawn of the *Age of Dialogue* (Leonard Swidler). Into this new Age of Dialogue Küng's Macro-Paradigm-Shift and Cousins's Second Axial Period are being recapitulated, sublated (*aufgehoben,* in Hegel's terminology)—that is, taken up and transformed. Moreover, humankind's consciousness is becoming increasingly global. Hence, our partners in dialogue must also be increasingly global. In this new Age of Dialogue, dialogue on a global basis is now not only a possibility, it is a necessity. As noted in the title of a recent book, humankind is faced ultimately with two choices: global dialogue or global death.[20]

6   Anthropology and Sociology of Religion

DESCRIPTION OF ANTHROPOLOGY AND SOCIOLOGY

ANTHROPOLOGY, as the name indicates etymologically, is the *logos* of *anthropos*, the study of humanity. In fact, however, it is a discipline that is necessarily considerably narrower than that all-embracing term would seem to indicate. Although many divisions of the social science of anthropology have been developed (e.g., physical, cultural), it has for the most part meant the study of humanity as it was and is as nearly as possible before it was socialized by civilization. That has been done mostly by studying "primitive" or traditional societies as they have continued to exist in isolated spots around the globe.

The use of the term *primitive* in relation to earlier forms of societal structure has gone out of fashion because many feel that it is used pejoratively. Mary Douglas, a very sensitive and renowned anthropologist pondered this move: "We feel there is something discourteous in the term 'primitive' and so we avoid it and the whole subject too." She suspected, however, that "our professional delicacy in avoiding the term 'primitive' is the product of secret convictions of superiority. The physical anthropologists have a similar problem when they attempt to substitute 'ethnic group' for the word 'race.'"

She went on to argue: "Finally we should revive the question of whether the word 'primitive' should be abandoned. I hope not. It can be given a valid meaning for technology and possibly for economics." She then asked, "What is the objection to saying that a personal, anthropocentric, undifferentiated worldview characterizes a primitive culture?" She suggested that the only source of objection "could be from the notion that it has a pejorative sense in relation to religious beliefs which it does not carry in technology and art. There may be something in this for a certain section of the English-speaking world." She might have noted, however, that when Christian church historians speak of the "Primitive Church," they often do so in rather glowing terms.[1] In this book we will, somewhat reluctantly, follow the contemporary custom

91

and use the term "traditional" religions—except when speaking within the context of a particular scholar's views.

The systematic study of "traditional" societies and religions—that is, the social science of anthropology—began in earnest in the second half of the nineteenth and beginning of the twentieth century. Some formative pioneers were Auguste Comte (1798–1857) of France,[2] N. D. Fustel de Coulanges (1830–89) of France,[3] Max Müller (1823–1900) of Germany and England,[4] William G. Sumner (1840–1910) of America,[5] Edward Burnett Tylor (1832–1917),[6] and James George Frazer (1854–1941) of England,[7] Emile Durkheim (1858–1917) of France,[8] and Bronislaw Malinowski (1884–1942) of Poland and England.[9]

Sociology is the *logos* of the *socios*, the *study* of *society*—that is, how humans live in relation to one another. What is sought is the existence and influence of the patterns of interrelationships among groups of humans. For the most part, this is done by studying contemporary communities or subsections of communities, although communities of the past can also be studied profitably this way, as long as there is enough data to do so. A major difference, of course, is that the sociologist can no longer put certain questions to dead societies and hope to receive answers.

One might say that anthropologists are basically sociologists of "traditional" societies. In fact, in the classics of both disciplines, it is often difficult to distinguish between the two. Was Durkheim an anthropologist or a sociologist, or both, and when was he one and when the other? For the purposes of the studying religion, it is perhaps not so vital to know which "hat" some of these formative scholars were wearing when they articulated important insights as it is to grasp the insights.

One of the objections to the anthropological and sociological study of religion—indeed, the social-scientific study of religion in general—that is raised by some religious people is that the social sciences cannot properly understand religion. Rather, they can only undermine it. However, almost a hundred years ago, Durkheim, the "father of the sociology of religion," warned against viewing knowledge as the source of evil. Rather, he states: "It is its remedy, the only remedy we have. Once established beliefs have been carried away by the current of affairs, they cannot be artificially reestablished; only reflection can guide us in life, after this." He argued that "once the social instinct is blunted, intelligence is the only guide left us and we have to reconstruct a conscience by its means." He advised those "who view anxiously and sadly the ruins of ancient beliefs, who feel all the difficulties of these critical times, not to ascribe to science an evil it has not caused but rather which it tries to cure! Beware of treating it as an enemy!"[10]

Douglas, a contemporary Catholic anthropologist, has pointed out that thought can advance only on the Kantian principle of freeing itself from the shackles of its own subjective conditions. The first Copernican revolution, the discovery that only humanity's subjective viewpoint made the sun seem to revolve round the Earth, has been continually renewed since that fifteenth-century "paradigm-shift." In our own Western culture, mathematics first and later logic, then history, then language, and now increasingly our very thought processes themselves, as well as even knowledge of the self and of society—all are fields of knowledge progressively freed from the subjective limitations of the mind.

Douglas points out how our contemporary culture is different from all previous cultures because of our new self-consciousness. "To the extent to which sociology, anthropology and psychology are possible in it, our own type of culture needs to be distinguished from others which lack this self-awareness and conscious reaching for objectivity."[11]

Gerd Theissen, a Protestant biblical expert in the sociology of the New Testament, makes an even stronger plea for utilizing social-scientific tools in the study of religion, including Christianity:

> Once we stop assuming that Christianity is a privileged tradition, and give up the claim that the truth is contained, once and for all, in one particular tradition, what is left? . . . What is left once we stop playing the defensive trick of declaring our own particular sanctuaries out of bounds to psychological and sociological criticisms. . . . For all its obscenities, illusions and daydreams, I believe that Christianity has an authenticity which can make it supremely significant for human life. Most Christians are not so confident. As a result, they are allergic to historical, empiricist and ideological criticism. They mistrust arguments. They prefer to say that faith is a miracle which defies all argument.[12]

MAGIC AND RELIGION

One of the first items students of religion must face is the relationship between magic and religion, which has been a much debated topic since the beginning of the social-scientific study of religion. It appears that magic is the ability to attain a goal through means outside those available to normal human knowledge; magical rituals offer ways of manipulating forces outside normal human control to bring about effects in the empirical world. However, it also appears that "magic differs from religion in that it is manipulative in essence. Religion offers what is felt to be a way of entering into a relationship with the supra-empirical aspects of reality, be they conceived as God, gods, or otherwise."[13] The greater the uncertainty and lack of knowledge, the more magic is likely to be employed.[14]

Some early anthropologists claimed that humankind first used magic to deal with forces beyond its control, then advanced to religion and gradually dropped magic. Religion related humans to the transcendent, however understood, in a much broader way than magic attempts to do and is not necessarily manipulative as magic is. But it has become clear that, even though the areas of human uncertainties shrink and the need for the manipulations of magic correspondingly shrivel, magic to some extent has tended to continue to exist alongside religion, depending on the maturity of the people involved.

Thus, according to Ronald Johnstone, there are a number of similarities between magic and religion:

1) Both are serious attempts to deal with and solve fundamental human problems;
2) Both are founded on faith in the existence and effectiveness of unseen powers;
3) Both engage in ritualistic activity;
4) Both are accepted elements of the larger culture.

At the same time, however, there are also significant differences:

1) Religion tends to deal with long-term issues, such as the meaning of life, existence after death, whereas magic handles immediate affairs, such as devising a love potion or bringing rain;
2) Religion is usually concerned with the future, whereas magic focuses on the present;
3) Religion is usually in awe of the transcendent, whereas magic tries to manipulate the supernatural to serve its own purposes;
4) Religion is largely, though not solely, a collective activity, with group beliefs, liturgies, codes of ethics, whereas magic is performed by the individual, but, of course, with the approval of the group.[15]

Hence, in Johnstone's view, "Magic is probably best seen neither as a competitor with religion nor as an alternative to it, but as a specialized subunit of religion. In fact, rarely is religion without at least some magical elements."[16]

FASCINATION WITH THREE

Something about the number three seems to be profoundly attractive to humans. The fact that religious and non-religious traditions speak of Ultimate Reality in terms of a trinity tells us that something very deep in our human experience is being expressed in these triadic images and language. There are divine trinities in at least five major world religions: Judaism, Hinduism, Christianity, Mahayana Buddhism, and Taoism.

While it is true that the Hebrew Bible insists on monotheism ("Hear, O Israel, Yahweh our God is one": Deuteronomy 6:5), there is also much talk of God as "Our Father" (*Abinu*), of God's Word (*Dabar*), and of God's Spirit (*Ruach*). But it is also equally true that these three were never thought of as ontologically existent; rather, they were thought of as metaphorical images of aspects of Yahweh as encountered by the Jews—not God in self (*Deus in se*), but God facing us (*Deus ad nos*).

Besides the—albeit metaphorical—Hebraic trinity and the well-known Christian Trinity of the Father, Son (Word), and Holy Spirit, an ancient form of Hinduism depicted Ultimate Reality as the *Trimurti* (One in Three): *Brahma* (a creator god, not to be confused with *Brahman*, the "Absolute"), *Vishnu*, and *Shiva*. In Mahayana Buddhism, Ultimate Reality is also conceived of as triadic in the *Trikaya* (the Threefold Body of the Buddha): *Dharma-kaya*, *Sambhoga-kaya*, and *Nirmana-kaya*. Taoism also sees Ultimate Reality as triune: *T'ai I* (Grand Unity), *T'ien I* (Heavenly Unity), and *Ti I* (Earthly Unity).

Many Western thinkers have a penchant for thinking of human history in three stages. For example, in the twelfth century Joachim de Fiore wrote of three ages: the Age of the Father (which lasted until the birth of Jesus), the Age of the Son (from Jesus's birth to the time of Joachim), and the Age of the Spirit (from Joachim's time to Christ's Second Coming). In the seventeenth century, the historian Giovanni Baptisia Vico also wrote of three ages: the Age of Gods (referred to in the great myths), the Age of Heroes (when grand models, such as Achilles, were held up to emulate), and the Age of Men (when historical human

reality was accepted for its own self). Even in nineteenth-century philosophy, triadic thinking holds a prominent place, most evidently in
Hegelian dialectical idealism and, in inverted fashion, in Marxist dialectical materialism: thesis, antithesis, synthesis.

We find this triadic approach at the foundation of the nineteenth-
century invention of the disciplines of anthropology and sociology. It
began with Auguste Comte, who wrote of the "Law of Three Stages":
the Religious Stage (when life's puzzles were explained with recourse
to spirits and gods), the Metaphysical Stage (when abstract rational
principles explained life), and the Positive Stage (when science solves
all problems). This three-stage explanation, which relegated religion to
the dustbin of history, was continued by the initially highly influential
pioneer anthropologists Edward B. Tylor and James G. Frazer.

REDUCTIONISM: RELIGION IS ONLY . . .

Many of the early writers in the area of the social-scientific study of religion were one or a combination of the following: 1) "reductionists"—
that is, they reduced religion to being only one thing, usually rather
covert. These writers also tended to be 2) "functionalists"—that is, they
explained religion only in terms of how it functioned in human life,
whether individual or societal. Several of them likewise tended to be
3) "projectionists"—that is, they claimed that religion is a transfer of
some individual or societal experience into a "projected" transcendental sphere. Finally, many of these writers tended to be 4) "evolution-
ists"—that is, they saw religion coming into existence at a certain stage
of development or evolution of humankind, and then disappearing as
the evolutionary process continued and the need for religion proportionately atrophied, and will eventually disappear altogether.

Ludwig Feuerbach

The first of the great reductionists was the German Ludwig Feuerbach
(1804–72), who published *Das Wesen des Christentums* (*The Essence of
Christianity* [1853]) in 1841. This work's popularity catapulted him into
sudden, temporary fame. He claimed that religion is "nothing but" a
psychological trick humans play on themselves, attaching all their
hopes, ideals, and virtues to an imaginary transcendental being called
"god." Hence, Feuerbach was not only a reductionist but likewise

"might well be called the first modern thinker to offer a purely 'projectionist' explanation of religion."[17] He did not stay popular for very long, but he has been assured historical notoriety by the fact that he greatly influenced Marx in his later, very influential theory of religion.

Karl Marx

Marx carried Feuerbach's functional reductionist–projectionist idea of religion even further. Marx "presents us less with a theory of religion than a total system of thought that itself resembles a religion":[18]

Founder: Marx
Scripture: Works of Marx
Saints/Heroes: Lenin, Mao (embalmed in "sacred" tombs)
Liturgy: May Day Parades
Clergy: Politburo, Commissars
"Heavenly" goal: The State of Communism—with the "withering away of the state," clearly a condition beyond history.

Let it be noted, however, that perhaps no other modern thinker "discusses religion in quite the same mood of sarcastic contempt as Marx":[19] "The social principles of Christianity declare all vile acts of the oppressors against the oppressed to be either the just punishment of original sin and other sins or trials that the Lord in his infinite wisdom imposes on those redeemed. The social principles of Christianity preach cowardice, self-contempt, abasement, submission, dejection."[20]

As we will see, a fellow projectionist, Sigmund Freud, believed that people would be much better off without their neurotic illusions of religion, but he apparently presumes that many will nevertheless cling to them. Marx, however, goes still further and insists that people "*cannot* be better off *until* they are without them—that is, until revolution has done away with the exploitation and misery that have created religion in the first place"[21]—which revolution will be brought about by the "*dictatorship* of the proletariat," meaning the small cadre of Communist Party members. As Marx put it: "The abolition of religion as the *illusory* happiness of the people is required for their *real* happiness."[22]

Sigmund Freud

Marx's functional reductionist–projectionist ideas on religion, however, were likewise largely ignored in his day in the mid-nineteenth century and became influential only in the twentieth century. However, a third great functional reductionist–projectionist, Sigmund Freud (who is treated in greater detail in the chapter on religion and psychology), picked up on the same idea from Feuerbach, and this time it attained great popularity. The reason is that in the latter part of the nineteenth century, two English anthropologists—Tylor and Frazer—made a large impression on the social-scientific world with their major writings on early humankind, very much including religion.

Tylor and Frazer argued that religion was basically a set of ideas explaining the meaning of all aspects of life; many of these ideas were subsequently seen to be quite absurd and superstitious. That, however, raised the question: Why had humankind believed such a lot of non-sense for such a long time, and worse still, why did so many hold on to it even in the "Scientific Age"? Freud provided a brilliant answer: Religion arises from emotions and conflicts that originate in early child-hood and are hidden deep below the surface of the rational personal-ity, which lead women and men to neuroses—that is, badly unbalanced responses to everyday reality. The reaction to those neuroses is religion. It is important to note that, for Freud, religion is *only* a psychological response—nothing more. Once the unhealthy neuroses have been elim-inated by psychoanalysis, the reason for, and reality of, religion will disappear. Freud does not venture into hand-to-hand combat with reli-gion by attempting to disprove the truth of its claims. He attempts to obliterate it by firing a long-distance missile at it: "To assess the truth-value of religious doctrines does not lie within the scope of the present enquiry. It is enough for us that we have recognized them as being, in their psychological nature, illusions."[23]

Nevertheless, for Freud, religion is a childhood illness that human-ity, like most children, will leave behind as it matures. In fact, human-ity is now in the midst of that process of outgrowing the disease of reli-gion: "Religion would thus be the universal obsessional neurosis of humanity.... A turning-away from religion is bound to occur with the fatal inevitability of a process of growth, and we find ourselves at this very juncture in the middle of that phase of development."[24]

Emile Durkheim

A last great reductionist who deserves to be mentioned here is Emile Durkheim. He claims that religion is rooted in the basic distinction that all societies make between the sacred and the profane, and that religion is concerned with the former. The sacred is always intimately connected with the great social events of the clan, whereas the profane is limited to day-to-day private affairs. Hence, for Durkheim religion is nothing but the projection of the clan, of society, into the supernatural realm. God is in reality the symbol of the society; when worshiping God, humans are really worshiping society.

The laws that God is said to issue are really issued by society for its own existence and well-being. Why do most, if not all, societies have something like the core of the Ten Commandments—honor parents; do not kill, steal, lie, commit sexual transgressions? Because those societies that did not have them self-destructed and disappeared. Hence, those commandments are really from society, which is projected into the supernatural realm and given the symbolic name of God: If the totem— that is, a mascot, a flag, or the like—"is at once the symbol of the god and the society, is that not because the god and society are only one?"[25]

Unlike the above reductionists—Feuerbach, Marx, and Freud—however, Durkheim did not look or work for the elimination of religion. As long as there is human society, he argued, there will be religion or its functional equivalent: "Religion's true purpose is not intellectual but social. It serves as the carrier of social sentiments, providing symbols and rituals that enable people to express the deep emotions which anchor them to their community. Insofar as it does this, religion, or some substitute for it, will always be with us."[26]

Critique of the Major Reductionists

To begin with, students of religion have learned a great deal about religion from these major reductionists, who have played a formative role in the founding and early direction of the social-scientific study of religion. For example, Feuerbach and, later, Freud made it clear that the divine is in many respects projected outwardly in human terms. There also can be no doubt that economics has a profound influence in human lives, as Marx stressed, and hence also on religion in a great variety of ways. The new nineteenth-century social sciences of anthropology and sociology have increasingly demonstrated the fundamental role that society plays in the lives of individual women and men, and Durkheim brought home how intimately society is connected with religion.

However, the main difficulty with the position of the reductionists, who argue that "religion is *nothing* but . . . ," is that human life is "anything but simple." To insist on a "simple" answer to a complex problem is simplistic—that is, *overly* simple. The point was made strongly by a major twentieth-century student of religion, Mircea Eliade (1907–86), who was adamantly opposed to the reductionism he found so dominant early in the twentieth century. He insisted that: "A religious phenomenon will only be recognized as such if it is grasped at its own level, that is to say, if it is studied *as* something religious. To try to grasp the essence of such a phenomenon by means of physiology, psychology, sociology, economics, linguistics, art, or any other study is false; it misses the one unique and irreducible element in it—the element of the sacred."[27]

All of the reductionists named earlier are also "projectionists"—that is, they argue that "religion is nothing but a projection" by individuals or society of a need into an external realm. They insist, for example, that whereas the beginning of the Bible states that "humanity [*anthropos,* or *ha adam* in Hebrew] is made in the image of God [*Theos*]," it is really the other way around: "God is made in the image of humanity." The projectionists reduce *theo*logy to *anthro*pology.

However, as critics of the projectionist position point out, if humans are in some significant sense "images," reflections, of Ultimate Reality, of God, then it is to be expected that humans will conceive of God in humanlike terms, for that is how God really would be since humans are "images" of God. So yes, these critics continue: Not only is it true to say that "the image of God is a human projection, *and* humans are images of God," but it is also true to say that "the image of God is a human projection, *because* humans are images of God." The sociologist of religion Peter L. Berger pointed that out when he wrote, "To say that religion is a human projection does not logically preclude the possibility that the projected meanings may have an ultimate status independent of man."[28]

Marx wrote that, after having been impressed with Hegel's dynamic scheme of history proceeding in dialectic fashion, he accepted Feuerbach's projectionist theory and "stood Hegel on his head" by rejecting his historical idealism in favor of historical materialism (and privileged material economic conditions as *the* fundamentally determining factor). Berger took this page from Marx's book and suggested that one could also "stand Marx on *his* head":

Put simply, this would imply that man projects ultimate meanings into reality because that reality is, indeed, ultimately meaningful, and because his own being (the empirical ground of these projections) contains and intends these same ultimate meanings. Such a theological procedure, if feasible, would be an interesting ploy on Feuerbach—the reduction of theology to anthropology would end in the reconstruction of anthropology in a theological mode.[29]

The great German social theorist Max Weber likewise turned Marx at least partially on his head (though without using such terms). He argued that instead of economics determining everything else, including religion, the new religion of Protestantism (especially the Calvinist version), while influenced by capitalism, also helped substantially to create the spirit of capitalism, rather than simply the other way around.[30] Elsewhere, he also commented contra-Marx:

It is not our thesis that the specific nature of a religion is a simple "function" of the social situation. . . . On the contrary, a more basic misunderstanding of the standpoint of these discussions would hardly be possible. However incisive the social influences, economically and politically determined, may have been upon a religious ethic in a particular case, it receives its stamp primarily from religious sources.[31]

The (mistaken) understanding of Weber's theory[32] in *The Protestant Ethic and the Spirit of Capitalism* as meaning that—as a converse of Marx's economic determinism—Protestantism was the determining force of capitalism has in turn been criticized. This, of course, simply reinforces the key point that there can be no simple solution to a complex human reality.

One of the reductionists themselves, Durkheim, was likewise critical of Marx's particular reductionist solution of historical materialism. Durkheim argued that his own reductionism was not so "materialistic" as Marx's (although he did not mention Marx's name):

Therefore it is necessary to avoid seeing in this theory of religion [Durkheim's own] a simple restatement of historical materialism: that would be misunderstanding our thought to an extreme degree. In showing that religion is something essentially social, we do not mean to say that it confines itself to translating into another language the material forms of society and its immediate vital necessities.[33]

Even though he continues to have a great influence on those studying the phenomenon of religion, Durkheim as a reductionist also comes in for severe criticism: "It is one thing to say that *alongside* its other claims and purposes, religion *also* has a social function; it quite another to say that religion has *only* a social function."[34] Durkheim, as we have seen, claims that all societies make a sharp distinction between the profane and the sacred, and the latter, which is religion's domain, is where all the great social events of society occur. But that means that at the beginning of his argument, Durkheim already assumes that society is identified with religion—a logical flaw customarily known as "begging the question."

> The inquiry would seem to begin at the very place where Durkheim wants to finish. The sacred is the social, he writes, and the religious is the sacred; therefore, the religious is the social. To be sure, Durkheim is not the only theorist whose reasoning tends toward a certain circularity; we have seen something of the same in Freud, and others, too.[35]

P. Worsley affirms that sociology of religion contributes greatly to our understanding of religion by tracing the effects of religion on the behavior of collectivities, and vice versa, and the ways in which religious institutions condition the behavior of individuals. But he is also critical of Durkheim's limiting the function of religion to societal level:

> Collectivities do not think, or undergo religious experiences; men do. Even Durkheim's occasions of collective ritual are situations in which men respond to the situation. Their behaviour is, to be sure, profoundly and directly conditioned by the presence of many others.... Even so, the required or resultant religious behaviour is still mediated through and only meaningful within the individual psyche. There is no group psyche.[36]

One of the greatest admirers of Durkheim's manifold contributions to a deeper understanding of the role of society in religion, and at the same time one of the severest critics of his reductionist approach, was the great Polish anthropologist Bronislaw Malinowski. When referring to Durkheim's theory of religion being "nothing more or less than Society divinized," Malinowski commented that his theory, which focuses so exclusively on the collective's being the very essence of religion, "seems very well to explain the public nature of cult, the inspiration and comfort drawn by man, the social animal, from congregation, the intolerance shown by religion, especially in its early manifestations, the cogency of morals and other similar facts." He added that this theory, which makes the ancient proverb *vox populi vox Dei* (the voice of the people is the voice of God) appear to be a sober, scientific truth, doubt-less would be congenial to modern people.

However, he insisted that, upon reflection, serious critical misgiv-ings arise: "Everyone who has experienced religion deeply and sin-cerely knows that the strongest religious moments come in solitude, in turning away from the world, in concentration and in mental detach-ment, and not in the distraction of a crowd." Moreover, "though most ceremonies are carried out in public, much of religious revelation takes place in solitude." In the end, society exercises great influence on in-dividuals, but "it works in the individual and through forces of the individual mind." Thus, Malinowski concluded that religion is "nei-ther exclusively social nor individual, but a mixture of both." Mali-nowski: "To sum up, the views of Durkheim and his school cannot be accepted."[37]

Let this suffice for a critique of the reductionist approach to religion. (Freud's insights and flaws in this regard are dealt with in the chapter on psychology and religion.)

CHURCH–DENOMINATION–SECT–CULT TYPES

One of the important distinctions in the discipline of sociology of reli-gion was initiated by the German sociologist of religion Max Weber, and developed more fully by his student Ernst Troeltsch (1865–1923)—namely, the distinction between the "church type" religious commu-nity and the "sect type." It should be noted that the church and the sect are types at two ends of a continuum, with real religious groups spread all along the space in between. Nevertheless, it is useful to look first at these two extreme types. Also, it should be borne in mind that, although it is drawn up on the basis of Christian history, this distinction has appli-cation far beyond Christianity.[38]

Church Type

The church type in its fullest form has the following marks:

1) It claims universality so that all members of the society (usually a nation) would automatically be considered members of the church;
2) Related to that, it tries to maintain a religious monopoly, brooking no competition;

3) Hence, it is very closely allied with the state and shares responsibilities with it;
4) It is highly organized and bureaucratized;
5) It has a full-time, educated, professional clergy;
6) It gains members automatically by natural reproduction and socialization of children;
7) It has more formal worship practices;
8) It is concerned with both otherworldly (e.g., salvation) and this-worldly (e.g., schools, hospitals) matters.

Examples of the church type would be the medieval Catholic church in Western Europe and Islam in present-day Iran.

Sect Type

The sect type arises in protest to the church type because the church is seen as having fallen from pristine purity in doctrine, practice, or the like. In its fullest form, the sect type has the following marks:

1) It understands itself as the fellowship of the elect;
2) It stresses spontaneity of expression;
3) It de-emphasizes organization and bureaucracy;
4) It is deliberately small in size;
5) It has no trained professional clergy;
6) It stresses purity of doctrine, usually by a return to the original teachings;
7) It emphasizes traditional ethics;
8) It concentrates on otherworldly issues, such as heaven, hell, salvation;
9) It gains members through conversion;
10) It comes largely from the lower social classes.

An example of the sect type are the Amish (Pennsylvania Dutch).
Set in contrast to each other, the characteristics of the church and sect types might be listed as follows:

Church	*Sect*
1) Membership by birth	Voluntary membership
2) Open to converting all	Must have conversion experience before becoming member

1) Understanding based on the most extensive available data, including information provided from all scholarly disciplines and studies of as many pertinent languages as possible.
2) An emotional attitude of appreciation (rather than indifference) of how religion encompasses the entire person.
3) The will to be constructive and to attempt to comprehend various types of religiosity.
4) The broadest possible experience—that is, varied engagement in as many different religious experiences as may be obtained by the scholar. It is important to be aware that there are different kinds of religious experiences.[5]

Wach pointed out that comparative religionists divided themselves as to the method of study: One group suggested that religion ought to be studied in the very same scientific manner as any other phenomenon, while the other group favored developing a method applicable only to the study of religion.[6] Since both of those approaches were found wanting, a third, a synthesis, was attempted which would take the uniqueness of religion into account but also follow the basic insight that the world is one and therefore the same methods of studying all phenomena may be used (methodological monism and the principle of coherence). One such system developed by Alfred North Whitehead attempts to relate and understand nature, mind, and spirit (often called process theology). The main characteristic of this method is the conviction that a phenomenon cannot necessarily be accounted for by the preceding stages of a process but unforeseeable and new phenomena may appear from time to time.

Comparative religion also insists on the validity of the hermeneutical principle arising out of Plato's affirmation that it is the kinship between the knower and the known which makes understanding possible. If the object of study in religion is in no way associated with the one who studies it, then no knowledge would be possible. In addition, Wach points out that Western thinkers who limit the study of religion simply to perception and inference can learn a great deal from the "Eastern" insistence "that there is an immediate awareness of an inclination toward truth, although the sources of religious insight have been differently conceived in different communities of faith."[7] If, as "the East" insists, the highest goal of life is to attain truth and truth is God's, then human beings in all communities of faith can know the truth only partially, and yet even that partial truth can be completely liberating.

Two tendencies arose in comparative religious studies, one of them being cultural and religious relativism. Here the claim is made that the differences from one culture and one religion to another are so deep that it is not possible to develop criteria of judgment that will legitimately belong to both. Hence, one can only clarify similarities and differences, but because cultures and religions operate as wholes, the differences also give even the similarities a differing "valence" within each of the separate cultures and religions. There are also discernible "strong" and "weak" relativisms; the former claims that each culture, each religion, is true, good in itself, and judgment about one but not the other being true or good is mistaken. The latter grants that one might be true and good, and the other not, but it is not possible to know that.

The second tendency in comparative religious studies wanted to overcome the relativist claim of the impossibility of locating general comparative criteria. The scholars of this camp of comparativists (e.g., Rudolf Otto, Mircea Eliade—more about them later) sought "universal, or nearly universal, revelatory structures that were supposed to take particular forms in particular religious traditions. The most important category employed was the concept of the sacred or the holy." In turn, in their attempt to overcome the provincialism of the relativist comparativists, the opponents of the universalist comparativists accused them "of imposing a universal theological category. It purchased universality at the expense of scientific plausibility."[8]

A recent development in the scientific study of cultural systems, however, has forced comparativists to rethink their provincialisms, whether of cultural relativism or theological universalism. Techniques have been developed indicating that cultures were neither as variable nor universal as previously thought. Comparative linguistics led the way in showing that although no two languages are alike on the usual levels of comparison such as grammar and syntax, it is possible to discern on very highly abstract levels that all languages are constrained by certain fundamental principles. Among students of culture, structuralists (who claim that there are certain fundamental structures pervading basic human activities: Claude Levy-Strauss was the foremost promoter of structuralism) began to apply the same method to the comparative study of religion, focusing especially on myth and ritual systems.

It has been pointed out, however, that this move to read religion like a linguistic text is problematic in that "the metaphor of culture [religion] as text has had the unintended consequence of imposing a greater unity on religious traditions than is warranted." Rather, "[a] religious tradition is something like a group of second-rate musicians performing a poorly remembered symphony without a score and without a conductor. Music gets played, and there is some continuity, but attempting to reconstruct the symphony from the performance will hardly disclose an unambiguous structure."[9]

10 Phenomenology of Religion

ONE OF THE more recent approaches to the study of religion includes one in which the scholar, whether philosopher or religious-studies expert, tries to describe, though not necessarily explain, the essence of religion—that is, the core of religion that distinguishes religious from non-religious phenomena. The American scholar Joseph Dabney Bettis explains that phenomenology of religion has three meanings.

The first meaning is the phenomenological–philosophical study of religion, of which the most famous protagonists are Edmund Husserl, Martin Heidegger, Jean-Paul Sartre, Maurice Merleau-Ponty, and Paul Ricoeur.[1]

The second meaning is the application of phenomenological methods to the study of the history of religion, of which the best known protagonists are Joachim Wach, Mircea Eliade, Gerardus van der Leeuw, and W. Brede Kristensen. Paying attention mostly to primitive religions, they were interested in the mythological and ritualistic elements of religion. Thus,

> The phenomenology of religion does not attempt to get beneath the cultural forms of expression to a common ground. When it seeks to describe the essence of religion the phenomenology of religion does not look to a common "natural" religion beneath the various culturally conditioned forms. It recognizes that culturally conditioned forms are the only forms of expression men have. What it seeks to do, however, is to raise to the level of conscious, reflective awareness what is actually taking place in religious activity.[2]

Phenomenology does attempt to point to common elements of in what may at first seem only disparate units. The data must be respected and not explained away by some grand theory.

Third, and most broadly, phenomenology of religion consists of the use of phenomenological methods to describe the essence of religion as it explores the entire range of religious activities, symbols, institutions, ideas, and rituals.[3]

Van der Leeuw provides a good discussion of the phenomenon and phenomenology in the epilogue of his book *Religion in Essence and Manifestation*,[4] the title of which is indeed a succinct statement of what phenomenology of religion is—namely, the attempt to understand the essence and appearance of something believed to exist, in this case, religion. That which is first experienced, then understood, and finally testified to is the phenomenon, which often, at least at first, is partially concealed, then revealed, and finally made clear.[5]

Phenomenology depends on data discovered by the history, philosophy, psychology, sociology of religions, theology, and similar branches of knowledge.[6] It arose as a rejection of comparative religion, which, at least in Europe, was practiced in such a way that it attempted to create a classification of all religions and religious phenomena in order to determine which religions were "higher" than others. In the nineteenth century, the idea of the evolutionary development of all religions was dominant and, comparative-religion scholars tried to establish hierarchies of religions, from primitive to advanced.

The phenomenologists of religion rejected this typology and attempted to study and understand religion as the followers of the religion experienced it, taking seriously their claims without attempting a value judgment. No attempts are made to judge whether they are existent or not, important or not; the scholar aims solely to describe and classify the reported or observed items, systematizing them and aiming at an understanding of the essence of the reported phenomena, all the while suspending judgment about its validity. The scholar may divide the reported religious data into, for example, the object of religion, the subject of religion, and the reciprocal relationship between the object and subject, the perceptions of the world and the forms of religion. This is done, for instance, by van der Leeuw. Or else one may, as Kristensen did, deal with the ancient religions of the Egyptians, Babylonians, Persians, Greeks, and Romans, and classify all the data into cosmology, anthropology, cultus, and cultic acts.[7] This is a difficult endeavor regardless of the object of study, but it is particularly difficult regarding claims of ultimate validity that tend to agitate the ones who experience them and who are by no means objective about it.

Phenomenology of religion first names the various phenomena, such as prayer, savior, purification rituals, national religions, revivals, and so on, following which "it must interpolate these appearances within its own life and experience them systematically."[8] It then observes them while abstaining from intellectual judgment. Then it attempts to clarify what has been observed and comprehend what has appeared, and finally to explain this to listeners amid the multiplicity of unexplained data. Phenomenology does not attempt to speculate about the origins and development of a religion.

In his introduction to Kristensen's book, Hendrik Kraemer states that phenomenologists such as Kristensen interpreted the constantly expanding data on cultus, myth, understanding of the world, and attitudes toward life of the various cultures, some preferring to restrict their investigation to certain historical periods and geographical areas, with others attempting a more comprehensive approach. Phenomenologists attempt, not wholly successfully, to bring a scientific objectivity and detachment to the study of religion, which scholars such as Kraemer consider unattainable.[9] Yet it is both a gratifying and necessary approach that is as much an art of uncovering the inner meaning of religion as it is a method to understand its various facets.

Kristensen regarded it as "the systematically pursued, comparative endeavour to interpret and understand (not explain) religious phenomena of the same category (sacrifice, prayer, sacraments, etc.), appearing in different religions, to get at their inner meaning."[10] In order to do this, one must meticulously respect the data and understand them sympathetically. One needs to understand religion as the believer understands it or intends to practice it. Many phenomenologists believe that, with this approach, as with the other approaches of studying religion, it is possible for scholars not only to gain the benefit of understanding the other religion but also to grow in their own personal religion, though this is not universally the case.

The American philosopher Frederick Streng adds that in phenomenological study, one looks for dominant or organizing patterns, going on the assumption that "the outward forms of human expression have an inner organizing pattern or configuration, with power to order the meaning for the person participating in this expression."[11] When the scholar links together the different perceptions of participants in religious practices, she or he can gain an understanding that goes beyond the individual facts.

Some phenomenologists, such as Rudolf Otto in his famous book *The Idea of the Holy*, started with the philosophical presupposition that behind religious phenomena there is the encounter with the "wholly other." Studying this notion, to which he attached the Latin term *numen*, he found that numenous experiences gives rise to a sense of tremendous mystery that is expressed in a simultaneous fascination and fear, attraction and repulsion: *Mysterium tremendum et fascinans*.[12]

Most phenomenologists refuse to start out with such a philosophical presupposition, although they admit the need to work with concepts from the philosophy of religion. They would agree with Otto, however, that one must not reduce the religious experience to other, non-religious human experience, arguing that religion is a distinct experience of awe, mystery, sacredness, and ultimacy.

A key phenomenologist of religion prior to 1950 was the Dutchman Gerardus van der Leeuw, whose best-known work was *Phänomenologie der Religion*. According to van der Leeuw, phenomenology studies things just as they are observed by people. He highlighted how people relate to the religious aspects of "power," a wholly other power that invades human affairs. He, like the philosopher Husserl, emphasized that the scholar should practice *epochê*—an intellectual suspension of one's own views, which, however, does not mean that the same scholar may not also be a person of faith.

One of the best-known scholars of the phenomenological orientation was Mircea Eliade, who focused mostly on the manner in which people relate to the universe. Eliade held that modern people relate to the world around them in a "scientific" or profane way, while many previous cultures had a notion of awe and wonder about the object of their apprehension that can be described as sacred. The religious impulse may be described as *"the desire to live in a pure and holy cosmos, as it was in the beginning, when it came fresh from the Creator's hands."*[13] Religion, then, is the appearance of the sacred, of the real that is opposite from the profane. Eliade pointed out the existence of sacred space and sacred time as religious phenomena and the periodic becoming contemporary with God or gods by means of symbolic behavior. Religions also have sacred history that is expressed in mythological terms.[14] Religious people become human by imitating the divine beings—namely, by conforming to the lessons found in the myth. In such manner, Eliade explored what he believed to be the realities of the religious vision of life.

The division of the world into sacred and profane is not unique to Eliade's scheme. Otto also posited a division into these two spheres and came to the conclusion that the word *holy* is appropriate only to religion in its pure form.

A Jewish scholar, Martin Buber, likewise noticed the division into the sacred and the everyday, but insisted that religion could be found not just in the sacred but also in the everyday in the encounter of the I and the Thou, which is where the sacred encroaches on daily reality. He denied that the I–Thou is a numenous reality, saying instead that in genuine encounters of the I with any Thou, the I also encounters the eternal Thou, which is thus a profound religious experience.[15]

Several scholars have warned against the generalization of human religious experience. Wach insisted that one must not neglect the particular cultural expression of each religion. The Canadian scholar Wilfred Cantwell Smith, on the other hand, emphasized the personal aspect of the faith of each individual that is distinct from the impersonal concept of religion.[16]

It is evident that the phenomenological approach exercised in the abstract, without interaction with historians of religion, would lead to abstractions. Phenomenologists try to intuit the essence of religious phenomena and, in doing so may, insert too many of their own normative and subjective conclusions. But the phenomenologist has contributed greatly to the general study of religion by stressing the importance of a sympathetic understanding for religious phenomena, an empathy with the alleged religious experience, and an appreciation of religious claims.

11   From the Age of Monologue to the Age of Global Dialogue

DIALOGUE: THE WAY FORWARD

IN THE PAST, it was possible—indeed, unavoidable—for most human beings to live out their lives in isolation from the vast majority of their fellows, without even having a faint awareness of, let alone interest in, their very existence. At most, and for most, the occasional tale with distorted descriptions of faraway foreigners satisfied their curiosity. Everyone for the most part talked to his or her own cultural "self." Even the rare descriptions of the "Other" hardly ever came from that Other; rather, it came from some of their own who had heard, or heard of, the Other. Put briefly, until the edge of the present era, humans lived in the *Age of Monologue.* That age is now passing.

As noted earlier, we are now poised at the entrance to the *Age of Dialogue.* We travel all over the globe, and large elements of the entire globe come to us. Hardly a large city in the world does not echo with foreign accents and languages. Our streets, businesses, and homes are filled with foreign products. Through our television sets, we invite into our living rooms myriad people of strange nations, cultures, and religions.

We can no longer ignore the Other, but we can close our minds and spirits to them, look at them with fear and misunderstanding, come to resent them and, perhaps, even hate them. This way of encounter can all too easily lead to hostility and eventually war and death.

Today nuclear, ecological, or other catastrophic devastation lies just a little farther down the path of monologue. It is only by struggling out of the self-centered monologic mindset into dialogue with the Other as she or he really is, and not as we have projected her or him in our monologues, that we can avoid such cataclysmic disasters. In brief: We must move quickly from the *Age of Monologue* to the *Age of Dialogue.*

As stated earlier, what we understand to be the "explanation of the ultimate meaning of life and how to live accordingly" is what we call

145

our religion—or, if that explanation is not based on a notion of the transcendent, we can call it an ideology or belief. Because our religion or ideology is so comprehensive, so all-inclusive, it is the most fundamental area in which the Other is likely to be different from us and hence possibly seen as the most threatening. This is not over-dramatization. The current catalogue of conflicts that have religion or ideology as a constituent element is staggering, including such obvious neuralgic flashpoints as Northern Ireland, Lebanon, Israel, Sri Lanka, Pakistan–India, Tibet, Afghanistan, Sudan, and Armenia–Azerbaijan.

Hence, if humankind is to move from the Age of Monologue into the Age of Dialogue, the religions and ideologies must enter into that transition full-force. They have, in fact, begun to make serious progress along this path, though the journey stretches far ahead indeed.

DIALOGUE: A WAY OF THINKING

Dialogue, especially in the religious and ideological area, is not simply a series of conversations. It is a whole new way of thinking, a way of seeing and reflecting on the world and its meaning.

If we were writing just for Christians, we would use the term *theology* to name what we are talking about here. But the dialogical way of thinking is not peculiarly Christian. Rather, it is a way for all human beings to reflect on the ultimate meaning of life. Regardless of whether one is a theist or whether one is given to using Greek thought categories, as Christians have been wont to do in their "theologizing," dialogue is ever more clearly the way of the future in religious and ideological reflection on the ultimate meaning of life and how to live accordingly.

We are convinced that it is necessary to try to think beyond the absolutes that we as Christians, Muslims, Buddhists, and others in our own ways have increasingly found "de-absolutized" in our modern thought world. Hence, we would like to reflect here on the ways all humans need to think about the world and its meaning now that more and more individuals, and even institutions, are gaining enough maturity to notice that there are ways to integrate an understanding of the world other than the way that they and their forebears grew up in.

Beyond the absolute way of understanding the world and its meaning, beyond the absolute way of thinking, a much richer, "truer" way to understand the world is beginning to emerge: the dialogical way of thinking. It is this dialogical way of thinking particularly in the area of religion and ideology that we turn to now.

Each person's dialogue partners in this new paradigm, or model, of understanding the world are in fact all the ways of understanding the world and its meaning—all the world's religions and ideologies. And so, each should strive eventually to engage in dialogue with at least the world's major religions and ideologies, reflecting on what can be learned about and from each. But beyond all these dialogue partners is the often unconscious but always pervasive dialogue partner for all reading this book and an ever increasing number of contemporaries: *modern critical thought.*

Those who are open to dialogue—that is, those who are open to going beyond prior absolutes to learn from one another—live in a de-absolutized, "relationized," modern, critical-thinking thought world, a thought world in which they no longer can live on the level of the first naivete, but are at least striving to live on the level of the second naivete. On this level, they see their root symbols and metaphors *as* symbols and metaphors; hence, they do not mistake them for empirical, ontological realities, but they also do not simply reject them as fantasies and fairy tales. Rather, because they see them as root symbols and metaphors, they correctly appreciate them as indispensable vehicles for communicating profound realities that go beyond the capacity of everyday language to communicate.

DIALOGUE: ITS MEANING

Dialogue is conversation between two or more persons with differing views, the *primary* purpose of which for each participant is to learn from the other so that he or she can change and grow. Of course, both partners will also want to share their understanding with their partners. We enter into dialogue, however, primarily so we can learn, change, and grow, not so we can force change on the other.

In the past, when we encountered those who differed from us in the religious and ideological sphere, we did so usually to defeat them as opponents or to learn about them in order to deal with them more effectively. In other words, we usually faced those who differed with us in a confrontation—sometimes openly polemically, sometimes more subtly so, but usually with the ultimate goal of overcoming the other because we were convinced that we alone had the truth.

But that is not what dialogue is. Dialogue is not debate. In dialogue, each partner listens to the other as openly and sympathetically as possible in an attempt to understand the other's position as precisely and, as it were, as much from within as possible. Such an attitude automatically assumes that, at any point, we might find the partner's position under discussion so persuasive that, if we were to act with integrity, we ourselves would have to change.

Until quite recently in almost all religious traditions, the idea of seeking religious or ideological wisdom, insight, or truth through dialogue, occurred to very few people, except in a very initial and rudimentary fashion. It certainly had no influence in the major religious or ideological communities. The further idea of pursuing religious or ideological truth through dialogue with other religions and ideologies was even less thinkable.

Today, the situation is dramatically reversed. One example of this literal revolution comes from an unexpected source: Catholicism. In 1964, Pope Paul VI's first encyclical focused on dialogue:

> Dialogue is *demanded* nowadays. . . . [It] is *demanded* by the dynamic course of action which is changing the face of modern society. It is *demanded* by the pluralism of society and by the maturity man has reached in this day and age. Be he religious or not, his secular education has enabled him to think and speak, and to conduct dialogue with dignity.[1]

Further official words of encouragement came from the Vatican Secretariat for Dialogue with Non-believers: "All Christians should do their best to promote dialogue . . . as a duty of fraternal charity suited to our progressive and adult age."[2]

When we speak of "dialogue" here, we do not mean just another discussion, as valuable as that might be. We mean an experience of meeting with people of different fundamental convictions in such a way that each one's assumptions come to light, and that all can move ahead in reciprocal learning. We mean strengthening and affirming fundamental beliefs and practices, and transforming them.

The evolution of religions and cultures points toward a process that is essential to healing the deep problems that inhere in all aspects of our human cultures and even threaten our very survival—namely, the awakening of human beings to the power of dialogue. Something remarkable happens when we experience the depth of personal and communal dialogical awakening. There is a profound shift in how we perceive our selves, our lives, our priorities, our relationships, our world. The dialogical awakening removes obstructions that tend to cloud our global vision as it releases passionate moral energy, intensifies social responsibility, and deepens spirituality. Such intensive encounters energize participants to translate dialogical potency and passion into socially responsible action.

DIALOGUE: REASONS FOR ITS RISE

Why this dramatic change? Why should we pursue the truth in the area of religion and ideology by way of dialogue?

Many "external" factors have appeared in the past century and a half that have contributed constitutively to the creation of what we today call the "global village." In the past, the vast majority of people were born, lived, and died within the village or valley of their origin. Now, however, hundreds of millions of people in many countries have left their homes not only once or a few times; they do so frequently. Consequently, they experience customs and cultures other than their own. Moreover, the world comes to us through the mass media. All our economies are fast becoming highly interdependent global economies.

All these external factors have made it increasingly impossible for Westerners, and then gradually everyone, to live in isolation. We meet the other willy-nilly, and after two catastrophic world wars, a world depression, a threat of nuclear holocaust, and now ecological disaster, we are learning that our meeting can no longer be in indifference, for that leads to encounters in ignorance and prejudice, which is the tinder of hostility, and then violence. But if this violence were to lead to World War III or ecological catastrophe, it would be the end of human history. Hence, for the sake of survival, meeting in dialogue and cooperation is the only alternative to global disaster.

The twentieth century's global-catastrophic events had a profound impact on precisely the institutions most responsible for those events: Western modernity and the major religious institution therein, Christianity. Stanley Samartha, the first director of the World Council of Churches' division on interreligious dialogue, for example, noted that

"It is not without significance that only after the second world war (1945), when, with the dismantling of colonialism, new nations emerged on the stage of history and asserted their identity through their own religions and cultures, that both the Vatican and World Council of Churches began to articulate a more positive attitude toward the peoples of other religious traditions."[3]

DIALOGUE: A PARADIGM SHIFT IN EPISTEMOLOGY

Paralleling the rise of these extraordinary "external" factors was the rise of "internal" ones, which might be described succinctly as the even more dramatic shift in the understanding of the structure of reality, and especially the understanding of truth, that has taken place in Western civilization and beyond throughout the nineteenth and twentieth centuries. This shift has made dialogue not only possible but necessary. Where such words as *immutability, simplicity,* and *monologue* largely characterized our Western understanding of reality in an earlier day, in the past 150 years, *mutuality, relationality,* and *dialogue* have come to be understood as constitutive elements of the very structure of our human reality.

This substantive shift has been both very penetrating and broad, profoundly affecting both our understanding of what it means to be human and our systematic reflection on that meaning—in traditional Christian terms, *theologizing.* It is important, therefore, to examine this sea change in our understanding of reality and truth—this fundamental paradigm shift—and the implications it has for our systematic reflection.

From a certain perspective, how we conceive the ultimate structure of the universe—as static or dynamic, for example—is the most fundamental dimension of our human thought. Everything else is built upon and stems from it. Even those who claim to have no ultimate view of the universe, no metaphysics, do in fact have the most elusive kind of metaphysics, a covert one.

However, from another perspective, that of origin and development, it is how we understand our process of understanding and what meaning and status we attribute to our statements about reality—in other words, our epistemology—that is primary. It will profoundly determine how we conceive our view of the ultimate structure of reality, or our metaphysics; what value we place on it; and how we can use it. The same is true of everything else we perceive, conceive, and think of, and how we subsequently decide on things and act. For this reason, the revolutionary changes in our understanding of our understanding, in our understanding of truth—that is, in our epistemology—that have occurred in the West since the eighteenth-century Enlightenment have been extremely pervasive and radically influential.

As noted earlier in some detail, whereas our Western notion of truth was largely absolute, static, and monologic or exclusive up to the nineteenth century, it has since become de-absolutized, dynamic and dialogic—or, to use another word, *relational.*

THE IMPORTANCE OF 'DEEP-DIALOGUE' AND 'CRITICAL-THINKING'

'Deep-Dialogue' is something far beyond mere conversation between two or more persons. It means to stand on our position, and at the same time seek self-transformation through opening ourselves to those who think differently. Together with its counterpart, 'Critical-Thinking,' it is *a whole new way of thinking.* To open ourselves to 'Deep-Dialogue,' however, we must at the same time also develop the skills of thinking carefully and clearly, of 'Critical-Thinking' (*critical,* from the Greek, *krinein,* to choose, to judge). However, because 'Deep-Dialogue' and 'Critical-Thinking' are in fact necessarily two sides of one reality, whenever we speak of 'Deep-Dialogue,' we automatically mean to include 'Critical-Thinking.' This should be borne in mind when reading this book. In brief, for the sake of simplicity, we will normally use the term 'Deep-Dialogue' alone, and include within that term the meaning of 'Critical-Thinking' as well. Further, however, beyond being a whole new way of thinking, we see the dialogical principle at the very basis of *all* reality.

The Foundation of 'Deep-Dialogue'

'Deep-Dialogue' is grounded in the primal field of Reality itself. All through the ages, across all traditions and worldviews, the greatest minds have sought to name and articulate the primal principle of life and existence. Many alternative, profound strategies have been developed through millennia, each recognizing in one way or another that the way we conduct our mind, our thinking, is central to encountering this primal principle authentically. The diverse explanations of "what is first" made it virtually impossible for the different worldviews to converge on a truly global name or universal explanation of all Reality. Nevertheless, people have been convinced through the centuries that there must be one originating principle underlying all realities, all worldviews, including those of the sciences, insisting that there must be a primal principle as the source of all unity and diversity, a unifying force that both generates and holds together all realities.

However, precisely because of the widely variant languages of experience, a truly global name and narrative are only now emerging from the heart of human and cultural evolution. Only now is the form of consciousness and pattern of thinking beginning to mature globally which makes it possible to conceive, experience, name, and articulate the global essence of this infinite origin. This new and higher form of thinking moves beyond the older monocentric habits of thought which localized, and hence both obstructed and deformed the access to, the primal principle. Our patterns of thinking, language, and world-making had first to break the monocentric barriers and evolve into a more open space for language, experience, and thought to become truly global.

This fundamental advance in human consciousness which opens access to the primal principle is the result of experiencing the awakening power of 'Deep-Dialogue' and 'Critical-Thinking.' This is the "dialogical/critical turn" in human evolution. It opens the way to a global consciousness that can adequately reach the common ground between worldviews and perspectives. This awakened global dialogical/critical perspective between worlds is a profound revolution in how we see, experience, and process reality in every aspect of our cultural life. It gives us the capacity to hold widely variant worldviews together in creative communion. This dramatic shift in thinking discloses deeper global patterns of reality that could not be detected or processed in the monocentric habits of thinking. We now begin to see an open and global narrative which situates all worldviews and perspectives within the infinite primal field.

The deep drive in diverse worldviews to express, and even name, the primal infinite principle is apparent from the primal names presented by the great enduring traditions—for example: In Africa, Traditional Religion spoke of *Nomo* (Infinite Word); in China, Taoism and Confucianism wrote of *Tao* (Way); in India, Hinduism wrote of *Aum* (Infinite Word), and Buddhism talked of *Sunyata* (Void); in the Near East,

Judaism spoke of *Hohmah* (Lady Wisdom); in Europe the Greeks wrote of *Logos* (Word, Reason); Christianity also spoke of *Logos* (ἐν ἀρχῇ ἦν ὁ λόγοσ, "In the beginning was the Word," [John 1:1]); contemporary science speaks of a *Field of Energy*. All these are understood as the Source or Ultimate Principle (which etymologically literally means the "Final First").

In developing the global perspective it becomes more urgent than ever at this moment in history to recognize that these limitless alternative primal names do in fact co-arise from the same infinite source and co-express the same universal origin, which, because it is seen from variant cultural perspectives, gives rise to the various names. This intuition follows immediately from rigorous reflection on the nature of the infinite Ultimate Principle. Such a principle must be infinitely unitive and also infinitely generative of boundless primal names.

No global name has until now emerged as a candidate that can truly help the wide spectrum of worldviews and traditions of primal names come together in celebration of this common global origin. Now at the beginning of the third millennium as the process of globalization is exploding with exponential rapidity, it becomes more important than ever that a way be found to express the Ultimate Principle which will draw all peoples together, rather than split them into their cultural individualities. In fact, advances in recent decades in our understanding of how we humans understand have pointed the way to this global understanding and naming of the "Final First" which both preserves and celebrates the many particular cultural namings, and at the same time celebrates the unity underlying them all.

Beginning especially in the early nineteenth century with the growth of a strong sense of history, followed by the development of a series of "hermeneutics of suspicion," it has become increasingly clear that all statements about reality, including Ultimate Reality, are necessarily limited: spoken always in particular contexts, addressing particular questions, utilizing particular thought categories, employing particular kinds of language, viewing all from particular viewpoints of social place, gender, religious conviction, etc. However, there cannot be *just* particular views, for then we would have no way to speak with an other; we can speak to each other only on the basis of what we have in common (beginning with our common language), of what unites us. There clearly is also an underlying commonality; otherwise we would not even be able to discern that there was difference—difference from what? The very fact that we can differ is built on a fundamental commonality, a unity, within which context we can perceive differences, particularities.

To be fully human, then, it is vital that we be aware of both the limited, particular character of all statements, *and* at the same time the underlying unity within which differences can even appear. Therefore, because no single narrative, no single name can fully comprehend or name the Final First (thus *recognizing the particularity* of all language), we humans must also be in endless dialogue with each other in order to approach endlessly the infinite Ultimate Principle as an ever visible, yet ever receding, horizon (thus *recognizing the underlying unifying dialogic* context within which all language should ultimately be placed).

Thus, we are speaking about the *concept Dia-Logos* (Greek: word/reason-*across*) as a global expression of the Ultimate Principle. Therefore, when speaking English or other Indo-European languages we will use the *term Dia-Logos*. Other languages will use their own corresponding terms to express the concept, e.g., Chinese *duihwa*, Hebrew *dosioch*.

We know that from subatomic physics, to astronomical cosmology, to the inner and inter workings of humanity, all reality is not static (Greek: *stasis:* standing still), but dynamic (*dynamis:* movement, energy). Hence, at the foundation of all reality is not just *Logos,* as expressed in the specific Greek and Christian cultural languages, but on a global inter-cultural, inter-language level: **Dia-Logos.**

In the Indo-European language family the term *Dia-Logos* of course can draw on the rich heritage of the Greek/Christian term *Logos* and help us global humans come together in the recognition of our common ground. For one thing, its cognate, "logic" helps us to realize that there is a deep logic, an onto-logic, of this Ultimate Principle. Further, the myriad words ending in "logy": geology, technology, psychology, sociology, ecology, biology, theology . . . carry the classical force of cognition, of giving an account, of a rigorous discipline or science, and this too can help us enter a rigorous path with ecumenical power across our diverse worldviews.

But it is vital here to recall again that as a global name for "what is first," *Dia-Logos,* does not compete with or displace the many primal names that have emerged through the ages across cultures. Rather, the global force of *Dia-Logos* must help us to be mindful that the Ultimate

Principle inherently generates alternative primal names, each of which has unique creative force. Thus *Dia-Logos* designates the *plurality* which must resonate: *Tao, Aum, Sunyata, Hohmah, Logos, Nomo, Energy Field* . . . the boundless range of genuine primal names. Nor does this suggest that these diverse primal names for the Ultimate Principle are "synonymous" or "equivalent" in any naive or uncritical sense. For the deep logic of *Dia-Logos* opens space for profound multiplicity and diversity— which nevertheless co-arise in Unity. This "unity in plurality," *e pluribus unum*, is the power of *Dia-Logos*.

As we enter the global dialogical/critical way of thinking and using language, we gain deeper access to the common grounds between worlds. However, it takes the awakening process of 'Deep-Dialogue' to expand human thought to the global level and to encounter the various primal names: *Logos, Tao, Hohmah* . . . ; but at the same time it takes the clarifying power of *Logos, Tao, Hohmah* . . . to move us into effective *Dia-Logos*, 'Deep-Dialogue.' In this natural evolutionary circularity of "unity in plurality" we see that the emergence in humanity of a dialogical/critical consciousness, of an *awareness* of *Logos, Tao, Hohmah* . . . and hence *Dia-Logos,* has been millennia in the making. The dynamics of 'Deep-Dialogue' are classically grounded in the evolutionary process itself, now clarified as the emergence of the *awareness* of the global *Dia-Logos* in human and cultural evolution.

The breakthrough in thinking to a globalized way of being has been a long painful process in our evolution. 'Deep-Dialogue' is the awakening process which both recapitulates the stages of the global turn and enables us to encounter the truly global, universal character of *Dia-Logos*. In the historic drama of *Dia-Logos* emerging we see that human cultures have been in inter-cultural interaction since the dawn of civilizations, but in contemporary times this globalizing dynamic has so accelerated that it is now precipitating an explosive "chain reaction," opening thereby space for a truly global disclosure of *Dia-Logos*.

When we attain an awareness that our particular naming of the Ultimate Principle is ultimate *within* its religious/cultural context, we reach the dialogical perspective. *Then* our particular naming can *for us* become truly globally ultimate. We can then affirm that *Aum, Tao, Logos* . . . is ultimate, because it is open-ended, because it is in dialogue with all other ultimate namings.

Principles Underlying 'Deep-Dialogue'

The following principles seek to capture and express some of the prominent dimensions of 'Deep-Dialogue.' Obviously there are other alternative formulations of principles of 'Deep-Dialogue' which would stress other aspects and articulate certain features of 'Deep-Dialogue' not here explicated. Nor does this initial experimental formulation seek to be comprehensive or conclusive. In the spirit of 'Deep-Dialogue' it remains under revision and subject to ongoing amendment. Underlying all reality we can see at least ten theoretical dialogic principles.

1) THE CONTINUUM PRINCIPLE.   All reality is dialogic/critical, operating on a continuum:

Destructive Dialogue	→	Disinterested Dialogue	→	Dialogical Dialogue	→	'Deep-Dialogue'
Elements are polarized against each other		Elements are tolerant of each other		Elements learn from each other		Elements are mutually transformed

2) THE DIALOGUE-ON-DIALOGUE PRINCIPLE.   A primary way, a "Royal Road," to the Dialogical/Critical Awakening is an extended dialogue on 'Deep-Dialogue' itself. Such an intense dialogue lays bare all the underlying issues—religious, philosophical, psychological, etc.—which, when resolved, when integrated, will together serve as a locomotive pulling forward all other issues submitted to dialogue.

3) THE REALITY-IS-DIALOGIC PRINCIPLE.   All reality is fundamentally inter-active, mutual, "dialogic." This dialogic structure is present from the sub-atomic to the cosmic (where on both levels matter and energy are convertible; and further, a growing number of thinkers believe that the binary structure of computers—that is, an endless series of 1's and 0's in "dialogue" with each other—is reflective of the fundamental nature of all reality), through the *intra*-personal to the *inter*-personal, still further to the inter-communal, and ultimately the global—and beyond to the Source and Goal of all reality.

4) THE INTEGRATIVE PRINCIPLE.   Not only is all reality "dialogic," it is also *integrative*. This "dialogue" of all reality oscillates in polar tension between the destructive and the integrative. For example, when the dialogic relationship between the electrons, protons, neutrons and other

"particles" and "waves" in an atom is not "integrated," when the centrifugal and centripetal forces are not balanced in creative polar tension, the atom will "dis-integrate" into either a black hole or a nuclear explosion. As matter becomes ever more complex, the integration of the "dialogue" becomes more and more that of a delicately balanced network, which makes a qualitative leap when it reaches living matter, and a still greater leap when it arrives at reflexive, rational/intuitive, affective, "spiritual" human beings.

5) The 'Critical-Thinking' is the Obverse of 'Deep-Dialogue' Principle.   In order to open oneself to 'Deep-Dialogue' it is vital to likewise develop the skills of thinking carefully and clearly, that is, of 'Critical-Thinking.' We need to learn how to understand what we, and others, really mean when we say something, and why we say it, in order to "choose," to "judge" (*krinein*) where we believe the truth lies. 'Critical-Thinking,' thus, entails at least these four elements:

a) That we work to raise our pre-suppostions from the un-conscious level—where by definition they reside—to the conscious level. Only then can we deal with them fully humanly, that is, rationally reflect on and decide for, against, or partly-partly concerning them.

b) That we realize that *our* view of reality is *a* view of reality, that though it shares much with others' views of reality, it is also partially shaped by our personal lenses through which we experience and interpret reality, and hence is not absolute but perspectival.

c) That we learn to understand all statements, whether from ourselves or others, in *their* context, that is, a text can be correctly understood in *its con*-text. Only then will we be able to translate the original core of the statements/texts into *our* context.

d) That we learn to probe with great precision *every* statement, first of our own, but also of all others, to learn *precisely* what they *really* mean. This is particularly important to do concerning simple statements, terms, and cliches because very often unconscious presuppositions lie beneath them.

This process of 'Critical-Thinking' obviously entails a mental dialogue within our own mind. Thus, at its root 'Critical-Thinking' is dialogic—and 'Deep-Dialogue' at its root entails clear, critical thought! They are two sides of the coin of Humanity: They must become *virtues,* that is, *habits of mind and spirit.*

6) THE KNOWING-IS-DIALOGIC-INTEGRATIVE PRINCIPLE.   All knowing is both inter-active, mutual, dialogic *and* integrative between the known and the knower. For knowing is a kind of unifying of the object and the subject—a kind of "integration." Example: the surface of a table becomes one with, "integrated with," the surface of my fingers. The inter-active, mutual, unifying, dialogic-integrative character is doubly true when the knower is also the known, as in my learning about what it means to be human. This is very especially true when *I* learn what it means *for me* to be human. That dialogic-integrative character, then, is endlessly, infinitely, true of all knowing: From

a) when the known and the knower are separate object and subject, through
b) when the known and knower are *inter*-personal, further through
c) when the known and knower are communities of persons, to ultimately
d) when they embrace the whole globe—and beyond
e) to the Source/Goal of all reality.

7) THE DIALOGUE-IS-COMMUNION PRINCIPLE.   Dialogue is a "coming together," a "conversation" with those who think differently from us *primarily* so *we* can learn. Because all reality is mutual, in a full dialogue *both* participants must come *primarily* to learn. Hence secondarily, but essentially, our partners must also teach if we are to learn, and vice versa. When "Destructive Dialogue" moves toward integration, it becomes the attitudinally indifferent "Disinterested Dialogue," then progresses toward learning "Dialogical Dialogue," and ultimately reaches 'Deep-Dialogue,' when the learning from each other attains the level which transforms our consciousness.

8) THE PLURALIZING-AUTHENTICATING PRINCIPLE.   Dialogue *can* occur when I realize that my view of reality is *a* view, not *the* only view. Dialogue *will* occur when I perceive persons with views different from mine who are living what I (and obviously also they) think are authentic human lives—I will then necessarily want to know how they do it!

9) THE WHOLENESS-AS-INNER/INTER-DIALOGUE PRINCIPLE.   Dialogue engages the whole person: the mind, emotions, action. It spills over from the cognitive into the affective area of life, and from there into the practical area both on the inter-personal and the communal, and then further into the inter-communal, levels. This naturally leads to networking, alliances, and cooperative activities, which are dialogue-integration in action. Thus Dialogue heals, makes whole (holy), persons and *polis*.

10) THE DIALOGUE-AS-ONTOLOGY-OF-RIGHTNESS PRINCIPLE.   When one successfully experiences dialogue, 'Deep-Dialogue,' it *feels* right. We feel *integrated*. 'Deep-Dialogue' feels right, integrated, because human dialogue is "in sync" with not only our whole humanity, body and spirit, but also with the whole of reality from the sub-atomic through the cosmic to Ultimate Reality, Which/Who is "in dialogue-integration" with the World.

Three Dynamics Operating in 'Deep-Dialogue'

It should be apparent that the ten principles articulated above are deeply integral to one another in the living praxis of 'Deep-Dialogue.' In the following articulation of three fundamental dynamics of 'Deep-Dialogue' we see that the diverse principles actually arise together and cooperate in the living process of 'Deep-Dialogue.'

1) THE REALITY DYNAMIC.   'Deep-Dialogue' is the human art of life that is grounded in the reality process itself. It is primarily the art of being, the art of conducting our minds in harmony with the process of reality itself. This awakening of awareness to a deeper encounter with reality is itself a natural evolution of our human condition. In the light of the *Dia-Logos* principle we see how and why objective reality is a dynamic dialogic or interactive process in which all existence is in a boundless, evolving interplay. Thus, the very fabric of reality is a dynamic drama of relations held together by the unifying power of *Dia-Logos*. All life is an unfolding dialogic process. Nature unfolds in dialogue, and so we may speak of "natural dialogue."

2) THE MUTUALITY DYNAMIC.   The magic and mystery of dialogue is that as the natural pulse of *Dia-Logos* is at once the binding force that holds diverse things together in primal relationality and the differential

force that generates and encourages the flourishing of multiplicity and differentiation. In brief: the primal force of existence is dialogic—i.e., the primal force is relational in that it allows things to be boundlessly differentiated, and yet totally unified in an integral whole. This is why all things essentially arise out of dialogical force, find their identity and inner integrity in and through this force, and are held together externally in a binding force that forms an integrating *continuum*, an external integrity. The very pulse of existence is a natural dialogic process. This *Dia-Logos* force, then, is the reason why existence is a *continuum* of boundlessly differentiated beings, each evolving in inner unity and outer integrity.

3) THE REFLEXIVE-AWAKENING DYNAMIC.   Human evolution has arisen out of the natural evolutionary dialogue in which consciousness moves increasingly in a dialogic/critical awakening—a self-reflexive dynamic in which life becomes self-aware of the dialogic/critical principle of *Dia-Logos* itself. This is the driving *logo*-motive of human life and the dynamics of 'Deep-Dialogue.' The awakening life process is the dialogic/critical impulse, the dialogical/critical imperative, awakening us to the living of the *Dia-Logos*. Thus, there is a deep circularity in the dynamics of 'Deep-Dialogue.' It takes 'Deep-Dialogue' to awaken to the moving force of life, which is realized in the reflexive awareness of 'Deep-Dialogue.'

'Critical-Thinking' as well as 'Deep-Dialogue'

'Deep-Dialogue,' thus, is a powerful transformative process that eventually must become a habit of mind and spirit, which is traditionally known as a *virtue*—grounded in classical philosophical and spiritual traditions in a global context. It has been experimentally developed and distilled over many years through a wide range of interworld encounters (interreligious, intercultural, interideological . . .). It is a method of entering other worlds or perspectives and returning mutually transformed, having gained a deepened sense of one's own worldview and an awakened awareness of the worldviews of others. Through this awakening power of 'Deep-Dialogue,' individuals and communities are able to experience common ground between worlds and across differences, and thus achieve deeper personal integrity and community-building.

At the same time, as noted earlier very briefly, in order to open one-self to 'Deep-Dialogue,' it is vital to develop the skills of thinking care-fully and clearly—that is, of thinking *critically*. We need to learn how to understand what we really mean when we say something, and why we said it, in order to "choose," to "judge" where we believe the truth lies. This process obviously entails a mental dialogue within one's own mind.

At the beginning of the third millennium, what is needed is a reno-vation of all education—from the cradle to the grave—through 'Deep-Dialogue' and 'Critical-Thinking' based on a *Global Ethic*, within an emerging *Global Civilization* (not a monolithic one, but one that is a "unity in diversity"—as the U.S. penny has it, *e pluribus unum*, "out of many, one"). It has become increasingly clear that one of the greatest challenges facing contemporary cultures and all levels of education is coping creatively with the powerful forces that arise when diverse worldviews and perspectives encounter one another. The most chronic, intractable, and devastating problems facing cultures today center on the breakdown of human relations in the collision of worldviews and differences in all aspects of our lives.

'Deep-Dialogue' and 'Critical-Thinking' are core human competen-cies that function at the foundation of all human life and experience. This key advance flows from the insight that reality itself, and therefore our thinking about it, is a dynamic, unified field of interrelations—a pro-found dialogic process in which all things are interconnected. From the wealth of cultural experiments through the ages the realization has emerged that human reason, 'Critical-Thinking,' is dialogical at its core. 'Deep-Dialogue' is thus the heart of our rational capacity to negotiate reality, to be in touch with the ever-changing worlds around us. To-gether, 'Deep-Dialogue' and 'Critical-Thinking' are vital in the art of being human.

This insight that the dynamics of dialogue permeate our life in every way is reflected in the ancient, perennial awareness that we humans play a vital role in co-shaping our living realities. Now, the most advanced research has made it clear that we humans inhabit worlds that we ourselves shape (and that reciprocally shape us) through our thought processes. We humans inhabit worldviews that we make through dia-logical processes of conceptualization, interpretation, imagination, con-struction, revision—all of which are integral to the rational enterprise.

In this way, every aspect of our lives, our experience, and the world around us arises in the context of a worldview or complex of "life worlds" that we inhabit, and that inhabit us. It has become clear that at the core of this human art of world-making, which shapes all our experience, is a fundamental dialogic dynamic between the self, or subject, and the realities that surround us. At the very foundation of our lives, we are situated in an interrelational structure of self and other (subject and object), which always involves modes of dialogue, interpretation, and critical thought.

Thus, it may be said that we humans are dialogical rational beings, world-makers, interpretive beings who directly co-shape and participate in all phenomena that appear to us. In this deeper and expanded sense of the rational enterprise, we can see that natural reason is essentially our capacity to shape our life worlds, to make our experience, to recognize analytically and clarify differences, and to cope with multiplicity and diversity. At the same time, it is also a capacity synthetically to discern fundamental unities and common ground, to harmonize differences into coherent order, and to negotiate complex factors in the forging of our individuality, personal identity, and integrity.

Further, the dialogic structure of humanity entails not only thinking and speaking dialogically, but also acting toward and with others—persons and things—in ways that are dialogic. Because the principles on which we base our actions are called *ethics,* and given that we are living increasingly in a single world, we are correspondingly moving toward a common basis, a *Global Ethic,* that shapes how we treat ourselves, one another, and the world we all inhabit.

These fundamental skills and competencies in the art of being a person exhibit diverse dimensions in the dynamics of 'Deep-Dialogue' and 'Critical-Thinking.' In this respect, the virtues of 'Deep-Dialogue' and 'Critical-Thinking' are at work in every aspect of our lives—in our passions and emotions; in our cognition, understanding, judgment, deliberation; in our relations with self, others, and the world around us, i.e., the "ecology." In the art of becoming a person, an integral being (an *in*-dividual—i.e., *un*-divided), it is now more urgent than ever for us to cultivate core competencies in the dynamics of 'Deep-Dialogue' and 'Critical-Thinking.' For these skills enable us to become whole persons, integral beings, who can not only harmonize a boundless diversity of worldviews, perspectives, and identities into a coherent inner life, but who can also negotiate our outer life, our ethics, in peaceful and non-violent ways of communion and community with others and the ecology.

SEVEN STAGES OF 'DEEP-DIALOGUE'

Stage One: Radical Encountering of Difference (Self Faces the Other)

This first encounter comes with a certain shock, with a realization of an Other, a different way of life, a different worldview, an alien Other that resists, interrupts, disrupts my settled patterns of interpretation. With this primal encounter there is a new realization that my habits of mind cannot make sense of this Other. This radical encounter with difference—a different world, a different way of making sense of and experiencing the world—is disconcerting, sometimes threatening, and evokes a vulnerability to this alien presence. I have a new sense of delimitation, and I feel challenged to change, to revise my way of relating to this Other. I realize now that my habit of translating the Other into my pattern of "minding," of appropriating the Other to my worldview, is dysfunctional. So I face a sudden silence, pause, opening—an open horizon of uncertainty and risk. I must make a decision to move forward, or draw back.

Stage Two: Crossing Over—Letting Go and Entering the World of the Other (Self Transformed Through Empathy)

After the initial shock and realization that I now face an alien world, a worldview very different from my own, I feel challenged to inquire, investigate, engage, and enter this new world. As I open my self to this Other, I realize that I need to stand back and distance myself from my former habits and patterns of minding the world. I begin to realize that this other world organizes and processes the world very differently from my way. I realize that I must learn new habits and ways of interpretation to make sense of this different world. I must learn a "new language." Indeed, I must translate myself into a different form of life that sees the world differently. This involves a bracketing of my prejudices.

Stage Three: Inhabiting and Experiencing the World of the Other (Self Transformed into the Other)

I begin to feel a new and deep empathy for my new habitat. I want to let myself go—free myself to enter, experiment, learn, and grow in this new way of being. I hold on to my prior views as much as I can, but I do advance in a conservative fashion. Still, I experience an excitement in discovering, in inhabiting a new and different worldview. I have a new profound realization of *an-Other*, an alternative reality and form of life. But in the end, I realize that this is not my home.

Stage Four: Crossing Back with an Expanded Vision
(Self Returns Home with New Knowledge)

I now cross back, return, to my own world, bringing back new knowledge of how to think and act—and may even wish to adopt or adapt some of it for myself. As a result of this primary encounter with the world of the Other, I now realize that there are other ways to understand reality. I am therefore open to rethinking how I see myself, others, and the world. I encounter my self and culture anew, with a newly opened mind. My encounter with radical difference now challenges my former identity, and everything begins to appear in a new light. A dramatic deepening now begins in my sense of my self, my identity, my ethnicity, my life world, my religion, my culture. There is no return to my former unilateral way of minding.

Stage Five: The Dialogical Awakening—A Radical Paradigm Shift
(Self Inwardly Transformed)

As a result of this new encounter with self, I begin when I cross back from my deep encounter with an Other to experience a profound shift in all aspects of my world—in my inner experience, in my encounter with others, in my relating to the world. I begin to realize that my encounter with the Other has shaken the foundation of my former worldview, my former identity. For now that I am mindful of the living reality of other worlds, other perspectives, I can no longer return to my former identity and forget this living presence of the Other. Indeed, I now begin to realize that there are many other worlds, other forms of life, other perspectives that surround me. I now open to a plurality of other worlds and perspectives, and this irrevocably changes my sense of self. I feel transformed to a deeper sense of relation and connection with my ecology. I feel more deeply rooted in this experience of relationality and community. I now see that my true identity is essentially connected with this expansive network of relations with Others. This is the ignition of the Dialogical Awakening.

Stage Six: The Global Awakening—The Paradigm Shift Matures
(Self Related to Self, Others, the World)

In my transformed dialogical awakening, I discover a deeper common ground between the multiple worlds and perspectives that surround me. I have a new sense that self and others are inseparably bound together in a boundless interrelational web. I realize that multiplicity and diversity enriches my self and my world. I now see that all worlds are situated in a common ground of reality and that radical differences are nevertheless situated in a field of unity.

I experience three related dimensions of global dialogical awakening:

1) An ever-deepening discovery of self: I become aware of a deep inner dialogue within my self. I discover a rich multiplicity and diversity of perspectives within my own inner world. In this inner dialogue, I feel increasingly deeply rooted and grounded in my world. My identity is enriched with multiplicity, and I experience a more potent sense of my uniqueness as I celebrate my expanded world of relationality with others and with the ecology.

2) A dynamic dialogue opens with others in my community: As my new inner dialogue evolves, I find myself in a new and transformed relationship with others who share my world, my tradition, my religion, my culture. This new phase of relations with my peers can be disorienting and disconcerting, for as I now dramatically grow in my identity, I find myself in an estranged distance from many of my peers, even as I discover a deeper affinity and embrace of my community, my *polis*. I face a new turbulence—miscommunication and misunderstanding with my colleagues—and a challenging and dramatic dialogue unfolds in my *polis*.

3) A global awakening emerges in all aspects of my life: As this inner and outer dialogue matures, I realize that my understanding of my world enters a new "global" light. I realize that I am surrounded with many worldviews. I enter a global horizon and a global consciousness in which inter-religious, inter-cultural, inter-ideological, inter-disciplinary, inter-personal dialogues abound in all directions. I now have a new globalized sense of reality—a dialogical domain in which multiple alternative worlds are situated in dynamic, ever-deepening relations. With this understanding comes a new attitude toward life and toward ethics.

Stage Seven: Personal and Global Transforming of Life and Behavior
(Self Lives and Acts in a New Global Dialogical Consciousness)

As this paradigm shift in my life matures, I realize that a deep change has taken place in all aspects of my life—a new moral consciousness and a *new practice*. As my new dialogical consciousness becomes a habit of life, I find that my behavior and my disposition toward self and other has blossomed. I feel a new sense of communion with my self, with others, and with the ecology. I realize that the deepest care for my self essentially involves my care for others and for the environment. I have a deeper sense of belonging to my world and to my community, and with this comes a boundless sense of responsibility in all of my conduct. I now realize that I am transformed in the deepest habits of mind and behavior. I find a deeper sense of self-realization and fulfillment and meaning in my life and my relationships with others and the world around me.

RESULTS OF INTERRELIGIOUS, INTERIDEOLOGICAL DIALOGUE

What results of the dialogue among religions, and ideologies, can be looked for? In general, we can expect not only a proportional cessation of violence—physical, verbal, economic, and so on—but also a burst of creativity. It is obvious that the diminishing of hostility in the world will automatically raise the level of "happiness" in the world. But beyond that, it is also true that the energy—particularly the psychic and intellectual energy—otherwise poured into overt and covert polemics will be released for constructive rather than destructive purposes. But will these newly freed forces be turned to other wasteful or even destructive uses? Possibly.

However, the overwhelming likelihood is that they will be focused on a creative expansion of the individual's authentic self, which very much includes relations with others—other persons, animals, inanimate things, and, finally, Ultimate Reality. The reasons for this are several:

Dialogue Partners Serve as Mirrors

First, in dialogue the partners serve as mirrors for each other. The same basic human law of becoming more wholly human through mutuality referred to earlier operates very centrally in dialogue. Every person entering dialogue will have a certain self-understanding. However, in the dialogue, people will not only learn more about their partners, they will also learn how their partners have perceived them.

Even if the first dialogue partners claim that the second have misunderstood them—which to a greater or lesser extent normally happens—the first partners will learn how they de facto have been seen by at least some of the others. This "relationship" of being perceived by others is also very much a part of their own reality. Relationships are essential, constitutive elements of each human (of every being, for that matter). Humans live not as atomized "monads," but in groups. As Aristotle noted, humans are gregarious animals (as in the Latin *gregis*, "flock"). Through their dialogue partners, humans learn an additional piece of "how they are in the world," as Heidegger might put it.

Because in dialogue people come primarily to learn from the other and to change accordingly, this learning to know how others perceive them will also tend to have a transformative effect on the first partners. For example, if the first partners understand themselves to be tolerant, but they frequently learn that others perceive them as intolerant, they will perhaps try to change their way of acting so as to communicate what they believe is their authentic self. Or they may be forced, after reflection, to admit to themselves that they were not in fact as tolerant as they thought they were and then move to change their inner reality and become more tolerant, or change their understanding of tolerance, or perhaps decide they are being as "tolerant" as they believe they, with integrity, ought to be (e.g., they judge they should not be "tolerant" of racism).

Shift from Inward to Outward Looking

Second, entering into serious interreligious, interideological dialogue entails shifting from a kind of inward staring—whose concomitant move is to sally forth to persuade or attack the outsider—to a looking outward. This is a fundamental, radical shift that normally will utterly transform the dialogue partners. The outside religious world is no longer perceived as essentially hostile and the locus of evil and error—or, at best, as the locus of ignorance—as it has been throughout the Age of Monologue. Rather, the outside religious and ideological world is now perceived as a possible source of knowledge, wisdom, insight, inspiration, edification—though one does not, of course, naively think that everything in other religions and ideologies is inspiration and wisdom.

But by approaching the outside world with positive expectations, the dialogue partners are inevitably amazed at the extraordinary quantity and quality of inspiration and wisdom that is found there. Both were there all along; the monologists were deaf to them, but the dialogists—as Jesus observed of the authentic seekers among his listeners—"have the ears to hear" (Matthew 13:9).

Dialogical "Chain Reaction"

Third, the turning of one's gaze from inward to outward toward a dialogue partner creates a kind of chain reaction. For example, the Catholic Church long was stolidly engaged in "navel-gazing" until the Second Vatican Council (1962–65). In the early 1920s, Pope Benedict XV refused to join with those Protestant and Orthodox Christians who invited him (and Catholicism) to help form the Ecumenical Movement, a movement of dialogue among Christians to work for Christian unity. His successor, Pope Pius XI, forbade Catholics to participate in the first world meeting of the Faith and Order Movement (for Christian unity) in 1927, and his successor Pope Pius XII did the same sort of thing again in 1948 and 1954.

However, Pius XII's successor, "Good Pope John" (Pope John XXIII), called the Second Vatican Council in 1959 "to renew the Catholic Church so it could work for Christian unity." The Council went on to insist officially on the absolute necessity of Catholics' entering into dialogue not only with Protestants and Orthodox Christians, but also with Jews, Muslims, Hindus, Buddhists, and other religionists, as well as non-believers.

Once the turn to dialogue with the first logical partners for Catholics—Protestants and Orthodox Christians—was made, the inner logic of that turn continued the dialogic move to each next "logical" partner: If inspiration and wisdom could be found in dialogue with non-Catholic Christians, should it not also be possible with those espousing Judaism, Christianity's "source"? Why not, then, the other Semitic religion, Islam? The religions of the East, Hinduism, Buddhism, Confucianism, Taoism, and so on? Why not "All men of good will"? as John XXIII put it in his moving encyclical *Pacem in terris*.[4]

The spiritual "fission and fusion" that has occurred as a result of this chain reaction in the Catholic Church has been nothing short of "thermonuclear." The Council itself stated that "All Christians should do their best to promote dialogue ... as a duty of fraternal charity suited to our progressive and adult age."[5] As noted previously, in his first encyclical (1964), Pope Paul VI wrote: "Dialogue is demanded nowadays. . . . It is demanded . . . by the maturity man has reached in this day and age," and in 1968 the Vatican Secretariat for Dialogue with Unbelievers wrote that, "Doctrinal dialogue should be initiated with courage and sincerity, with the greatest freedom. . . . Doctrinal discussion [must] recognize the truth everywhere, even if the truth demolishes one so that one is forced to reconsider one's own position, in theory and in practice."[6]

Adapt Elements from Our Dialogue Partners

Fourth, in dialogue we will not only learn to know our partners more accurately; we will also find things in their tradition that we find admirable, even to the point that we will want to adopt them for ourselves. For example, some Buddhist traditions of meditation have made a strong impression on many Christians. Conversely, some Buddhists have been greatly impressed by the Christian commitment to social justice, even to the point of going to prison or dying for social justice. The result has been that some Christians have taken up meditation methods they learned from Buddhists, and some Buddhists have become deeply involved in social-justice actions.

However, interreligious dialogue should not lead to a kind of syncretism in the sense of an eclectic mixture of elements from here and there. Rather, dialogue should, and does, lead one to "adapt" rather than simply "adopt" elements from our dialogue partners. This means that the adapted element is modified to fit with integrity into the first partner's tradition. For example, a Christian does not become a nontheist by adapting Zen meditation, and a Buddhist engages in social-justice action not despite the fact that he or she is Buddhist, but because of it!—as was vigorously stated by the Theravada Buddhist Sulak Sivaraksa from Bangkok.

Dialogue Needs to Result in Practice

Fifth, dialogue needs to result in joint action in the practical area. Such joint religious action began to develop in earnest in the West only in the nineteenth century. Until that time, efforts to help disadvantaged human beings were pretty much done on a remedial, individualistic basis. "Charitable" institutions were founded—actually in quite extraordinary richness. The situation began to change drastically, however, with the coming of the Industrial Revolution in England in the late eighteenth century and elsewhere in Europe and in America starting in the nineteenth century. The old guild and feudal systems no longer functioned for the increasing millions caught in the transfer of populations to the cities.

Before the nineteenth century, most people died quite young, and a much smaller population lived in relative social and geographical stability. Then, a massive and exploding population problem burst upon the world for which neither civil society nor religion was prepared. Individual acts of charity and charitable institutions were increasingly swamped in the growing flood of social misery that rose as the nineteenth and twentieth centuries wore on. At the same time, the structures of society and their workings were being studied. Plans for shaping and reshaping those structures were laid and tested, adjusted, and retested. Such awareness, planning, and action also took place within Western religions.

Around the globe today, Christian and Jewish institutions spend billions of dollars annually on social-justice issues, a significant portion of which is aimed at changing the structures of society to benefit more people. The notion is spreading among Christians that the mission of the Church is to preach the Good News of the Gospel to all humanity, not just quantitatively in terms of individual persons, but also qualitatively in terms of every portion of the human beings: The human patterns one lives in are an essential part of one's humanity. The message of the *relationality* of all reality, very much including humankind, has struck home.

A similar phenomenon is also beginning to take place in some dimensions of Buddhism. One very striking example is Won Buddhism, which sprang up in Korea early in the twentieth century. Won Buddhism works to combine the principles of Gautama Buddha with an affirmation of modern science and technology in working for the betterment of men and women, individually and collectively. Hence, it is not surprising that the Won Buddhists also have a very strong commitment to interreligious dialogue.

A similar development has taken place in Japan—namely, in some of the so-called new religions that are Buddhist-based. For example, the Rissho Kosei-Kai—co-founded in the 1930s by Nikkyo Niwano—was initially very much an individualistically oriented branch of Buddhism. But in recent decades—significantly, as a result of dialogue with Catholics, and in particular a meeting with Pope Paul VI in 1965— Rissho Kosei-Kai has moved toward a strong commitment to social justice and interreligious dialogue.

At the same time, we would like to stress that joint religious action should not be limited to helping those who are in material need. Rather, we would like to suggest that the other toward whom our joint "altruistic" ethical action should reach might simply be named the oppressed, the unfree in any dimension—and who is completely free? Logic, of course, also directs that those in greatest need should receive the greatest attention, but it likewise directs that each should contribute according to her or his gifts, and in a preeminent, though not exclusive, way to those before them now in need, whether that be a material, spiritual, social, esthetic, or other need: for example, producing good material things for the well-to-do and the poor, teaching the poor as well as the well-to-do, making democracy work better for the well-to-do and the poor, creating beauty for the poor and the well-to-do.

In the United States, for example, the material poverty of the 30 million "poor" must be eradicated, but at the same time, the various spiritual poverties of the 220 million "well-to-do" must likewise be diminished. This "preferential option for the unfree" in no way rules out the "preferential option for the poor." Rather, it includes it—in eminent fashion—but expands it.

In conclusion, interreligious, interideological action that does not eventuate in dialogue will grow mindless, ineffective. Interreligious and interideological dialogue that does not eventuate in action will grow hypocritical, ineffective. Neither can survive singly.

New Questions Not Raised Before

Sixth, patiently pursued dialogue will eventually cast up new questions that neither of the dialogue partners had thought of on their own. Here is the area of the greatest potential creativity in dialogue. Of course, we won't know what the creative questions will be ahead of time. If we did, they would not be new or fully creative. Still, let me offer two examples of such questions that have already begun to arise from the Buddhist–Christian dialogue in one case and the Christian–Muslim dialogue in the other:

EFFECTS OF DESCRIBING ULTIMATE REALITY.   Earlier, we laid out something of our understanding of Christian (and one could perhaps also add Jewish and Muslim) and Buddhist understandings of Ultimate Reality. We, along with some other Christians engaged in dialogue with Buddhism, suggested that the Christian penchant for describing Ultimate Reality in positive terms (Being, Fullness, *Pleroma*) and the Buddhist tendency to describe it in negative terms (Emptiness, *Sunyata*) need not be understood as mutually exclusive contradictions, but perhaps more like complementary descriptions.

If this position is more or less accepted, it becomes extremely interesting and enlightening to investigate whether, and then how, these different descriptions of Ultimate Reality "make a difference in the world." The Semitic (Jewish, Christian, and Muslim) religions over the centuries have invested huge amounts of energy in trying to improve the human lot *in this world,* while Buddhism institutionally has been relatively uninterested. Is this difference in the world somehow connected with the differing understandings, and therefore descriptions, of Ultimate Reality? Is the fact that at least two of the Semitic religions have consistently been vastly more aggressive, intolerant, and violent than has Buddhism also connected with their particular—affirmative and negative, respectively—descriptions of Ultimate Reality?

If there is a connection, what are its mechanisms? What, if anything, can or should be done about it? These, we believe, could be extremely critical questions for the future of humanity and of the religions in questions, and for their mutual relationships.

HUMAN RIGHTS AND SEPARATION OF RELIGION AND STATE.   According to the first book of the Bible, Genesis, every human being was created by the one God as God's image (*imago Dei*); from this flows the biblical notion of the equal dignity of all human beings. This idea became one of the pillars of what is known today as "human rights" as they are enshrined in the United Nations' 1948 Declaration and subsequent documents. Two other pillars are the Greek concept of the political rule of the people (*demos-cratia,* "democracy") and the highly developed Roman system of universal law. It took a long and circuitous evolution of human history before Western civilization was able to establish on the foundation of these three pillars the modern concept and growing reality of human rights. However, particularly after the American and

French revolutions at the end of the eighteenth century, human rights began to become a conscious reality—unfortunately, a reality that the Christian churches often resisted until recent decades, when they became vigorous promoters of human rights.

One of the essential elements in the advances of Western civilization in the area of human rights, as well as in science, politics in general, and economic prosperity—the like of which was never before experienced in human history—is separation of state and religion. Of course, "religion" here includes any ideology that functions like a religion, such as atheistic Marxism.

In the Late Middle Ages, Western civilization's predecessor, Christendom, began reaching the cultural level of the earlier Greek and Roman and the then-contemporary Islamic civilizations. All historical data strongly suggest that Christendom would have plateaued at that approximate level for a longer or shorter period of time, then gone into decline—as had all other civilizations before then, and as eventually Islamic civilization did, as well. That did not happen, however. Why? One very fundamental reason is that, starting with the Renaissance, religion and the state slowly and very painfully began to be separated. This separation broke the forced quality of religion (ideology) and consequently freed the human spirit and mind to pursue its limitless urge to know ever more, to solve every problem it confronts.

This resulted in a series of what historians call *revolutions:* the Commercial Revolution (sixteenth–seventeenth centuries), the Scientific Revolution (seventeenth century), the Industrial Revolution (eighteenth century), the Political Revolution (eighteenth century, epitomized in the American and French Revolutions), and on into the nineteenth and twentieth centuries, with myriad revolutions of all sorts occurring at geometrically increasing speed and magnitude.

With these "exponential" advances in capabilities, the possibilities of destructiveness increased correspondingly. As the medieval philosophers said, *Corruptio optimae pessima* (The corruption of the best becomes the worst). Nevertheless, because freedom is of the essence of being human, even though we may well destroy ourselves if we do not learn wisdom and live virtuously, we can never turn back to an unfree stage of human development.

Hence, societies that try to reunite religion–ideology with the power of the state are doomed to remain third-class societies. That is why, for example, we are convinced that the present attempt of "Islamists" to reestablish the Muslim law, the *Shari'a,* in the Muslim world will condemn those countries to remaining always behind the "West." And given the Islamists' memory of the past medieval cultural glory and superiority of Islam over Christendom, it is precisely the present inferiority in every way of all Islamic countries vis-à-vis the West that infuriates them.

When they argue that Islam is different from Christianity because, unlike Christianity, it is a holistic religion that includes politics as well as all other aspects of life, they need to be reminded that Christendom was exactly the same for well over a millennium—during the Constantinian era. Only when the West broke out of that mischievous marriage of religion–ideology and state did it embark on the path of human freedom, with its limitless possibilities of creativity (and destruction).

DIALOGUE: ITS GROUND RULES

To engage in interreligious, interideological dialogue, it is not sufficient to discuss a religious or ideological subject—that is, "the ultimate meaning of life and how to live accordingly." The partners must come to the dialogue as people who are significantly identified with a religious or ideological community. If I were neither a Christian nor a Muslim, for example, I could not participate as a partner in a Christian–Muslim dialogue, though I might listen in, ask some questions for information, and make helpful comments. Of course, those who are not identified with a particular tradition can engage in a religious or ideological dialogue, but one simply would not call it an inter-religious or inter-ideological dialogue.

The following are some basic ground rules for authentic inter-religious and inter-ideological dialogue. These are not theoretical rules from an ivory tower. They have been learned through hard experience. To ignore them is to diminish or destroy the dialogue.

RULE 1. *The primary purpose of dialogue is to learn—that is, to change and grow in the perception and understanding of reality, and then to act accordingly.* We come to dialogue so that we ourselves can learn, change, and grow, not so we can force change on the other, our partner, as the old polemical debates hoped to do. On the other hand, because in dialogue both partners come with the intention of learning and changing themselves, each will in fact find that the partner has changed. Each partner will also have taught the other—but only because teaching was not the primary purpose of the encounter. Thus, the alleged goal of debate, and much more, is accomplished far more effectively by dialogue.

RULE 2. *Interreligious and interideological dialogue must be a two-sided project—within each religious or ideological community and between religious or ideological communities.* Because interreligious and interideological dialogue is corporate, and because its primary goal is for all partners to learn and change themselves, it is necessary that all the participants enter into dialogue not only with their partners across the faith line—the Catholic with the Protestant, for example—but also with their co-religionists to share the fruits of the interreligious dialogue. In this way, the whole community can eventually learn and change, together gaining ever-more-perceptive insights into reality.

RULE 3. *Each participant must come to the dialogue with complete honesty and sincerity.* It should be made clear in what direction the major and minor thrusts of the tradition move, what the future shifts might be, and even where the participants have difficulties with their own traditions. False fronts have no place in dialogue.

Conversely, each participant must assume the same complete honesty and sincerity in the other partners. Just as a failure in sincerity will prevent dialogue from happening, a failure to assume the partner's sincerity will do so, as well. In brief: no trust, no dialogue.

RULE 4. *In interreligious and interideological dialogue we must not compare our ideals with our partner's practice.* Rather, we must compare our ideals with our partner's ideals, and our practice with our partner's practice.

RULE 5. *Each participant must define herself or himself.* Only the Jew, for example, can define from the inside what it means to be a Jew. The rest of us can only describe what it looks like from the outside. Moreover, because dialogue is a dynamic medium, as each participant learns, she or he changes and hence continually deepens, expands, and modifies her or his self-definition as a Jew, being careful to remain in constant dialogue with fellow Jews. Thus, it is mandatory that each dialogue partner define what it can mean to be an authentic member of that tradition.

Conversely, the side being interpreted must be able to recognize itself in the interpretation. For the sake of clarity, the dialogue participants will naturally attempt to express for themselves what they believe to be the meaning of the partner's statement. The partner must be able to recognize herself or himself in that expression.

RULE 6.   *Each participant must come to the dialogue without hard-and-fast assumptions as to where the points of disagreement lie.* Both partners should not only listen to each other with openness and sympathy; they should also try to agree as far as is possible while still maintaining integrity with their own tradition. Where they absolutely cannot agree further without violating their own integrity—precisely there is the real point of disagreement—which most often turns out to be quite different from what was assumed beforehand.

RULE 7.   *Dialogue can take place only between equals, or par cum pari, as Vatican II put it.* Both must come to learn from each other. This means, for instance, that between a learned scholar and an uninformed person there can be no authentic, full dialogue. At most, there can be a gathering of information, as in a sociological interrogation.

At the same time, if a Muslim views Hinduism as inferior, or a Hindu views Islam as inferior, there will be no dialogue. For authentic interreligious dialogue between Muslims and Hindus, both partners must come mainly to learn from each other. Only then will they speak "equal with equal" (*par cum pari*).

This rule also indicates that there can be no such thing as a one-way dialogue. The Jewish–Christian discussions that began in the 1960s, for example, were on the whole only prolegomena to interreligious dialogue. Understandably and properly, the Jews came to those exchanges only to teach Christians, and the Christians came mainly to learn. But for authentic interreligious dialogue between Christians and Jews, the Jews must also come to learn. Only then will the conversation be *par cum pari.*

RULE 8.   *Dialogue can take place only on the basis of mutual trust.* Although interreligious and interideological dialogue has a kind of "corporate" dimension in that the participants must be involved as members of a religious or ideological community—for instance, as Taoists or Marxists—it is also fundamentally true that only *persons* can enter into dialogue. But a dialogue among persons can be built only on personal trust. Hence, it is wise not to tackle the most difficult problems in the beginning; instead, one shouldo seek issues that are most likely to provide common ground and establish a basis of human trust. As this personal trust deepens and expands, the more thorny matters can gradually be undertaken.

RULE 9.   *As we enter into interreligious and interideological dialogue, we must learn to be at least minimally self-critical of both our self and our own religious or ideological tradition.* A lack of such self-criticism implies that our own tradition already has all the correct answers. Such an attitude makes dialogue not only unnecessary, but even impossible, because we enter into dialogue primarily so *we* can learn—which obviously is impossible if our tradition has never made a misstep, if it has all the right answers. To be sure, participants in interreligious and interideological dialogue must stand within a religious or ideological tradition with integrity and conviction, but their integrity and conviction must include, not exclude, healthy self-criticism. Without it, there can be no dialogue—and, indeed, no integrity.

RULE 10.   *Each participant eventually must attempt to experience the partner's religion or ideology "from within."* A religion or ideology does not engage merely the head; it also engages the spirit, heart, and "whole being." It has both individual and communal dimensions. John S. Dunne speaks of "passing over" into another's religious or ideological experience, then coming back enlightened, broadened, and deepened.[7]

Interreligious and interideological dialogue operates in three areas: the practical, where we collaborate to help humanity; the depth or "spiritual" dimension, where we attempt to experience the partner's religion or ideology "from within"; and the cognitive, where we seek understanding and truth. Dialogue also has three phases. In the first phase, which we never completely outgrow, we unlearn misinformation about each other and begin to know each other as we truly are. In the second phase, we begin to discern values in our partner's tradition and wish to appropriate them into our own. If we are serious, persistent, and sensitive enough in the dialogue, we may at times enter into the third phase. Here, we together begin to explore new areas of reality, of meaning, of truth aspects of which neither of us had even been aware. We are brought face to face with these new, still unknown dimensions of reality through questions, insights, and probing produced in the dialogue. We will experience for ourselves that patiently pursued dialogue can become an instrument of new "re-velation" (*velare*, Latin "to cover, hence, to veil"), a further "un-veiling" of reality—on which we must act.

12 Universal Declaration of a Global Ethic

THE NEED FOR A GLOBAL ETHIC

WHEN THE FACT of the epistemological revolutions leading to the growing necessity for interreligious, interideological, and intercultural dialogue is coupled with the fact of all humankind's interdependence—such that any significant part of humanity could precipitate the whole of the globe into a social, economic, nuclear, environmental, or other catastrophe—a pressing need arises: to focus the energy of these dialogues not only on how humans perceive and understand the world and its meaning, but also on how they should act in relationship to themselves, to other persons, and to nature, within the context of reality's undergirding, pervasive, overarching source, energy, and goal, however understood. In brief, humankind needs increasingly desperately to engage in a dialogue on the development of not, say, a Buddhist, Christian, or Marxist ethic, but a Global Ethic. A key instrument in that direction will be the shaping of a "Universal Declaration of a Global Ethic."

Moreover, it is beyond the borders of sanity that Protestants and Catholics are blowing each other up in Northern Ireland; that Hindus and Buddhists wantonly massacre each other in Sri Lanka; that Jews and Muslims teeter on the abyss of war in the Near East; that Sikhs and Hindus terrorize each other in Punjab and Hindus and Muslims slaughter each other in India; that Muslims and Hindus are always in a state of hostile unrest in Kashmir; that Orthodox Christians, Catholics, and Muslims murder one another in Yugoslavia; and on and on. Only the religions themselves can put a stop to these perversions of religion.

Modern purely secular men and women often put religiously committed women and men to shame in their human love and compassion. The religions, however, also have profound answers to the fundamental human ethical questions. But they can no longer speak in multiple, confusing tongues about it. A worldwide dialogue, a global dialogue, needs to be initiated that will lead to the building of a minimal consensus on a Global Ethic, and we believe a key instrument in that direction will be the shaping of that Universal Declaration of a Global Ethic.

Ethic in the singular, rather than *ethics* in the plural, is used because what is needed is not a full-blown Global Ethical system in great detail—indeed, that would not even be possible—but a *global consensus on the fundamental attitude toward good and evil and the basic and middle principles* to put it into action.

Clearly also, this ethic must be global. It will not be sufficient to have a common ethic for, say, Westerners, or Africans, or Asians. The destruction of the ozone layer, for example, or the loosing of a destructive gene mutation by any one group will be disastrous for all. Bilateral dialogues between religions, vital as they are, are not sufficient for the world of today and tomorrow.

A beginning has been made, of course, through organizations such as the World Conference on Religion and Peace, but the occasional large meeting is far from sufficient. The situation is much too critical, and is becoming increasingly so at an almost geometric rate of acceleration. The world does not have the luxury of waiting patiently for a Global Ethic to grow slowly and haphazardly by itself, as will gradually happen if we do not destroy ourselves first. It is vital that there be a conscious focusing of energy on such a development now. Immediate action is necessary.

There needs to be conscious concentration of efforts to draw together research and reflection on a Global Ethic into a Universal Declaration of a Global Ethic to be circulated to the various forums of all religions and ethical groups for input and appropriate revisions, with a view toward eventual adoption by all the religions and ethical groups of the world. Such a Universal Declaration of a Global Ethic would then serve a function similar to that of the United Nations' 1948 Universal Declaration of Human Rights—a kind of minimal ethical standard that all will be committed to and, therefore, expected to live up to.

Such an undertaking by the world's religions and ethical groups would be different from, but complementary to, the work of the United Nations. The United Nations brings to bear the political force of all the nations of the world on the implementation of the Universal Declaration of Human Rights and subsequent U.N. documents. The Universal Declaration of a Global Ethic would in a major way bring to bear the moral and spiritual resources of all the religions and ethical groups on

the basic ethical problems of the world, which are not easily susceptible to political force.

It needs to be stressed, however, that such a project cannot be carried
out only by the scholars and leaders of the world's religious and ethical communities, though obviously the vigorous participation of these
elements is vital. The ideas and sensitivities must also come from the
grassroots.

Moreover, it is also at the grassroots, as well as at the level of scholars and leaders, that consciousness must first be raised regarding the
desperate need for the development of a Global Ethic. Conviction
regarding its validity will then follow. The most carefully thought out
and sensitively crafted declaration will be of no use if those who are to
adhere to it do not believe in it. In other words, a Global Ethic must work
on all three levels—scholars, leaders, grassroots—or it will not work at
all. It is on that vital grassroots level that we invite all to participate in
the shaping of a Universal Declaration of a Global Ethic.

This Universal Declaration of a Global Ethic must be arrived at by
consensus through *dialogue*. Attempts at imposing a unitary ethics by
various kinds of force have been made aplenty, and they have inevitably
fallen miserably short of globality. The most recent failures can be seen
in the widespread collapse of communism and, in an inverse way, in the
resounding rejection of secularism by resurgent Islamism.

Principles of a Universal Declaration of a Global Ethic

We will first outline some suggestions on the general notions that ought
to shape a Universal Declaration of a Global Ethic, then offer a tenta-
tive draft constructed in their light:

1) The declaration should use language and images that are acceptable to all major religions and ethical groups. Hence, its language
   ought to be "humanity-based" rather than drawn from authorita-
   tive religious books. That is, the language should come from
   "below," not from "above."
2) Therefore, the declaration should be anthropocentric—indeed more.
   It must be cosmo-anthropocentric, for we cannot be fully human
   except within the context of the whole of reality.

3) The affirmations should be dynamic in form in the sense that they will be susceptible to being sublated (*aufgehoben*). That is, they might properly be reinterpreted by being taken up into a larger framework.

4) The declaration needs to set not only inviolable minimums, but also open-ended maximums to be striven for. But maximums may not be required, for they might violate the freedom minimums of some persons.

5) The declaration could well start with—though not limit itself to—elements of the so-called Golden Rule: Treat others as we would be treated.

Excursus: The "Golden Rule"

A glimpse of just how pervasive the Golden Rule is, albeit in various forms and expressions, in the world's religions and ideologies, great and small, can be garnered from this partial listing:

i) *Perhaps the oldest recorded version that is cast in a positive form stems from Zoroaster (628–551 B.C.E.): "That which is good for all and any one, for whomsoever—that is good for me. . . . What I hold good for self, I should for all. Only Law Universal is true Law" (Gathas, 43.1).*

ii) *Confucius (551–479 B.C.E.), when asked "Is there one word which may serve as a rule of practice for all one's life?" said: "Do not to others what you do not want done to yourself" (Analects, 12.2 and 15.23). Confucius also stated in a variant version: "What I do not wish others to do to me, that also I wish not to do to them" (Analects, 5.11).*

iii) *The founder of Jainism was Vardhamana, known as Mahavira ("Great Hero"; 540–468 B.C.E.). The various scriptures of Jainism, however, derived from a later period: "A man should wander about treating all creatures as he himself would be treated" (Sutrakri-tanga 1.11.33); "One who you think should be hit is none else but you. . . . Therefore, neither does he cause violence to others nor does he make others do so" (Acaranga-sutra 5.101–1-2).*

iv) *The founder of Buddhism was Siddhartha Gautama, known as the Buddha ("Enlightened One"; 563–483 B.C.E.). The various scriptures of Buddhism also derived from a later period: "Comparing oneself to others in such terms as 'Just as I am so are they, just as they are so am I,' he should neither kill nor cause others to kill" (Sutta Nipata 705); "Here am I fond of my life, not wanting to die, fond of pleasure and averse from pain. Suppose someone should rob me of my life.... If I in turn should rob of his life one fond of his life.... How could I inflict that upon another?" (Samyutta Nikaya v. 353).*

v) *The third-century* B.C.E. *Hindu epic poem Mahabharata states that its Golden Rule, which is expressed in both positive and negative form, is the summary of all Hindu teaching ("the whole Dharma"): "Vyasa says: Do not to others what you do not wish done to yourself; and wish for others too what you desire and long for for yourself—this is the whole of Dharma; heed it well" (Mahabharata, Anusasana Parva 113.8).*

vi) *In the biblical book of Leviticus (composed in the fifth century* B.C.E., *though some of its material may be more ancient), the Hebrew version of the Golden Rule is stated positively: "You shall love your neighbor as yourself" (Leviticus 19:18).*

vii) *The deutero-canonical biblical Tobit was written around the year 200* B.C.E. *and contains a negative version—as most are—of the Golden Rule: "Never do to anyone else anything that you would not want someone to do to you" (Tobit 4:15).*

viii) *The major founder of Rabbinic Judaism, Hillel, who lived about a generation before Jesus (though he may also have been his teacher) taught that the Golden Rule—his version being both positive and negative—was the heart of the Torah, and "all the rest was commentary": "Do not do to others what you would not have done to yourself" (Btalmud, Shabbath 31a).*

ix) *Following in this Jewish tradition, Jesus stated the Golden Rule in a positive form, saying that it summed up the whole Torah and prophets: "Do for others just what you want them to do for you" (Luke 6:31); "Do for others what you want them to do for you: this is the meaning of the Law of Moses [Torah] and of the teachings of the prophets" (Matthew 7:12).*

x) *In the seventh century* C.E., *Muhammad is said to have claimed that the Golden Rule is the "noblest Religion": "Noblest Religion is this—that you should like for others what you like for yourself; and what you feel painful for yourself, hold that as painful for all others too." Again: "No man is a true believer unless he desires for his brother that which he desires for himself."*[1]

xi) *The Golden Rule is likewise found in some non-literate religions: "One going to take a pointed stick to pinch a baby bird should first try it on himself to feel how it hurts."*[2]

xii) The eighteenth-century Western philosopher Immanuel Kant provided a "rational" version of the Golden Rule in his famous "Categorical Imperative," or "Law of Universal Fairness": "Act on maxims which can at the same time have for their object themselves as universal laws of nature. . . . Treat humanity in every case as an end, never as a means only."[3]

xiii) The late-nineteenth-century founder of Baha'ism, Baha'ullah, wrote: "He should not wish for others that which he doth not wish for himself, nor promise that which he doth not fulfill."[4]

xiv) In 1915, a new version of Buddhism, Won Buddhism, was founded in Korea by the Great Master Sotaesan. In the teachings he left behind are found variants of the Golden Rule: "Be right yourself before you correct others. Instruct yourself first before you teach others. Do favors for others before you seek favors from them"; "Ordinary people may appear smart in doing things only for themselves, but they are really suffering a loss. Buddhas and Bodhisattvas may appear to be stupid in doing things only for others, but eventually they benefit themselves."[5]

It is clear that the core of the world's major religions, the Golden Rule, does not attempt the futile and impossible task of abolishing and annihilating the authentic ego. On the contrary, it tends to make concern for the authentic ego the measure of altruism. "Do not foster the ego more than the alter; care for the alter as much as for the ego"; "To abolish egoism is to abolish altruism also; and vice versa."[6]

Authentic egoism and authentic altruism then are not in conflict with each other; the former necessarily moves to the latter, even possibly "giving one's life for one's friend." This, however, is the last and highest stage of human development. It is the stage of a (w)holy person, the saint, the arahat, the bodhisattva, the sage. Such a stage cannot be the foundation of human society; it must be the goal of it. The foundation of human society must first be authentic self-love, which includes moving outward to loving others.

Not recognizing this foundation of authentic self-love is the fundamental flaw of those idealistic systems, such as communism, that try to build a society on the foundation of altruism. A human and humanizing society should lead toward (w)holiness, toward altruism, but it cannot be built on the assumption that its citizens are (w)holy and altruistic to start with. Such an altruism must grow out of an ever-developing authentic self-love. It cannot be assumed, and surely it cannot be forced, as has been tried for decades—with disastrous dehumanizing results.

To return from the excursus:

6) As humans ineluctably seek ever more knowledge and truth, so, too, do they seek to draw what they perceive as the good to themselves (that is, they *love*). Usually this self is expanded to include the family, then friends. It needs to continue its natural expansion to the community, nation, world, and cosmos, and the source and goal of all reality.

7) This human love must necessarily start with self-love, for one can love one's "neighbor" only *as* one loves oneself. But because one becomes human only through interhuman mutuality, loving others fulfills one's own humanity, and hence is the greatest act of authentic self-love.

8) Another aspect of the Golden Rule is that humans are always to be treated as ends, never as mere means—that is, as subjects, never as mere objects.

9) Yet another implication of the Golden Rule is that those who cannot protect themselves ought to be protected by those who can.

10) A further ring of the expanding circles of the Golden Rule is that non-human beings are also to be reverenced and treated with respect.

11) It is important that not only basic but also middle ethical principles be spelled out in this declaration. Although most of these middle ethical principles are already embedded in juridical form in the United Nations' Universal Declaration of Human Rights, it is vital that the religions and ethical traditions expressly state and approve them. Then the world, including both adherents and outsiders of the various religions and ethical traditions, will know what ethical standards all are committing themselves to.

If a Universal Declaration of a Global Ethic is to be meaningful and effective, its framers must resist the temptation to pack too many details and special interests into it. It can function best as a kind of "constitutional" set of basic and middle ethical principles from which more detailed applications can be drawn.

A PLAN OF ACTION

Such general suggestions need to be discussed, confirmed, rejected, modified, supplemented. Beyond that, it is vital that all the disciplines contribute what, from their perspectives, ought to be included in the Declaration, how it should be formulated, what is to be avoided. This is beginning to happen.

The year 1993 marked the one-hundredth anniversary of the 1893 World Parliament of Religions, which took place in Chicago and signaled the beginning of what would become a worldwide interreligious dialogue. As a consequence, a number of international conferences took place. At their center has been the development of a Universal Declaration of a Global Ethic.

The first conference was held in New Delhi, India, in February 1993; the second was held in August of the same year in Bangalore, India; and the third was held that year in September in Chicago. For the huge (more than 6,000 participants) September 1993 Chicago Parliament of the World's Religions, Hans Küng drafted a document titled, "Declaration Toward a Global Ethic," which the parliament adopted. The text is found in the Appendix.[7]

Beyond that, after having been commissioned by the January 1992 meeting in Atlanta, Georgia, of the International Scholars' Annual Trialogue (ISAT-Jewish-Christian-Muslim), a proposed declaration was drafted by Leonard Swidler and submitted to and analyzed at the January 1993 meeting of ISAT in Graz, Austria. This text, which is given in Chapter 13, was also a focus of "Global Ethics–Human Rights–World Religions," a graduate seminar that Swidler held in the spring of 1993 at Temple University; at the First International Conference on Universalism in August 1993, in Warsaw, Poland; at a Consultation of the American Academy of Religion in November 1993, in Washington, D.C.; and at the sixth International Scholars' Annual Trialogue in January 1994, in Jerusalem. In May 1994, the draft was also the subject of a conference sponsored by the International Association of Asian Philosophy and Religion (IAAPR) in Seoul, Korea. The World Conference on Religion and Peace (WCRP) in part focused on it in its fall 1994 World Assembly in Rome and Riva del Garda, Italy. And on June 20–21, 1995, it was the subject of Celebrating the Spirit: Toward a Global Ethic, a conference held in San Francisco in honor of the fiftieth anniversary of the founding of the United Nations. For further details see Leonard Swidler's two edited works *Theoria→Praxis: How Jews, Christians, and Muslims Can Together Move from Theory to Practice* (Leuven, Belgium: Peeters,

1998) and *For All Life. Toward a Universal Declaration of a Global Ethic: An Interreligious Dialogue* (Ashland, OR: White Cloud Press, 1999).

At the same time, it is imperative that various religious and ethical communities and geographical regions work on discussing and drafting their own versions of a possible text for a Universal Declaration of a Global Ethic. The Swidler draft given in Chapter 13 and the one drawn up by Küng, which is given in the appendix, should certainly be used in this process. But all communities and regions need to make their own contributions to the final declaration. In the process of wrestling with the issue and forging the wording, they will make the concern for a Global Ethic their own and will thus better be able to mediate it to their "constituents" and enhance the likelihood of the declaration's being adhered to in practice.

Send comments to Prof. Leonard Swidler, Religion Department, Temple University, Philadelphia, PA 19122, USA; Fax: 215-477-5928; E-mail: dialogue@vm.temple.edu; Web: http:// blue.temple.edu/~dialogue.

13   A Proposed Draft

A Universal Declaration of a Global Ethic

RATIONALE

WE WOMEN AND MEN from various ethical and religious traditions commit ourselves to the following Universal Declaration of a Global Ethic. We speak here not of *ethics* in the plural, which implies rather great detail, but of *ethic* in the singular—that is, the fundamental attitude toward good and evil, and the basic and middle principles needed to put it into action.

We make this commitment not despite our differences but arising out of our distinct perspectives, recognizing nevertheless in our diverse ethical and religious traditions common convictions that lead us to speak out *against* all forms of inhumanity and *for* humaneness in our treatment of ourselves, one another, and the world around us. We find in each of our traditions: 1) grounds in support of universal human rights; 2) a call to work for justice and peace; and 3) concern for conservation of the Earth.

We confirm and applaud the positive human values that increasingly are becoming universally accepted and advocated in our world: freedom, equality, democracy, recognition of interdependence, commitment to justice and human rights. We also believe that conditions in our world encourage—indeed, require—us to look beyond what divides us and to speak as one on matters that are crucial for the survival of and respect for the Earth. Therefore, we advocate movement toward a global order that reflects the best values found in our myriad traditions.

We are convinced that a just global order can be built only upon a global ethic that clearly states universally recognized norms and principles, and that such an ethic presumes a readiness and intention on the part of people to act justly—that is, a movement of the heart. Second, a global ethic requires a thoughtful presentation of principles that are held up to open investigation and critique—that is, a movement of the head.

Each of our traditions holds commitments beyond what is expressed here, but we find that within our ethical and religious traditions the world community has discovered elements of a fundamental minimal consensus on ethics that is convincing to all women and men of good will, religious and non-religious alike, and that provides us with a moral framework within which we can relate to ourselves, each other, and the world in a just and respectful manner.

In order to build a humanity-wide consensus, we find it is essential to develop and use a language that is humanity-based, though each religious and ethical tradition also has its own language for what is expressed in this declaration.

Furthermore, none of our traditions, ethical or religious, is satisfied with minimums, vital as they are; rather, because humans are endlessly self-transcending, our traditions also provide maximums to be striven for. Consequently, this declaration does the same. The maximums, however, clearly are ideals to be striven for, and therefore cannot be required, lest the essential freedoms and rights of some thereby be violated.

PRESUPPOSITIONS

As a Universal Declaration of a Global Ethic, which we believe must undergird any affirmation of human rights and respect for the Earth, this document affirms and supports the rights and corresponding responsibilities enumerated in the 1948 Universal Declaration of Human Rights of the United Nations. Along with that first United Nations declaration we believe there are five general presuppositions that are indispensable for a global ethic:

1) Every human possesses inalienable and inviolable dignity; individuals, states, and other social entities are obliged to respect and protect the dignity of each person.
2) No person or social entity exists beyond the scope of morality; everyone—individuals and social organizations—is obliged to do good and avoid evil.
3) Humans are endowed with reason and conscience. The great challenge of being human is to act conscientiously. Communities, states, and other social organizations are obliged to protect and foster these capabilities.

4) Communities, states, and other social organizations that contribute to the good of humans and the world have a right to exist and flourish. This right should be respected by all.

5) Humans are a part of nature, not apart from nature; ethical concerns extend beyond the human community to the rest of the Earth and the cosmos. In brief, this declaration, in reflection of reality, is not just anthropocentric, but cosmo-anthropocentric.

A FUNDAMENTAL RULE

We propose the Golden Rule, which for thousands of years has been affirmed in many religious and ethical traditions, as a fundamental principle upon which to base a global ethic: "What you do not wish done to yourself, do not do to others," or, in positive terms, "What you wish done to yourself, do to others." This rule should be valid not only for one's own family, friends, community, and nation, but also for all other individuals, families, communities, nations, the entire world, the cosmos.

Basic Principles

PRINCIPLE 1.   Because freedom is of the essence of being human, every person is free to exercise and develop every capacity, so long as it does not infringe on the rights of other persons or express a lack of due respect for things living or non-living. In addition, human freedom should be exercised in such a way as to enhance both the freedom of all humans and due respect for all things, living and non-living.

PRINCIPLE 2.   Because of their inherent equal dignity, all humans should always be treated as ends, never as mere means. In addition, all humans in every encounter with others should strive to enhance to the fullest the intrinsic dignity of all involved.

PRINCIPLE 3.   Although humans have greater intrinsic value than non-humans, all such things, living and non-living, do possess intrinsic value simply because of their existence. As such, they are to be treated with due respect. In addition, all humans in every encounter with non-humans, living and non-living, should strive to respect them to the fullest of their intrinsic value.

PRINCIPLE 4.   As humans necessarily seek ever more knowledge and truth, so, too, they seek to unite themselves with what they perceive as the good—that is, they love. Usually, this self is expanded or transcended to include their own family and friends, seeking the good for them. In addition, as with the Golden Rule, this loving and loved "self" needs to continue its natural expansion and transcendence to embrace the community, nation, world, and cosmos.

PRINCIPLE 5.   Thus, true human love is authentic self-love and other-love co-relatively linked in such a way that it ultimately is drawn to become all-inclusive. This expansive and inclusive nature of love should be recognized as an active principle in personal and global interaction.

PRINCIPLE 6.   Those who hold responsibility for others are obliged to help those for whom they hold responsibility. In addition, the Golden Rule implies: If we were in serious difficulty wherein we could not help ourselves, we would want those who could help us to do so, even if they held no responsibility for us. Therefore, we should help others in serious difficulty who cannot help themselves, even though we hold no responsibility for them.

PRINCIPLE 7.   Because all humans are equally entitled to hold their religion or belief—that is, their explanation of the ultimate meaning of life and how to live accordingly—as true, every human's religion or belief should be granted its due freedom and respect.

PRINCIPLE 8.   In addition, dialogue—that is, conversation whose *primary* aim is to learn from the other is a necessary means whereby women and men ceaselessly expand and deepen their explanation of the meaning of life and develop an ever-broadening consensus whereby men and women can live together on this globe in an authentically human manner.

Middle Principles

1) LEGAL RESPONSIBILITIES.   Because all humans have an inherent equal dignity, all individuals and communities should treat everyone equally before the law, providing all with equal protection.

At the same time, all individuals and communities should follow all just laws, obeying not only the letter but most especially the spirit.

2) RESPONSIBILITIES CONCERNING CONSCIENCE AND RELIGION OR BELIEF. Because humans are thinking, and therefore essentially free-deciding, beings, all individuals and communities should respect this aspect of human nature, granting that all humans have the right to freedom of thought, speech, conscience, and religion or belief.

At the same time, all humans should exercise their rights of freedom of thought, speech, conscience, and religion or belief in ways that will show respect for themselves and all others and strive to produce maximum benefit, broadly understood, for both themselves and their fellow humans.

3) RESPONSIBILITIES CONCERNING SPEECH AND INFORMATION. Because humans are thinking beings with the capacity to perceive reality and express their perceptions of it, all individuals and communities should respect this aspect of human nature, granting that all individuals and communities have both the right and the responsibility, as far as possible, to learn the truth and express it honestly.

At the same time, everyone should avoid cover-ups, distortions, manipulations of others, and inappropriate intrusions into personal privacy. This freedom and responsibility is especially true for the mass media, artists, scientists, politicians, and religious leaders.

4) RESPONSIBILITIES CONCERNING PARTICIPATION IN ALL DECISION-MAKING AFFECTING ONESELF OR THOSE FOR WHOM ONE IS RESPONSIBLE. Because humans are free-deciding beings, all individuals and communities should respect this aspect of human nature, granting that all humans have the right to a voice, direct or indirect, in all decisions that affect them, including a meaningful participation in the choosing of their leaders and holding them accountable, as well as the right of equal access to all leadership positions for which their talents qualify them.

At the same time, all humans should strive to exercise their right, and obligation, to participate in self-governance to produce maximum benefit, widely understood, for both themselves and their fellow humans.

5) RESPONSIBILITIES CONCERNING RELATIONSHIP OF WOMEN AND MEN. Because women and men are inherently equal and are frequently attracted to each other, all individuals and communities should respect these aspects of human nature, granting that all humans have a right to an equal development of their talents as well as the freedom to

marry, with equal rights for all women and men in living out or dissolving marriage.

At the same time, all men and women should act toward each other outside of and within marriage in ways that will respect the intrinsic dignity, freedom, and responsibilities of themselves and others.

6) RESPONSIBILITIES CONCERNING PROPERTY.   Because humans are free, bodily and social in nature, all individuals and communities should respect these dimensions of human nature, granting that all individual humans and communities have the right to own property of various sorts.

At the same time, society should be so organized that property will be dealt with respectfully, striving to produce maximum benefit not only for the owners but also for their fellow humans, as well as for the world at large.

7) RESPONSIBILITIES CONCERNING WORK AND LEISURE.   Because to lead an authentic human life all humans should normally have both meaningful work and recreative leisure, all individuals and communities should respect these dimensions of human nature and strive to organize society so as to provide these two dimensions of an authentic human life for themselves and for all the members of their communities.

At the same time, all individuals have an obligation to work appropriately for their recompense, and, with all communities, to strive for ever more creative work and recreative leisure for themselves, their communities, and other individuals and communities.

8) RESPONSIBILITIES CONCERNING EDUCATION.   Because humans can become authentically human only through education in the broad sense—and today, increasingly in the formal sense—all individuals and communities should respect this dimension of human development and strive to provide an education directed to the full development of the human person; respect for human rights and fundamental freedoms; and the promotion of understanding, dialogue, and friendship among all humans, regardless of racial, ethnic, religious, belief, sexual, or other differences, and respect for the Earth.

At the same time, all individuals and communities have the obligation to contribute appropriately to providing the means necessary for this education for themselves and their communities, and beyond that to strive to provide the same for all humans.

9) RESPONSIBILITIES CONCERNING PEACE.   Because peace as both the absence of violence and the presence of justice for all humans is the necessary condition for the complete development of the full humanity of all humans, individually and communally, all individuals and communities should respect this human need and strive constantly to further the growth of peace on all levels—personal, interpersonal, local, regional, national, and international—granting that

a) the necessary basis of peace is justice for all concerned;
b) violence is to be vigorously avoided, being resorted to only when its absence would cause a greater evil;
c) when peace is ruptured, all efforts should be bent to its rapid restoration on the necessary basis of justice for all.

At the same time, it should be recognized that peace, like liberty, is a positive value that should be constantly cultivated, and therefore all individuals and communities should make the necessary prior efforts not only to avoid its breakdown but also to strengthen its steady development and growth.

10) RESPONSIBILITIES CONCERNING PRESERVATION OF THE ENVIRONMENT. Because things, living and non-living, have an intrinsic value simply because of their existence, and also because humans cannot develop fully as humans, or even survive, if the environment is severely damaged, all individuals and communities should respect the ecosphere within which "we all live, move and have our being," and act so that

a) nothing, living or non-living, will be destroyed in its natural form except when used for some greater good, such as the use of plants and animals for food;
b) if at all possible, only replaceable material will be destroyed in its natural form.

At the same time, all individuals and communities should constantly be vigilant to protect our fragile universe, particularly from the exploding human population and increasing technological possibilities that threaten it in an ever-expanding fashion.

Conclusion

WE STARTED OUT by noting that the study of religion is not peripheral if we wish to understand ourselves individually and communally. Rather, it is at the very heart of our being human. Even those of us who claim that we are not religious have the functional equivalent of a religion—that is, an explanation of the ultimate meaning of life and how to live accordingly. The explanation may be very crude and undeveloped, but it will direct our actions and provide us with whatever vague meaning we attribute to life (including the very negative versions of total confusion and sheer despair). Beyond that, most people live in societies that have been, and usually still are, fundamentally formed by one religion or another. Thus, to understand being human entails understanding the religions that shape individuals and civilizations.

We then traversed the many disciplines and methods that have been painstakingly developed over the centuries, especially the last two, to learn how we best can delve into this core study of humanness. These techniques included those in the humanities, but in recent decades especially those from the relatively new social sciences. We likewise have seen that the greatest advance in this study of the meaning of life has come in our understanding of how we understand, of how we think.

It is most particularly in this last area, our epistemology—the study of understanding—that the greatest revolutions have taken place. We have increasingly moved from an absolutized understanding of statements about reality (truth) to a de-absolutized understanding of truth. All statements about something, even though true—that is, that accurately describe something—are necessarily limited, that is, "not absolute" ("un-limited" being the literal meaning of "ab-solute"). Something else can also be said of the object in question, depending on the questions the thinker has put to it, the thought categories she or he has used to speak about it (e.g., physical, legal, metaphorical, psychological), the perspective from which the thinker has experienced the object (e.g., as a white, black, Asian, male, rich person, slave, German, uneducated person). All this is true when speaking about things in general, and most abundantly true when speaking about the ultimate meaning of life, about religion.

Otherwise, how can one explain the fact most people born in China are Confucianists, that most people born in Italy are Catholic, that most people born in Arabia are Muslim? Clearly, the "explanation of the ultimate meaning of life and how to live accordingly" is intimately related to the individual believer and the circumstances in which she or he has been formed. As more and more people become experientially aware of this obvious fact, they are increasingly drawn—nay, driven—by the never-ending human search for ever more truth, to dialogue with those from whom they are different.

Thus, we arrived at the core characteristic that is shaping the next millennium: *dialogue.* We probed rather deeply into what dialogue is and used the term "Deep-Dialogue' to name the transforming process that is involved when one ventures seriously onto the path of dialogue. Further, we found that dialogue is not only something psychological; it is also at the very heart of all reality: *Dia-Logos.* Thus, our human evolution in the direction toward dialogue, toward 'Deep-Dialogue,' is really an unfolding of a natural orientation built into the subatomic structure of physical reality and is relayed upward to the non-material level, the spiritual level, in humanity.

On that human level, we learned that the other side of the human coin of 'Deep-Dialogue' is its counterpart, 'Critical-Thinking.' If we do not develop our human skills of thinking clearly and logically, our "dialogue" will be not a 'Deep-Dialogue' or a mutual advance toward an ever-increasing understanding of reality, of truth; it will simply be a sharing of muddle. It is toward that end of an endlessly increasing, enriching, deepening understanding of reality and its meaning that the study of religion is directed.

Finally, our move into an Age of Global Dialogue inevitably leads to the need to develop a global dialogical way of acting toward ourselves, other humans, the world around us, and ultimately whatever or whomever we understand to be Ultimate Reality. Thus, we have ended by advancing the notion—and we hope, the reality—of a Global Ethic for our emerging Global Civilization.

Appendix

Explanatory Remarks Concerning the
"Declaration Toward a Global Ethic"

THE COUNCIL for a Parliament of the World's Religions in Chicago commissioned Professor Hans Küng of the University of Tübingen to develop a draft of a "Declaration of the Religions for a Global Ethic" to be submitted to the September 1993 Parliament of the World's Religions. Küng was able to deal with the problems of such a declaration throughout the entire summer semester (1992) in an interdisciplinary colloquium with participants from various religions and continents. He produced an initial draft that was sent to various colleagues and friends for correction. The first draft received broad agreement from all those to whom it was sent. At the same time, dozens of formal as well as material suggestions for correction were submitted, which were taken into account in producing a revised draft.

The following are the principles that guided Küng:

1) The document would in the first place be a declaration of the *religions,* which could later be followed by a general declaration (for example, within the framework of UNESCO).

2) In a Declaration for a World Ethic, the focus cannot be on the *juridical* level of laws, codified rights, and appealable paragraphs (e.g., human rights), or on the *political* level of concrete suggested solutions (e.g., in reference to the debt crisis of the Third World). Rather, the focus must be only on the ethical level: the level of *binding values, irrevocable standards* and *interior fundamental attitudes.* These three levels of course are related to one another.

3) Such a declaration must be *capable of producing a consensus.* Hence, statements must be avoided that would be rejected a priori by one of the great religions. As a consequence, disputed moral questions (such as abortion and euthanasia) had to be excluded.

This declaration was signed by most of the nearly two hundred "delegates" of the world's religions who attended the Parliament of the World's Religions held in 1993, the centenary of the first World Parliament of Religions, which was held in Chicago in 1893. The 1993 Parliament of the World's Religions (attended by more than 6,000 persons) was held in Chicago from August 28 to September 4, 1993, and this declaration was solemnly proclaimed on September 4, 1993.

PARLIAMENT OF WORLD'S RELIGIONS DECLARATION OF A GLOBAL ETHIC

INTRODUCTION

The world is in agony. The agony is so pervasive and urgent that we are compelled to name its manifestations so that the depth of this pain may be made clear.

Peace eludes us ... the planet is being destroyed ... neighbors live in fear ... women and men are estranged from each other ... children die!

This is abhorrent!

We condemn the abuses of Earth's ecosystems.

We condemn the poverty that stifles life's potential; the hunger that weakens the human body; the economic disparities that threaten so many families with ruin.

We condemn the social disarray of the nations; the disregard for justice that pushes citizens to the margin; the anarchy overtaking our communities; and the insane death of children from violence. In particular, we condemn aggression and hatred in the name of religion.

But this agony need not be.

It need not be because the basis for an ethic already exists. This ethic offers the possibility of a better individual and global order, and leads individuals away from despair and societies away from chaos.

We are women and men who have embraced the precepts and practices of the world's religions:

We affirm that a common set of core values is found in the teachings of the religions, and that these form the basis of a global ethic.

We affirm that this truth is already known, but yet to be lived in heart and action.

We affirm that there is an irrevocable, unconditional norm for all areas of life, for families and communities, for races, nations and religions. There already exist ancient guidelines for human behavior which are found in the teachings of the religions of the world and which are the condition for a sustainable world order.

WE DECLARE

We are interdependent. Each of us depends on the well-being of the whole, and so we have respect for the community of living beings, for people, animals, and plants, and for the preservation of Earth, the air, water and soil.

We take individual responsibility for all we do. All our decisions, actions and failures to act have consequences.

We must treat others as we wish others to treat us. We make a commitment to respect life and dignity, individuality and diversity, so that every person is treated humanely, without exception. We must have patience and acceptance. We must be able to forgive, learning from the past but never allowing ourselves to be enslaved by memories of hate. Opening our hearts to one another, we must sink our narrow differences for the cause of the world community, practicing a culture of solidarity and relatedness.

We consider humankind our family. We must strive to be kind and generous. We must not live for ourselves alone, but should also serve others, never forgetting the children, the aged, the poor, the suffering, the disabled, the refugees and the lonely. No person should ever be considered or treated as a second-class citizen, or be exploited in any way whatsoever. There should be equal partnership between men and women. We must not commit any kind of sexual immorality. We must put behind us all forms of domination or abuse.

We commit ourselves to a culture of nonviolence, respect, justice and peace. We shall not oppress, injure, torture or kill other human beings, forsaking violence as a means of settling differences.

We must strive for a just social and economic order, in which everyone has an equal chance to reach full potential as a human being. We must speak and act truthfully and with compassion, dealing fairly with all, and avoiding prejudice and hatred. We must not steal. We must move beyond the dominance of greed for power, prestige, money and consumption to make a just peaceful world.

Earth cannot be changed for the better unless the consciousness of individuals is changed first. We pledge to increase our awareness by disciplining our minds, by meditation, by prayer, or by positive thinking. Without risk and a readiness to sacrifice there can be no fundamental change in our situation. Therefore, we commit ourselves to this global ethic, to understanding one another, and to socially beneficial, peace-fostering and nature-friendly ways of life.

We invite all people, whether religious or not, to do the same.

THE PRINCIPLES OF A GLOBAL ETHIC

Our world is experiencing a *fundamental crisis:* a crisis in global economy, ecology and politics. The lack of a grand vision, the tangle of unresolved problems, political paralysis, mediocre political leadership with little insight or foresight, and in general too little sense for the commonweal are seen everywhere: Too many old answers to new challenges.

Hundreds of millions of human beings increasingly suffer unemployment, poverty, hunger, destruction of their families. Hope for a lasting peace among nations slips away. There are tensions between the sexes and generations. Children die, kill and are killed. More and more countries are shaken by corruption in politics and business. It is increasingly difficult to live together peacefully in our cities because of social, racial and ethnic conflicts, the abuse of drugs, organized crime and even anarchy. Even neighbors often live in fear of one another. Our planet continues to be ruthlessly plundered. A collapse of the ecosystem threatens us.

Time and again we see leaders and members of *religions* incite aggression, fanaticism, hate and xenophobia—even inspire and legitimate violent and bloody conflicts. Religion often is misused for purely power-political goals, including war. We are filled with disgust.

We condemn these blights and declare that they need not be. An *ethic* already exists within the religious teachings of the world that can counter the global distress. Of course this ethic provides no direct solution for all the immense problems of the world, but it does supply the moral foundation for a better individual and global order: a *vision* which can lead women and men away from despair and society away from chaos.

We are persons who have committed ourselves to the precepts and practices of the world's religions. We confirm that there is already a consensus among the religions that can be the basis for a global ethic— a minimal, *fundamental consensus* concerning *binding values, irrevocable standards* and *fundamental moral attitudes.*

I. NO NEW GLOBAL ORDER WITHOUT A NEW GLOBAL ETHIC!

We women and men of various religions and regions of Earth therefore address all people—religious and nonreligious. We wish to express the following convictions that we hold in common:

- We all have a *responsibility for a better global order.*
- Our involvement for the sake of human rights, freedom, justice, peace and the preservation of the Earth is absolutely necessary.
- Our different religious and cultural traditions must not prevent our common involvement in opposing all forms of inhumanity and working for greater humaneness.
- The principles expressed in this Global Ethic can be affirmed by all persons with ethical convictions whether religiously grounded or not.
- As *religious and spiritual* persons, we base our lives on an Ultimate Reality and draw spiritual power and hope therefrom, in trust, in prayer or meditation, in word or silence. We have a special responsibility for the welfare of all humanity and care for the planet Earth. We do not consider ourselves better than other women and men, but we trust that the ancient wisdom of our religions can point the way for the future.

After two world wars and the end of the Cold War, the collapse of fascism and Nazism, the shaking to the foundations of communism and colonialism, humanity has entered a new phase of its history. Today we possess sufficient economic, cultural and spiritual resources to introduce a better global order. But old and new *ethnic, national, social, economic and religious tensions* threaten the peaceful building of a better world. We have experienced greater technological progress than ever before, yet we see that worldwide poverty, hunger, death of children, unemployment, misery and the destruction of nature have not diminished but rather have increased. Many peoples are threatened with economic ruin, social disarray, political marginalization, ecological catastrophe and national collapse.

In such a dramatic global situation, humanity needs a *vision of peoples living peacefully together,* or ethnic and ethical groupings and of religions sharing responsibility for the care of Earth. A vision rests on hopes, goals, ideals, standards. But all over the world these have slipped from our hands. Yet we are convinced that, despite their frequent abuses and failures, it is the communities of faith who bear a responsibility to demonstrate that such hopes, ideals and standards can be guarded, grounded and lived. This is especially true in the modern state. Guarantees of freedom of conscience and religion are necessary but they do not substitute for binding values, convictions and norms that are valid for all humans regardless of their social origin, sex, skin color, language or religion.

We are convinced of the fundamental unity of the human family on Earth. We recall the 1948 Universal Declaration of Human Rights of the United Nations. What it formally proclaimed on the level of *rights,* we wish to confirm and deepen here from the perspective of an *ethic:* The full realization of the intrinsic dignity of the human person, the inalienable freedom and equality in principle of all humans, and the necessary solidarity and interdependence of all humans with each other.

On the basis of personal experiences and the burdensome history of our planet we have learned:

- That a better global order cannot be created or enforced by laws, prescriptions and conventions alone;
- That the realization of peace, justice and the protection of Earth depends on the insight and readiness of men and women to act justly;
- That action in favor of rights and freedoms presumes a consciousness of responsibility and duty, and that, therefore, both the minds and hearts of women and men must be addressed;
- That rights without morality cannot long endure, and that *there will be no better global order without a global ethic.*

By a *global ethic* we do not mean a global ideology or a *single unified religion* beyond all existing religions, and certainly not the domination of one religion over all others. By a global ethic we mean a *fundamental consensus on binding values, irrevocable standards and personal attitudes.* Without such a fundamental consensus on an ethic, sooner or later every community will be threatened by chaos or dictatorship and individuals will despair.

II. A FUNDAMENTAL DEMAND: EVERY HUMAN BEING MUST BE TREATED HUMANELY

We are all fallible, imperfect men and women with limitations and defects. We know the reality of evil. Precisely because of this, we feel compelled for the sake of global welfare to express what the fundamental elements of a global ethic should be—for individuals as well as for communities and organizations, for states as well as for the religions themselves. We trust that our often millennia-old religious and ethical traditions provide an *ethic* that is *convincing and practicable for all women and men of goodwill,* religious and nonreligious.

At the same time, we know that our various religious and ethical traditions often offer very different bases for what is helpful and what is unhelpful for men and women, what is right and what is wrong, what is good and what is evil. We do not wish to gloss over or ignore the serious differences among the individual religions. However, they should not hinder us from proclaiming publicly those things that we a*lready hold in common* and that we jointly affirm, each on the basis of our own religious or ethical grounds.

We know that religions cannot solve the environmental, economic, political and social problems of the earth. However, they can provide what obviously cannot be attained by economic plans, political programs, or legal regulations alone: A *change* in the inner orientation, the whole mentality, *the "hearts" of people,* and a conversion from a false path to a new orientation for life. Humankind urgently needs social and ecological reforms, but it needs *spiritual renewal* just as urgently. As religious or spiritual persons, we commit ourselves to this task. The spiritual powers of the religions can offer a fundamental sense of trust, a ground of meaning, ultimate standards and a spiritual home. Of course religions are credible only when they eliminate those conflicts that spring from the religions themselves, dismantling mutual arrogance, mistrust, prejudice and even hostile images, and thus demonstrates respect for the traditions, holy places, feasts and rituals of people who believe differently.

Now as before, *women and men are treated inhumanely* all over the world. They are robbed of their opportunities and their freedom; their human rights are trampled underfoot; their dignity is disregarded. But might does not make right! In the face of all inhumanity our religious and ethical convictions demand that *every human being must be treated humanely!*

This means that every human being without distinction of age, sex, race, skin color, physical or mental ability, language, religions, political view, or national or social origin possesses an inalienable and *untouchable dignity* And everyone, the individual as well as the state, is therefore obliged to honor this dignity and protect it. Humans must always be the subjects of rights, must be ends, never mere means, never objects of commercialization and industrialization in economics, politics and media, in research institutes and industrial corporations. No one stands "above good and evil"—no human being, no social class, no influential interest group, no cartel, no police apparatus, no army and no state. On the contrary: Possessed of reason and conscience, every human is obliged to behave in a genuinely human fashion, *to do good and avoid evil!*

It is the intention of this Global Ethic to clarify what this means. In it we wish to recall irrevocable, unconditional ethical norms. These should not be bonds and chains, but helps and supports for people to find and realize once again their lives' direction, values, orientations and meaning.

There is a principle that is found and has persisted in many religious and ethical traditions of humankind for thousands of years: *What you do not wish done to yourself, do not do to others.* Or in positive terms: *What you wish done to yourself, do to others!* This should be the irrevocable, unconditional norm for all areas of life, for families and communities, for races, nations and religions.

Every form of egoism should be rejected: All selfishness, whether individual or collective, whether in the form of class thinking, racism, nationalism or sexism. We condemn these because they prevent humans from being authentically human. Self-determination and self-realization are thoroughly legitimate so long as they are not separated from human self- responsibility and global responsibility, that is, from responsibility for fellow humans and for the planet Earth.

This principle implies very concrete standards to which we humans should hold firm. From it arise *four broad, ancient guidelines* for human behavior that are found in most of the religions of the world.

III. Irrevocable Directives

1. Commitment to a Culture of Nonviolence and Respect for Life

Numberless women and men of all regions and religions strive to lead lives not determined by egoism but by commitment to their fellow humans and to the world around them. Nevertheless, all over the world we find endless hatred, envy, jealousy and violence, not only between individuals but also between social and ethnic groups, between classes, races, nations and religions. The use of violence, drug trafficking and organized crime, often equipped with new technical possibilities, has reached global proportions. Many places still are ruled by terror "from above," dictators oppress their own people, and institutional violence is widespread. Even in some countries where laws exist to protect individual freedoms, prisoners are tortured, men and women are mutilated, hostages are killed.

A. In the great, ancient religious and ethical traditions of humankind we find the directive: *You shall not kill!* Or in positive terms: *Have respect for life!* Let us reflect anew on the consequences of this ancient directive: All people have a right to life, safety and the free development of personality insofar as they do not injure the rights of others. No one has the right physically or psychically to torture, injure, much less to kill, any other human being. And no people, no state, no race, no religion has the right to hate, to discriminate against, to "cleanse," to exile, much less to liquidate a "foreign" minority that is different in behavior or holds different beliefs.

B. Of course, wherever there are humans, there will be conflicts. Such conflicts, however, should be resolved without violence within a framework of justice. This is true for states as well as for individuals. Persons who hold political power must work within the framework of a just order and commit themselves to the most nonviolent, peaceful solutions possible. And they should work for this within an international order of peace, which itself has need of protection and defense against perpetrators of violence. Armament is a mistaken path; disarmament is the commandment of the times. Let no one be deceived: There is no survival for humanity without global peace!

C. Young people must learn at home and in school that violence may not be a means of settling differences with others. Only thus can a *culture of nonviolence* be created.

D. A human person is infinitely precious and must be unconditionally protected. But likewise the *lives of animals and plants,* which inhabit this planet with us, deserve protection, preservation and care. Limitless exploitation of the natural foundations of life, ruthless destruction of the biosphere and militarization of the cosmos are all outrages. As human beings, we have a special responsibility—especially with a view to future generations—for Earth; and the cosmos, for the air, water and soil. We are *all intertwined together* in this cosmos and we are all dependent on each other. Each one of us depends on the welfare of all.

Therefore, the dominance of humanity over nature and the cosmos must not be encouraged. Instead, we must cultivate living in harmony with nature and the cosmos.

E. To be authentically human, in the spirit of our great religious and ethical traditions, means that in public as well as in private life we must be concerned for others and ready to help. We must never be ruthless and brutal. Every people, every race, every religion must show tolerance and respect—indeed high appreciation—for every other. Minorities need protection and support, whether they be racial, ethnic or religious.

2. Commitment to a Culture of Solidarity and a Just Economic Order

Numberless men and women of all regions and religions strive to live their lives in solidarity with one another and to work for authentic fulfillment of their vocations. Nevertheless, all over the world we find endless hunger, deficiency and need. Not only individuals, but especially unjust institutions and structures are responsible for these tragedies. Millions of people are without work; millions are exploited by poor wages, forced to the edges of society, with their possibilities for the future destroyed. In many lands the gap between the poor and the rich, between the powerful and the powerless is immense. We live in a world in which totalitarian state socialism as well as unbridled capitalism have hollowed out and destroyed many ethical and spiritual values. A materialistic mentality breeds greed for unlimited profit and a grasping for endless plunder. These demands claim more and more of the community's resources without obliging the individual to contribute more. The cancerous social evil of corruption thrives in the developing countries and in the developed countries alike.

A. In the great, ancient religious and ethical traditions of humankind we find the directive: *You shall not steal!* Or in positive terms: *Deal honestly and fairly!* Let us reflect anew on the consequences of this ancient directive: No one has the right to rob or dispossess in any way whatsoever any other person or the commonweal. Further, no one has the right to use her or his possessions without concern for the needs of society and Earth.

B. Where extreme poverty reigns, helplessness and despair spread and theft occurs again and again for the sake of survival. Where power and wealth are accumulated ruthlessly, feelings of envy, resentment and deadly hatred and rebellion inevitably well up in the disadvantaged and marginalized. This leads to a vicious circle of violence and counter-violence. Let no one be deceived: There is no global peace without global justice!

C. Young people must learn at home and in school that property, limited though it may be, carries with it an obligation, and that its uses should, at the same time, serve the common good. Only thus can a *just economic order* be built up.

D. If the plight of the poorest billions of humans on this planet, particularly women and children, is to be improved, the world economy must be structured more justly. Individual good deeds and assistance projects, indispensable though they be, are insufficient. The participation of all states and the authority of international organizations are needed to build just economic institutions.

A solution that can be supported by all sides must be sought for the debt crisis and the poverty of the dissolving Second World and, even more, the Third World. Of course conflicts of interest are unavoidable. In the developed countries, a distinction must be made between necessary and limitless consumption, between socially beneficial and nonbeneficial uses of property, between justified and unjustified uses of natural resources and between a profit-only and a socially beneficial and ecologically oriented market economy. Even the developing nations must search their national consciences.

Wherever those ruling threaten to repress those ruled, wherever institutions threaten persons, and wherever might oppresses right, we are obligated to resist—whenever possible nonviolently.

E. To be authentically human in the spirit of our great religious and ethical traditions means the following:

- We must utilize economic and political power for *service to humanity* instead of misusing it in ruthless battles for domination. We must develop a spirit of compassion with those who suffer, with special care for the children, the aged, the poor, the disabled, the refugees and the lonely.
- We must cultivate *mutual respect* and consideration, so as to reach a reasonable balance of interests, instead of thinking only of unlimited power and unavoidable competitive struggles.

- We must value a *sense of moderation* and modesty, instead of an unquenchable greed for money, prestige and consumption. In greed, humans lose their "souls," their freedom, their composure, their inner peace and thus that which makes them human.

3. Commitment to a Culture of Tolerance and a Life of Truthfulness

Numberless women and men of all regions and religions strive to lead lives of honesty and truthfulness. Nevertheless, all over the world we find endless lies and deceit, swindling and hypocrisy, ideology and demagoguery:

- Politicians and business people who use lies as a means to success;
- Mass media that spread ideological propaganda instead of accurate reporting, misinformation instead of information, cynical commercial interest instead of loyalty to the truth;
- Scientist and researchers who give themselves over to morally questionable ideological or political programs or to economic interest groups, or who justify research that violates fundamental ethical values;
- Representatives of religions who dismiss other religions as of little value and who preach fanaticism and intolerance, instead of respect and understanding.

A. In the great, ancient religious and ethical traditions of humankind we find the directive: *You shall not lie!* Or in positive terms: *Speak and act truthfully!* Let us reflect anew on the consequences of this ancient directive: No woman or man, no institution, no state or church or religious community has the right to speak lies to other humans.

B. This is especially true

- For those who work in the *mass media,* to whom we entrust the freedom to report for the sake of truth and to whom we, thus, grant the office of guardian. They do not stand above morality but have the obligation to respect human dignity, human rights and fundamental values. They are duty-bound to objectivity, fairness and the preservation of human dignity. They have no right to intrude into individuals' private spheres, to manipulate public opinion or to distort reality;
- For *artists, writers* and *scientists,* to whom we entrust artistic and academic freedom. They are not exempt from general ethical standards and must serve the truth;

- For the leaders of countries, *politicians* and *political parties,* to whom we entrust our own freedoms. When they lie in the faces of their people, when they manipulate the truth or when they are guilty of venality or ruthlessness in domestic or foreign affairs, they forsake their credibility and deserve to lose their offices and their voters. Conversely, public opinion should support those politicians who dare to speak the truth to the people at all times;
- Finally, for *representatives of religion.* When they stir up prejudice, hatred and enmity toward those of different belief or even incite or legitimate religious wars, they deserve the condemnation of humankind and the loss of their adherents.

Let no one be deceived: There is no global justice without truthfulness and humaneness!

C. Young people must learn at home and in school to think, speak and act *truthfully.* They have a right to information and education to be able to make the decisions that will form their lives. Without an ethical formation they will hardly be able to distinguish the important from the unimportant. In the daily flood of information, ethical standards will help them discern when opinions are portrayed as facts, interests veiled, tendencies exaggerated and facts twisted.

D. To be authentically human in the spirit of our great religious and ethical traditions means the following:

- We must not confuse freedom with arbitrariness or pluralism with indifference to truth.
- We must *cultivate truthfulness* in all our relationships instead of dishonesty, dissembling, and opportunism.
- We must *constantly seek truth* and incorruptible sincerity instead of spreading ideological or partisan half-truths.
- We must courageously *serve the truth* and we must remain *constant* and *trustworthy,* instead of yielding to opportunistic accommodation to life.

4. Commitment to a Culture of Equal Rights and Partnership Between Men and Women

Numberless men and women of all regions and religions strive to live their lives in a spirit of partnership and responsible action in the areas of love, sexuality and family. Nevertheless, all over the world there are condemnable forms of patriarchy, domination of one sex over the other, exploitation of women, sexual misuse of children and forced prostitution. Too frequently, social inequities force women and even children into prostitution as a means of survival—particularly in less developed countries.

A. In the great, ancient religious and ethical traditions of humankind we find the directive: *You shall not commit sexual immorality!* Or in positive terms: *Respect and love one another!* Let us reflect anew on the consequences of this ancient directive: No one has the right to degrade others to mere sex objects, to lead them into or hold them in sexual dependency.

B. We condemn sexual exploitation and sexual discrimination as one of the worst forms of human degradation. We have the duty to resist wherever the domination of one sex over the other is preached—even in the name of religious conviction; wherever sexual exploitation is tolerated, wherever prostitution is fostered or children are misused. Let no one be deceived: There is no authentic humaneness without a living together in partnership!

C. Young people must learn at home and in school that sexuality is not a negative, destructive or exploitative force, but creative and affirmative. Sexuality as a life-affirming shaper of community can only be effective when partners accept the responsibilities of caring for one another's happiness.

D. The relationship between women and men should be characterized not by patronizing behavior or exploitation, but by love, partnership and trustworthiness. Human fulfillment is not identical with sexual pleasure. Sexuality should express and reinforce a loving relationship lived by equal partners.

Some religious traditions know the ideal of a voluntary renunciation of the full use of sexuality. Voluntary renunciation also can be an expression of identity and meaningful fulfillment.

E. The social institution of marriage, despite all its cultural and religious variety, is characterized by love, loyalty and permanence. It aims at and should guarantee security and mutual support to husband, wife and child. It should secure the rights of all family members.

All lands and cultures should develop economic and social relationships that will enable marriage and family life worthy of human beings, especially for older people. Children have a right of access to education. Parents should not exploit children, nor children parents. Their relationships should reflect mutual respect, appreciation and concern.

F. To be authentically human in the spirit of our great religious and ethical traditions means the following:

- We need mutual respect, *partnership* and understanding, instead of patriarchal domination and degradation, which are expressions of violence and engender counter-violence.
- We need mutual concern, tolerance, readiness for reconciliation, and love, instead of any form of possessive lust or sexual misuse.

Only what has already been experienced in personal and familial relationships can be practiced on the level of nations and religions.

IV. A TRANSFORMATION OF CONSCIOUSNESS!

Historical experience demonstrates the following: Earth cannot be changed for the better unless we achieve a transformation in the consciousness of individuals and in public life. The possibilities for transformation have already been glimpsed in areas such as war and peace, economy, and ecology, where in recent decades fundamental changes have taken place. This transformation must also be achieved in the area of ethics and values!

Every individual has intrinsic dignity and inalienable rights, and each also has an inescapable responsibility for what she or he does and does not do. All our decisions and deeds, even our omissions and failures, have consequences.

Keeping this sense of responsibility alive, deepening it and passing it on to future generations, is the special task of religions.

We are realistic about what we have achieved in this consensus, and so we urge that the following be observed:

1) A universal consensus on many *disputed ethical questions* (from bioethics and sexual ethics through mass media and scientific ethics to economics and political ethics) will be difficult to attain. Nevertheless, even for many controversial questions, suitable solutions

should be attainable in the spirit of the fundamental principles we have jointly developed here.

2) In many areas of life a new consciousness of ethical responsibility has already risen. Therefore, we would be pleased if as many *professions* as possible, such as those of physicians, scientists, business people, journalists and politicians, would develop up-to-date *codes of ethics* that would provide specific guidelines for the vexing questions of these particular professions.

3) Above all, we urge the *various communities of faith* to formulate their very *specific ethics:* What does each faith tradition have to say, for example, about the meaning of life and death, the enduring of suffering and the forgiveness of guilt, about selfless sacrifice and the necessity of renunciation, about compassion and joy. These will deepen, and make more specific, the already discernible global ethic.

In conclusion, we appeal to all the inhabitants of this planet. Earth cannot be changed for the better unless the consciousness of individuals is changed. We pledge to work for such transformation in individual and collective consciousness, for the awakening of our spiritual powers through reflection, meditation, prayer or positive thinking, for a *conversion* of the heart. Together we can move mountains! Without a willingness to take risks and a readiness to sacrifice there can be no fundamental change in our situation! Therefore, we commit ourselves to a common global ethic, to better mutual understanding, as well as to socially beneficial, peace-fostering and Earth-friendly ways of life.

We invite all men and women, whether religious or not, to do the same!

Notes

INTRODUCTION

1. Emile Durkheim, *The Elementary Forms of the Religious Life,* trans. Joseph Swain (1912; Glencoe: Free Press, 1961), 48.

CHAPTER 1

1. Wilhelm Schmidt, *The Origin and Growth of Religion: Fact and Theories* (New York: Cooper Square Publishers, 1972).

2. Friedrich Schleiermacher, *The Christian Faith* (Edinburgh: T. & T. Clark, 1928), excerpted in Joseph D. Bellis, ed., *Phenomenology of Religion* (New York and Evanston: Harper Forum Books, 1969), 166.

3. Immanuel Kant, *Religion Within the Limits of Reason Alone,* 2nd ed., trans. T. M. Greene and H. H. Hudson (LaSalle, Ill.: Open Court Publishing, 1960), 142–43.

4. Branko Bosnjak, *Filozofija i krscanstvo* (Philosophy and Christianity) (Zagreb, Yogoslavia: Naprijed, 1966), 574.

5. Edward Scribner Ames in J. H. Leuba, *A Psychological Study of Religion* (New York: Macmillan, 1912), 53–54.

6. J. Milton Yinger, *Religion, Society, and the Individual* (New York: Macmillan, 1957), 9.

7. Mircea Eliade, *The Sacred and the Profane,* trans. Willard R. Trask (New York: Harcourt, 1957).

8. Rudolph Otto, *The Idea of the Holy,* trans. John Harvey (London: Oxford University Press, 1958).

9. Paul Tillich, *Theology of Culture,* ed. Robert C. Kimball (New York: Oxford University Press, 1964), 7.

10. Martin Buber, *Between Man and Man* (New York: Macmillan, 1965), 13–14.

11. Edgar Sheffield Brightman, *A Philosophy of Religion* (Englewood Cliffs, N.J.: Prentice-Hall, 1958), 17.

12. John F. Wilson, *Religion: A Preface* (Englewood Cliffs, N.J.: Prentice-Hall, 1982), 34.

13. William C. Tremmel, *Religion: What Is It?* 2nd ed. (New York: Holt, Rinehart and Winston, 1984), 7.

14. Niels C. Nielsen, Jr., Norvin Hein, Frank Reynolds, et al., *Religions of the World* (New York: St. Martin's Press, 1983), 7.

15. John Clark Archer, *Faiths Men Live By* (New York: Thomas Nelson and Sons, 1934), 12.

16. Karl Jaspers, *The Origin and Goal of History* (New Haven, Conn.: Yale University Press, 1953); idem, *Vom Ursprung und Ziel der Geschichte* (Zurich: Artemis Verlag, 1949). More about this later.

17. See James W. Fowler, *Stages of Faith* (New York: Harper & Row, 1981), 107; see also Leonard Swidler, *After the Absolute. The Dialogical Future of Religious Reflection* (Minneapolis: Fortress Press, 1990), 195–99.

18. The rabbis of Judaism spoke similarly in Hebrew of the *Malkut Shomaim*, the "Kingdom [or better, Reign] of Heaven." (*Heaven* is a euphemism for the name of God.) This is reflected in the use of "the Reign of *Heaven*" by Matthew, the most "Jewish" of the evangelists.

19. Roger Garaudy, *De l'anatheme au dialogue* (Paris: Plon, 1965); idem, *From Anathema to Dialogue* (New York: Herder and Herder, 1966), 90f.

20. Jean Jacques Rousseau, *The Social Contrast* (Oxford, U.K.: Oxford University Press, 1947), 239.

21. *Hsün Tzu—Basic Writings*, trans. by Burton Watson (New York: Columbia University Press, 1963), 157.

22. *The Works of Hsün Tzu*, trans. H. H. Dubs, vol. *Man's Nature Is Evil* (Taipei: Confucius Publishing Co., 1983).

23. Thomas Aquinas, *Summa Theologiae*, I–II, Q. 91, a. 2: "Inter cetera autem rationalis creatura excellentiori quondam modo divinae providentiae subiacet, inquantum et ipsa fit providentiae particeps, sibi ipsi et aliis providens."

24. Ibid., II–II, Q.1, a. 2.

25. In the early rabbinic period (around the beginning of the Common Era), a third term was also employed to denote God vis-à-vis humanity, God's presence (*Shekhinah*). Wisdom was further identified with another extremely important expression of the divine vis-à-vis humanity—namely, *Torah*, God's "instructions" to humans on how to live (see Ben Sira 24:1–3). The rabbis made the identification even closer (see *Genesis Rabbah* 1; 8[6a]).

26. Raimundo Panikkar, *The Unknown Christ in Hinduism*, rev. ed. (Maryknoll, N.Y.: Orbis, 1981), 9.

27. Gerhard Kittel, ed., *Theological Dictionary of the New Testament*, vol. 4 (Grand Rapids, Mich.: Eerdmans, 1968), 133ff.

28. Panikkar, *Unknown Christ*, 140.

29. Paul Tillich, *The Courage to Be* (New Haven, Conn.: Yale University Press, 1952), 190.

30. Cited in John Hick, *God Has Many Names* (Philadelphia: Westminster Press, 1982), 92.

31. Panikkar, *Unknown Christ*, 152f.

32. Hans Küng et al., *Christentum und Weltreligionen* (Munich: Piper Verlag, 1984), 491, 492.

33. Ibid., 551f.

34. Masao Abe, "A Dynamic Unity in Religious Pluralism: A Proposal from the Buddhist Point of View," in *The Experience of Religious Diversity*, ed. John Hick and Hasan Askari (Hants, England: Gower, 1985), 163–90.

35. John Hick, "Religious Diversity as Challenge and Promise," in ibid., 19.

36. Abe, "Dynamic Unity," 184.

37. Santosh Chandra Sengupta, "The Misunderstanding of Hinduism," in *Truth and Dialogue in World Religions: Conflicting Truth Claims*, ed. John Hick (Philadelphia: Westminster, 1974), 97.

38. See Tang Yi, "Taoism as a Living Philosophy," *Journal of Chinese Philosophy* 12, no. 4 (December 1985): 408.

39. Nagarjuna is cited in Paul O. Ingram's paper "Buddhist and Christian Paradigms of Selfhood," presented at the conference "Paradigm Shift in Buddhism and Christianity: Cultural Systems and the Self," Honolulu, January 3–11, 1984.

40. Jung Young-Lee, "Can God Be Change Itself?" *Journal of Ecumenical Studies* 10, no. 4 (fall 1973): 752–70.

41. Jay McDaniel, "The God of the Oppressed and the God Who Is Empty," *Journal of Ecumenical Studies* 23, no. 3 (fall 1985): 687.

42. Hans Küng and Julia Ching, *Christentum und chinesische Religion* (Munich: Piper Verlag, 1988), 95.

43. Ibid., 116.

44. As cited in ibid., 42.

45. Mou Tsung-san, *Chung-kuo che-hsüeh t'e-chi* {The Uniqueness of Chinese Philosophy} (Taipei: Student Book Co., 1974), as cited in John Berthrong's paper "Adjustments: Dual Transcendence and Fiduciary Community," delivered at the Hong Kong International Christian–Confucian Conference, June 8–15, 1988.

46. *Book of Mencius*, 7a, 1.

47. Tu Wei-ming, "On Confucian Religiousness," conference paper, Hong Kong International Confucian–Christian Conference, June 8–15, 1988.

48. Carsun Chang, *The Development of Neo-Confucian Thought*, vol. 2, appendix (New York, 1963), as cited in Küng and Ching, *Christentum*, 123f.

49. Tu, "On Confucian Religiousness," 2.

50. Berthrong, "Adjustments," 11.

51. Tu, "Confucian Religiousness," 8.

52. Ibid.

53. Berthrong, "Adjustments," 46.

54. Hans Küng and Julia Ching, *Christianity and Chinese Religions* (New York: Doubleday, 1989), 174. We are particularly grateful to Hans Küng in this section for his insight into Taoism.

55. G. H. Dunstheimer, *Histoire des religions*, vol. 3, ed. H. C. Puech (Paris, 1976), 389.

56. Küng and Ching, *Christianity*, 177.

57. Cited in Thomas Aquinas, *De Potentia*, q. 7, a. 5. English: *On the Power of God* (London, 1934), vol. 3, p. 33.

58. See, for example, Roger Garaudy, *De l'anatheme au dialogue* (Paris: Plon, 1965); idem, *From Anathema to Dialogue* (New York: Herder and Herder, 1966). See also Leonard Swidler, *After the Absolute. The Dialogical Future of Religious Reflection* (Minneapolis: Fortress Press, 1990), 165–89.

59. Garaudy, *Anathema*, 54. The several citations from Garaudy that follow are also taken from this book.

60. Hans Küng, *Does God Exist?* (New York: Doubleday, 1980).

61. See Anthony Matteo, "Joseph Marechal and the Transcendental Turn in Catholic Thought" (Ph.D. diss., Temple University, Philadelphia, 1985).

62. Pal Horvath, "Changes in the Evaluation of Religion and the Churches in the Last Decade in Hungary and the U.S.A.," paper delivered at the Christian–Marxist Dialogue, University of Budapest Law School, Budapest, Hungary, June 20–25, 1988.

63. See Leonard Swidler, ed., *Human Rights, Christians, Marxists and Others in Dialogue* (New York: Paragon House, 1991).

CHAPTER 2

1. Winston L. King, *Introduction to Religion* (New York; Evanston, Ill.; and London: Harper & Row, 1954), 80.

2. Ibid., 81.

3. William J. Abraham, *An Introduction to the Philosophy of Religion* (Englewood Cliffs, N.J.: Prentice-Hall, 1985), 6.

4. Ibid., 8.

5. Edgar S. Brightman, *A Philosophy of Religion* (Englewood Cliffs, N.J.: Prentice-Hall, 1940), 22.

6. Ibid., 26–30.

7. Boniface VIII, "Unam sanctam," in *The Teaching of the Catholic Church*, ed. J. Neuner and J. Depuis, no. 875 (Dublin: Mercier Press, 1972), 211.

8. Thomas Aquinas, *Summa Theologiae*, II–II, Q. 1, a. 2.

9. I am grateful to Henry Rosemont, Fulbright Professor of Philosophy at Fudan University, Shanghai, 1982–84, for this exemplary comparison.

10. Paul Knitter, *No Other Name?* (Maryknoll, N.Y.: Orbis, 1984), 219.

CHAPTER 3

1. They are the "Chronicle of Ancient Events" and "Chronicle of Japanese Events," respectively.

2. Recently, claims have arisen that some religions that have been considered uninterested in their history—Buddhism, for example—are in fact historical. See Whalen Lai, "Buddhism as a Historical Faith: Answer to John Cobb," *The Pacific World*, New Series no. 7 (Fall 1991), 1–13.

CHAPTER 4

1. The words *critical* and *criticism* in the context of scriptural studies should be understood analogously to the way they are used in music, art, and film criticism—that is, they do not mean expressing a negative attitude toward something, but following an analytical and evaluative procedure to help the listener or observer appreciate the place, significance, and meaning of a work. In scriptural studies, it is the text that is more adequately appreciated through historical and literary criticism.

2. Lawrence Boadt, *Reading the Old Testament: An Introduction* (New York and Mahwah, N.J.: Paulist Press, 1984), 79.

3. Ibid., 85.

4. Roger Schmidt, *Exploring Religion* (Belmont, Calif.: Wadsworth, 1988), 489.

CHAPTER 5

1. Robert N. Bellah, "Religious Evolution," *American Sociological Review* 29 (1964): 358–74, reproduced in Roland Robertson, ed., *Sociology of Religion* (Hammondsworth: Penguin Books, 1969).

2. Talcott Parsons, *The Structure of Social Action* (1937; New York: Free Press, 1968).

3. Mary Douglas, *Purity and Danger* (New York: Routledge and Kegan Paul, 1966), 82.

4. Bellah, "Religious Evolution," 263. The several following quotations from Bellah are from this essay.

5. The word *sacred* comes from the Latin *sacer,* meaning *separate, set aside* from the everyday for the divine. The word *profane* comes from the Latin *profanum*—literally, *in front of the temple,* or that which is not *set aside* for the divine, not placed in the temple.

6. See Leonard Swidler, "Liberal Catholicism—A Lesson from the Past," *Cross Currents* (Spring 1971); and idem, *Aufklärung Catholicism 1780–1850* (Missoula, Mon.: Scholars Press, 1978).

7. Karl Jaspers, *Vom Ursprung und Ziel der Geschichte* (Zurich: Artemis, 1949), 19–43; idem, *The Origin and Goal of History,* trans. Michael Bullock (New Haven, Conn.: Yale University Press, 1953).

8. We are in this section especially indebted to Ewert Cousins' essay "Judaism-Christianity-Islam: Facing Modernity Together, *Journal of Ecumenical Studies,* 30:3–4 (Summer–Fall, 1993), pp. 417–425.

9. Oswald Spengler, *Der Untergang des Abendlandes* (Munich: Beck, 1922–23), 2 vols.

10. Pitirim A. Sorokin, *The Crisis of Our Age* (New York: Dutton, 1941).

11. Samuel Huntington, "Clash of Civilizations," *Foreign Affairs,* 72, 3 (July 1993): 22–49.

12. See among others, Hans Küng, *Theologie im Aufbruch* (Munich: Piper Verlag, 1987), esp. 153ff.

13. See especially Ewert Cousins, "Judaism-Christianity-Islam," 417–25.

14. For a more comprehensive treatment of Cousins's concept of the Second Axial Period, see his book *Christ of the 21st Century* (Rockport, Mass.: Element, 1992).

15. Pierre Teilhard de Chardin, *Le Phénomène humain* (Paris: Editions du Seuil, 1955; idem, *The Phenomenon of Man*, trans. Bernard Wall (New York: Harper and Row, 1965). See also idem, *L'Activation de l'énergie* (Paris: Editions du Seuil, 1962); and idem, *L'Energie humaine* (Paris: Editions du Seuil, 1962). For a more detailed study of Teilhard's thought in relation to the Second Axial Period, see Ewert Cousins's paper "Teilhard de Chardin and the Religious Phenomenon," delivered at UNESCO's International Symposium on the Occasion of the Centenary of the Birth of Teilhard de Chardin, Paris, September 16–18, 1981, UNESCO Document Code SS.82/WS/36.

16. Teilhard, *Le Phénomène humain,* 268–69.

17. Ibid., 292; idem, *Phenomenon,* 262.

18. On the concept of dialogic dialogue, see Raimundo Panikkar, *Myth, Faith and Hermeneutics* (New York: Paulist Press, 1979), 241-45; see also his *The Intrareligious Dialogue* (New York: Paulist Press, 1978).

19. See Leonard Swidler, "The Age of Global Dialogue," *Marburg Zeitschrift für Religionswissenschaft* 1, no. 2 (July 1996). This article can be found on the Internet at http://www. marburguni.de/fb11/religionswissenschaft/journal/swidler.html.

20. Leonard Swidler et al., *Death or Dialogue* (Philadelphia: Trinity Press International, 1990).

CHAPTER 6

1. Mary Douglas, *Purity and Danger* (New York: Routledge and Kegan Paul, 1966), excerpted in *Sociology of Religion. Selected Readings,* ed. Roland Robertson (1915; Hammondsworth: Penguin Books, 1969), 79, 97.

2. Auguste Comte, *Cours de philosophie positive,* 6 vols. (Paris, 1831–42). The English translation is titled *The Positive Philosophy,* 6 vols. (London, 1853, 1875).

3. N. D. Fustel de Coulanges, *Ancient City* (1864; Garden City, NY: Doubleday, 1986).

4. Max Müller, *Lectures on the Origin and Growth of Religion* (London: Longmans, 1878).

5. William Graham Sumner, *Folkways* (New York, 1906).

6. Edward Burnett Tylor, *Primitive Culture* (London: Murray, 1871), 2 vols.

7. James G. Frazer, *The Golden Bough,* 3rd ed., 12 vols. (1911–14).

8. Emile Durkheim, *The Elementary Forms of Religious Life,* trans. Joseph Ward Swain (1912; New York: Macmillan, 1915).

9. Bronislaw Malinowski, "Magic, Science and Religion," in *Science, Religion and Reality*, ed. James Needham (New York: Macmillan, 1925), reproduced in Bronislaw Malinowski, *Magic, Science and Religion and Other Essays* (1948; New York: Doubleday, 1954).

10. Emile Durkheim, *Suicide: A Study in Sociology* (1897; London:Routledge, 1951), excerpted in Robin Gill, *Theology and Sociology: A Reader* (New York: Paulist Press, 1987), 54f.

11. Douglas, *Purity and Danger*, 83.

12. Gerd Theissen, *On Having a Critical Faith* (London: SCM Press, 1979), 1.

13. Thomas F. O'Dea, *The Sociology of Religion* (Englewood Cliffs, N.J: Prentice-Hall, 1966), 7.

14. Malinowski, *Magic, Science and Religion*, 30.

15. Ronald L. Johnstone, *Religion in Sociology. A Sociology of Religion*, 3rd ed. (Englewood Cliffs, N.J.: Prentice-Hall, 1988), 16.

16. Ibid., 17.

17. Daniel L. Pals, *Seven Theories of Religion* (New York: Oxford University Press, 1996), 78.

18. Ibid., 125.

19. Ibid., 139.

20. Karl Marx, "The Communism of the Paper *Rheinischer Beobachter*," in *Karl Marx and Friedrich Engels on Religion*, ed. Reinhold Niebuhr (New York: Schocken Books, 1964), 83f.

21. Pals, *Seven Theories*, 145.

22. Karl Marx and Friedrich Engels, *On Religion* (Atlanta: Scholar's Press, 1982), 42; excerpted in Andrew M. Greeley, ed., *Sociology and Religion* (New York: HarperCollins, 1995), 4.

23. Sigmund Freud, *The Future of an Illusion*, in *The Standard Edition of the Complete Psychological Works of Sigmund Freud*, ed. James Strachey with Anna Freud (London: Hogarth Press, 1961), 21:33.

24. Ibid., 43.

25. Durkheim, *The Elementary Forms of the Religious Life*, 206.

26. Pals, *Seven Theories*, 111.

27. Mircea Eliade, *Patterns in Comparative Religion*, trans. Rosemary Sheed (1949; New York: Meridian Books, 1963), xiii.

28. Peter L. Berger, *The Sacred Canopy* (New York: Doubleday, 1967), as excerpted in Gill, *Theology and Sociology*, 95.

29. Ibid.

30. Max Weber, *The Protestant Ethic and the Spirit of Capitalism*, trans. Talcott Parsons (1904–05; New York: Free Press, 1930).

31. Max Weber, "Major Features of World Religions," in *Sociology of Religion*, ed. Robertson, 22.

32. See Greeley, *Sociology and Religion*, 32f.

33. Durkheim, *The Elementary Forms of the Religious Life*, excerpted as "The Social Foundations of Religion," in *Sociology of Religion*, ed. Robertson, 53.

34. Pals, *Seven Theories*, 117.

35. Ibid., 115.

36. P. Worsley, *The Trumpet Shall Sound* (McGibbon and Kee, 1968), excerpted as "Religion as a Category," in *Sociology of Religion*, ed. Robertson, 231f.

37. Malinowski, *Magic, Science and Religion* (1954), 56–59.

38. We are particularly indebted in this section to Johnstone, *Religion in Society*, 72–95.

39. See J. Milton Yinger, *The Scientific Study of Religion* (New York: Macmillan, 1970), 266–68.

40. Jeannie Mills, *Six Years with God: Life Inside Rev. Jim Jones's Peoples Temple* (New York: A&W Publishers, 1979), 181.

41. Ibid., 151f.

42. See O'Dea, *Sociology of Religion*, 14f.

43. See ibid., 103f.

CHAPTER 7

1. William J. Abraham, *An Introduction to the Philosophy of Religion* (Englewood Cliffs, N.J.: Prentice-Hall, 1985), 58.

2. Sigmund Freud, *The Future of an Illusion*, trans. W. D. Robson-Scott, rev. ed., James Strachey (London: Hogarth Press and Institute of Psycho-Analysis, 1978), 29.

3. Erich Fromm, *Man for Himself* (New York: Rinehart, 1947).

4. C. G. Jung, *Symbols of Transformation*, 5 vols. (Princeton: Princeton University Press, 1976); see also Ninian Smart, *Worldviews: Crosscultural Explorations of Human Belief* (New York: Charles Scribner's Sons, 1983), 75.

5. William James, *Varieties of Religious Experience* (1902; New York: Macmillan, 1961).

6. A British psychoanalyst who should be distinguished from his better-known American behaviorist colleague B. F. Skinner.

7. Clement Reeves, *The Psychology of Rollo May* (San Francisco; Washington, D.C.; London: Jossey-Bass, 1977), 285.

8. H. Richard Niebuhr, *The Responsible Self* (New York: Harper & Row, 1963), 65.

9. James W. Fowler, *Stages of Faith* (New York: Harper & Row, 1981), 121. Italics added for emphasis.

10. Lawrence Kohlberg and Carol Gilligan, "The Adolescent as a Philosopher: The Discovery of the Self in a Postconventional World," *Daedalus* 100 (fall 1971): 1071.

11. Lawrence Kohlberg, "Education for Justice: A Modern Statement of the Platonic View," in *Moral Education*, ed. Nancy F. Sizer and Theodore R. Sizer (Cambridge, Mass.: Harvard University Press, 1970), 72.

12. Lawrence Kohlberg, "Moral Education in the Schools: A Developmental View," *The School Review* 74 (1966): 21.

13. Walter E. Conn, *Conscience: Development and Self-Transcendence* (Birmingham, Ala.: Religious Education Press, 1981), 79.

14. Jean Piaget, *The Construction of Reality in the Child,* trans. Margaret Cook (New York: Ballentine [1937], 1971), xii.

15. Bernard Lonergan, *Method in Theology* (New York: Herder and Herder, 1972), 253.

16. Erik Erikson, *Identity: Youth and Crisis* (New York: Norton, 1968), 138.

17. Conn, *Conscience,* 71.

18. Lonergan, *Method,* 241.

19. Bernard Lonergan, "Faith and Beliefs," paper presented at the Annual Meeting of the American Academy of Religion, Newton, Mass., October 1969, 9, quoted in Conn, *Conscience,* 186.

20. Conn, *Conscience,* 187.

21. Walter E. Conn, "Conversion: A Developmental Perspective," *Cross Currents* (Fall 1982): 326ff.

22. Seiichi Yagi, *Die Front-Struktur als Brücke vom buddhistischen zum christlichen Denken* (Munich: Kaiser, 1988), 74. English in Leonard Swidler (co-author with and translator of Seiichi Yagi) and Seiichi Yagi, *A Bridge to Buddhist-Christian Dialogue* (Mahwah, N.J.: Paulist Press, 1990).

23. Piangendo Francesco disse un Giorno a Gesu: / "Amo il sole, amo le stelle, / amo Chiara e le sorelle, / amo il cuore degli uomini, / amo tutte le cose belle. / O mio Signore, mi devi perdonare, / perche te solo io dovrei amare." / Sorridendo il Signore gli rispose cosi: / "Amo il sole, amo le stelle, / amo Chiara e le sorelle, / amo il cuore degli uomini, / amo tutte le cose belle. / O mio Francesco, non devi piangere piu, / perche io amo quel che ami tu." (Sung by Bernardino Greco, OFM, at the Institut für ökumenische Forschung, Tübingen, June 22, 1985).

24. O'Dea, *The Sociology of Religion,* 33.

25. Gordon W. Allport, *The Individual and His Religion* (New York: Macmillan, 1950; paperback ed., 1960), 52–54.

26. Ibid., 63.

27. Ibid., 70.

28. Ibid., 72.

29. Kohlberg and Gilligan, "The Adolescent as a Philosopher," 1072.

30. Fowler, *Stages of Faith,* 186f.

31. Ibid., 197.

32. Abraham Maslow, *The Farther Reaches of Human Nature* (New York: Viking Press, 1971). For an overview of "humanistic psychology," see Frank Gable, *The Third Force* (New York: Grossman Publishers, 1970).

33. Elizabeth Monroe Drews and Leslie Lipson, *Values and Humanity* (New York: St. Martin's Press, 1971), 40–41.

34. Margaret Cotroneo, "A Contextual Catholic Ethics" (Ph.D. diss., Temple University, Philadelphia, 1983), 213.

35. Ibid., 248.

36. Ibid.
37. Ibid.

Chapter 8

1. Roger Schmidt, *Exploring Religion,* 2nd ed. (Belmont, Calif.: Wadsworth, 1988), 303.

2. Max Weber, *The Protestant Ethic and the Spirit of Capitalism,* trans. Talcott Parsons (London: George Allen & Unwin, 1930).

3. Max Weber, "On the Social Psychology of the World Religions," in *Ways of Understanding Religion,* ed. Walter H. Capps (New York: Macmillan, 1972), 217–27.

4. Lawrence S. Cunningham et al., *The Sacred Quest: An Invitation to the Study of Religion* (New York: Macmillan, 1991), 4.

5. See, for example, the initiating publication Gustavo Gutierrez, *A Theology of Liberation: History, Politics and Salvation* (Maryknoll, N.Y.: Orbis Books, 1973); and later Jon Sobrino, *Christology at the Crossroads* (Maryknoll, N.Y.: Orbis Books, 1978); Leonardo Boff, *Church, Charism and Power: Liberation Theology and the Institutional Church* (New York: Crossroad, 1985). See also Michael Novak, *Will It Liberate? Questions about Liberation Theology* (New York: Paulist Press, 1986).

6. See Jose Miguez-Bonino, *An Emerging Theology in World Perspective: Commentary on Korean Minjung Theology* (Mystic, Conn.: Twenty-Third Publications, 1988).

7. See Peter Berger, *The Capitalist Revolution: Fifty Propositions about Prosperity, Equality, and Liberty* (New York: Basic Books, 1986).

8. These include the "Interfaith Declaration: A Code of Ethics on International Business for Christians, Muslims and Jews," "The Caux Round Table Principles for Business," the "Kyosei Principles," and the "CERES Principles." All can be found on the World Wide Web at http://astro.temple.edu/~dialogue.

9. See, for example, James C. Collins and Jerry I. Porras, *Built to Last. Successful Habits of Visionary Companies* (New York: HarperBusiness, 1994).

10. Karl Marx, "Contribution to the Critique of Hegel's Philosophy of Right," in *Marx and Engels on Religion,* ed. Reinhold Niebuhr (New York: Shocken Books, 1964), 41–58.

11. This Marxist economic-determinist view is explained and then rejected by Esad Cimic in *Socijalisticko drustvo i religija* (Sarajevo: Svjetlost, 1966), 13–23.

Chapter 9

1. John F. Wilson, *Religion: A Preface* (Englewood Cliffs, N.J.: Prentice-Hall, 1982), 15.

2. Max Müller, ed., *The Sacred Books of the East,* 51 vols. (Oxford, U.K.: Clarendon Press, 1889ff.).

3. William C. Tremmel, *Religion: What is It?* 2nd ed. (New York: Holt, Rinehart and Winston, 1984), 294.

4. Ibid., 295.

5. Joachim Wach, "Theology and the Scientific Study of Religion" in *Ways of Understanding Religion,* ed. Walter H. Capps (New York: Macmillan, 1972), 257–60; idem, *The Comparative Study of Religion,* ed. Joseph Kitagawa (New York: Columbia University Press, 1958), 9–21.

6. Wach, *Theology,* 260.

7. Ibid., 265.

8. Jonathan Z. Smith, ed., *The Harpercollins Dictionary of Religion* (San Francisco: Harper–San Francisco, 1995), 278, s.v. "comparative religion."

9. Ibid., 279.

CHAPTER 10

1. Joseph Dabney Bettis, ed., *Phenomenology of Religion* (New York and Evanston, Ill.: Harper & Row, 1969), 1.

2. Ibid., 3.

3. Ibid., 1–2.

4. Gerardus van der Leeuw, *Religion in Essence and Manifestation,* trans. J. E. Turner, 2nd ed. (London: George Allen & Unwin, 1938).

5. Ibid., 671.

6. For a concise history of phenomenological research up to the 1930s, see ibid., 690–95.

7. W. Brede Kristensen, *The Meaning of Religion: Lectures in the Phenomenology of Religion,* trans. John B. Carman (The Hague: Martinus Nijhoff, 1960).

8. Van der Leeuw, *Religion,* 688.

9. Hendrik Kraemer, "Introduction," in Kristensen, *The Meaning of Religion,* 13.

10. Ibid., xxi. The words are Kraemer's, not Kristensen's.

11. Frederick J. Streng, *Understanding Religious Man* (Belmont, Calif.: Dickenson, 1969), 40.

12. Rudolf Otto, *The Idea of the Holy,* trans. John Harvey (Oxford: Oxford University Press, 1958), 1–13, 25–32.

13. Mircea Eliade, *The Sacred and Profane,* trans. William R. Trask (New York: Harcourt, Brace & World, 1959), as quoted in Bettis, *Phenomenology of Religion,* 206. Italics are in the original.

14. Ibid., 209.

15. Martin Buber, *I and Thou,* trans. R. Gregor Smith, 2nd ed. (New York: Charles Scribners' Sons, 1958), 17; and idem, *Between Man and Man* (New York: Macmillan, 1965), 13–14.

16. Streng, *Understanding Religious Man,* 43. Wach's ideas come from his book *Comparative Study of Religion* (New York: Columbia University Press, 1958), while Wilfred Cantwell Smith's can be found in his *Meaning and End of Religion* (New York: Macmillan, 1962).

CHAPTER 11

1. *Ecclesiam suam*, no. 9, as cited in *Vatican Council II*, ed. Austin Flannery (Collegeville, Minn.: Liturgical Press, 1975), 1003.

2. *Humanae personae dignitatem*, August 28, 1968, cited in ibid.

3. Stanley Samartha, *One Christ—Many Religions* (Maryknoll, N.Y.: Orbis Books, 1991), 86.

4. Pope John XXIII, *Pacem in terris* (New York: Ridge Press, 1964).

5. Vatican II, *Decree on the Apostolate of the Laity*, n. 7.

6. *Humanae personae dignitatem*, 1007, 1010.

7. Cf. John S. Dunne, *The Way of All the Earth* (New York: Macmillan, 1972).

CHAPTER 12

Acknowledgment. The initial inspiration for this section came from Hans Küng's *Projekt Weltethos* (Munich: Piper Verlag, 1990); *Global Responsibility: In Search of a New World Ethic* (New York: Crossroad, 1991).

1. Hadith: Muslim, chapter on "iman," 71–72; Ibn Madja, introduction, 9; Al-Darimi, chapter on "riqaq"; Hambal 3, 1976. The first quotation is cited in Bhagavan Das, *The Essential Unity of All Religions* (1934), 298.

2. A Yoruba (Nigeria) proverb, cited in Andrew Wilson, ed., *World Scripture* (New York: Paragon House, 1991), 114.

3. Immanuel Kant, *Critique of Practical Reason*, trans. Lewis White Beck (Indianapolis: Bobbs-Merrill, 1956).

4. *Gleanings from the Writings of Baha'u'llah*, trans. Shoghi Effendi, 2nd ed. (Wilmette, Ill.: Baha'i Publishing Trust, 1976).

5. *The Scripture of Won Buddhism*, rev. ed. (Iri, Korea: Won Kwang Publishing Co., 1988), 309f.

6. Das, *Essential Unity*, 303.

7. Hans Küng and Karl-Josef Kuschel, ed., *A Global Ethic* (New York: Continuum, 1993).

Index

Abe, Masao, 27–29, 42, 215 (nn. 34, 36)
Abraham, William, J., 45, 216 (n. 3), 220 (n. 1)
Age of Global Dialogue, 2, 84, 89–90, 145–178, 196, 218 (n. 19)
Allport, Gordon W., 110, 120, 221 (n. 25)
Ames, Edward Scribner, 213 (n. 5)
Anthropology, 1, 55, 65, 73, 78, 91–109
Archer, John Clark, 7, 214 (n. 15)
Aristotle, 14, 43, 167
Askari, Hasan, 215 (n. 34)
Audience Criticism, 70
Axial Period, 11, 75, 80–84

Baha'i, 56, 107, 184, 187, 224 (n. 4)
Bellah, Robert, 73–90, 217 (nn. 1, 4)
Benedict XV (Pope), 168
Berger, Peter L., 219 (n. 28), 222 (n. 7)
Bergson, Henri, 46
Berthrong, John, 215 (nn. 45, 53)
Bettis, Joseph Dabney, 140, 223 (n. 1)
Boadt, Lawrence, 66, 69, 217 (n. 2)
Boff, Leonardo, 222 (n. 5)
Boniface VIII (Pope), 48, 216 (n. 7)
Bosnjak, Branko, 4, 213 (n. 4)
Boszormenyi-Nagy, Ivan, 114, 125
Bradley, F. H., 46
Brahman, 13, 23–29, 95
Brightman, Edgar Schefield, 6, 45, 213 (n. 11), 216 (n. 5)
Buber, Martin, 6, 144, 213 (n. 10), 223 (n. 15)
Buddha (Gautama), 10, 14, 16, 26–29, 82, 95, 107, 111, 170, 182, 184
Buddhism, 9–10, 13–14, 16, 22, 26–31, 39, 42, 60, 72, 75, 76–77, 95, 111, 127, 130–131, 146, 152, 168–172, 179, 182, 184, 187, 215 (nn. 34, 39), 216 (n. 2), 221 (n. 22)

Calvin(ism), John, 18, 77, 101
Capps, Walter H., 223 (n. 5)
Catholic(ism), 11, 16, 18–19, 26, 32–33, 37, 78, 93, 104, 116–117, 119, 125, 129, 131, 148, 168–169, 171, 175, 179, 187, 196, 216 (n. 61), 217 (n. 6), 221 (n. 34)
Chang, Carsun, 215 (n. 48)
Ching, Julia, 35, 214 (n. 42), 215 (nn. 42, 54)
Christianity, 8, 14, 16, 18–19, 21–28, 31–42, 54, 56–58, 62, 64, 69–72, 75, 78, 82, 91, 93, 95–97, 103, 106, 118–119, 125, 127, 129, 131–132, 136, 146, 148–150, 152, 154, 168, 174, 176, 179, 186, 215 (nn. 19, 45, 46, 54), 217 (n. 8), 221 (n. 22), 222 (n. 8)
Cimic, Esad, 222 (n. 11)
Collins, James C., 222 (n. 9)
Communis(t)m, 15, 36–41, 97, 132, 181, 184, 201, 219 (n. 20)
Comparativists, 136, 138
Comte, Auguste, 73, 92, 96, 218 (n. 2)
Confucian(ism), 9, 17, 22, 31–35, 59, 75, 77, 119, 131–132, 152, 168, 196, 215 (nn. 45, 47, 48)
Confucius, 9, 31–32, 182
Conn, Walter E., 116–118, 221 (nn. 13, 21)
Cotroneo, Margaret, 126, 221 (n. 34)
Coulanges, N. D. Fustel de, 92, 218 (n. 3)
Cousins, Ewert, 84–86, 88–90, 217 (n. 8), 218 (nn. 13, 14)
Critical-Thinking, 33, 147, 151–152, 157, 160–162, 196
Cunningham, Lawrence S., 222 (n. 4)

Das, Bhagavan, 224 (n. 1)
Deep-Dialogue, 151–178, 196
Dia-Logos, 154–155, 159–160, 196
Dialogue, 1–2, 26, 33, 36, 39–40, 42, 46–45, 51, 54, 84, 87–90, 114–116, 122–126, 133,

225

145–181, 186, 191, 193, 196, 214 (nn. 19, 37), 216 (nn. 58, 62), 218 (nn. 18, 19, 20), 221 (n. 22), 222 (n. 8)
Dostoyevsky, Fyodor, 132
Douglas, Mary, 73, 91, 93, 217 (n. 3), 218 (n. 1), 219 (n. 11)
Drews, Elizabeth Monroe, 221 (n. 33)
Dunne, John S., 177, 224 (n. 7)
Dunstheimer, G. H., 215 (n. 55)
Durkheim, Emile, 1, 4, 73, 92, 98–103, 218 (n. 8), 219 (nn. 10, 33)

Ecclesiam suam, 224 (n. 1)
Ecumenical Movement, 168
Effendi, Shoghi, 224 (n. 4)
Eliade, Mircea, 5, 100, 138, 140, 143, 213 (n. 7), 219 (n. 27), 223 (n. 13)
Enlightenment (*Aufklärung*), 13, 68, 76, 78, 82, 85, 151, 217 (n. 6)
Epistemology, 46, 53, 150, 179, 195
Erikson, Erik, 110, 221 (n. 16)

Feuerbach, Ludwig, 96–101
Form Criticism, 67–69
Fowler, James W., 12, 114–115, 118, 122–124, 214 (n. 17), 220 (n. 9)
Francis of Assisi, 119
Frazer, James G., 58, 92, 96, 98, 136, 218 (n. 7)
Freud, Sigmund, 4, 97–99, 102–103, 110–112, 119–120, 219 (n. 23), 220 (n. 2)
Fromm, Erich, 110, 112, 220 (n. 3)

Gable, Frank, 221 (n. 32)
Gadamer, Hans-Georg, 50
Garaudy, Roger, 15, 37–40, 214 (n. 19), 216 (nn. 58, 59)
Gill, Robin, 219 (n. 10)
Gilligan, Carol, 220 (n. 10)
Global Ethic, 1–2, 161–162, 179–194, 197–212, 224 (n. 7)
Golden Rule, 22, 182–185, 190–191
Greco, Bernadino, 221 (n. 23)
Greeley, Andrew, 219 (n. 22)
Gutierrez, Gustavo, 222 (n. 5)

Hadith, 224 (n. 1)
Halacha, 8–9, 34

Heaven, 9, 14–15, 27, 31–36, 70, 76, 95, 97, 104, 214 (n. 18)
Heidegger, Martin, 140, 167
Heraclitus, 29
Hermeneutics, 47, 50–52, 66, 70–71, 79, 85, 137, 153, 218 (n. 18)
Hick, John, 28, 214 (n. 30), 215 (nn. 34, 35)
Hillel, 183
Hinduism, 9, 12–13, 22–26, 28–29, 43, 60–61, 72, 75–76, 82, 95, 111, 118, 127, 130, 152, 168, 176, 179, 183, 196, 214 (n. 26), 215 (n. 37)
Historical criticism, 71–72
Historicism, 65–66
Hocking, William, 46
Horvath, Pal, 39, 216 (n. 62)
Hsün Tzu, 17, 214 (nn. 21, 22)
Human nature, 12, 17–22, 34, 192–193
Human rights, 172–174, 180, 185–186, 188–189, 193, 197, 201–203, 208
Humanae personae dignitatem, 224 (n. 2)
Hume, David, 46
Huntington, Samuel, 82, 217 (n. 11)
Husserl, Edmund, 140, 143

Ingram, Paul O., 215 (39)
Intentionality, 47, 49
Islam, 8–9, 14, 22, 24–26, 56, 60, 62, 77, 104, 127, 129, 168, 173–174, 176, 181, 217 (n. 8)

Jainism (Mahavira; Vardhamana), 13, 182
James, William, 4, 110, 113, 220 (n. 5)
Jaspers, Karl, 11, 75, 80–82, 214 (n. 16), 217 (n. 7)
Jastrow, Morris, Jr., 136
Joachim de Fiore, 95
John (the Evangelist), 20–21, 23, 116, 153
John XXIII (Pope), 168
Johnstone, Ronald L., 94, 219 (n. 15), 220 (n. 38)
Jones, Jim, 107–108, 220 (n. 40)
Judaism, 8–9, 14, 21–22, 26, 55, 57, 61, 64, 71, 75–76, 95, 125, 127, 129, 131, 136, 153, 168, 183, 214 (n. 18), 217 (n. 8)
Jung, Carl G., 110, 113, 220 (n. 4)

Kant, Immanuel, 4, 28, 46, 93, 114, 184, 213 (n. 3), 224 (n. 3)

Kashmir, 179
Kierkegaard, Søren, 46
King, Winston, L., 44, 216 (n. 1)
Kitagawa, Joseph, 223 (n. 5)
Kittel, Gerhard, 214 (n. 27)
Knitter, Paul, 54, 216 (n. 10)
Kohlberg, Lawrence, 114–118, 122–123, 220 (nn. 10, 11, 12)
Kraemer, Hendrik, 142, 223 (nn. 9, 10)
Kristensen, W. Brede, 141–142, 223 (n. 7)
Küng, Hans, 22–27, 35, 38, 84, 89–90, 195–197, 214 (nn. 32, 33), 215 (nn. 42, 54), 216 (n. 60), 218 (n. 12), 224, 224 (n. 7)
Kuschel, Karl-Josef, 224 (n. 7)

Lai, Whalen, 216 (n. 2)
Lao-tzu, 31
Leviticus, 21, 183
Levy-Strauss, Claude, 138
Liberation, 9, 12–13, 27, 31, 43–44, 124, 130–131, 222 (n. 5)
Lipson, Leslie, 221 (n. 33)
Literary criticism, 65–72, 2217 (n. 1)
Logos, 23, 26, 82, 91–92, 153–155
Lonergan, Bernard, 52, 114, 117–118, 221 (nn. 15, 19)
Lotze, Rudolf H., 46
Luke, 14, 67, 70, 183
Luther, Martin, 18
Lyon, Quinter Marcellus, 6

Mahabharata, 183
Malinowski, Bronislaw, 92, 102–103, 219 (n. 9), 220 (n. 37)
Mannheim, Karl, 49
Marechal, Joseph, 38, 216 (n. 61)
Mark, 67
Marx(ism), Karl, 4, 8, 15, 22, 36–41, 44, 56, 80, 96–97, 99–101, 132–134, 173, 177, 179, 219 (nn. 20, 22), 222 (n. 10)
Maslow, Abraham, 221 (n. 32)
Matteo, Anthony, 216 (n. 61)
Matthew, 23, 67, 70, 168, 183, 214 (n. 18)
May, Rollo, 110, 113, 220 (n. 7)
McDaniel, Jay, 215 (n. 41)
McGregor, Geddes, 6
Mencius, 17, 32, 215 (n. 46)
Merleau-Ponty, Maurice, 140

Miguez-Bonino, Jose, 222 (n. 6)
Mills, Jeannie, 220 (n. 40)
Mohammed, 28, 183
Mou Tsung-san, 32, 34, 215 (n. 45)
Müller, Max, 58, 92, 135, 218 (n. 4), 222 (n. 2)

Nagarjuna, 30, 215 (n. 39)
Needham, James, 219 (n. 10)
Niebuhr, H. Richard, 114, 129, 220 (n. 8)
Niebuhr, Reinhold, 219 (n. 20), 222 (n. 10)
Nielsen, Niels C., 7, 213 (n. 14)
Nirvana, 9, 13–14, 16, 26–27, 77
Niwano, Nikkyo, 170
Novak, Michael, 222 (n. 5)
Nyiri Tamas, 39

O'Dea, Thomas F., 119–120, 219 (n. 13)
Otto, Rudolf, 5, 120, 136, 138, 142, 213 (n. 8), 223 (n. 12)

Pacem in terris, 168
Pals, Daniel, L., 219 (n. 17)
Panikkar, Raimundo (Raimon), 214 (nn. 26, 31), 218 (n. 18)
Paradigm (shift), 47, 50–53, 84, 89–90, 93, 122, 147, 150, 164–166, 215 (n. 39)
Parliament of the World's Religions, 186, 197–198
Parsons, Talcott, 73, 217 (n. 2)
Paul VI (Pope), 148, 169, 171
Phenomenology, 140–144, 223 (nn. 1, 6, 7)
Piaget, Jean, 114–116, 122, 221 (n. 14)
Pius XI, (Pope), 168
Pius XII (Pope), 168
Plato, 43, 48, 120, 137, 220 (n. 11)
Pleroma, 28, 172
Porras, Jerry I., 222 (n. 9)
Post-Modernism, 84–85
Pratitya samutpada, 29
Pringle-Pattison, Andrew Seth, 46
Projectionists, 96–98, 100
Pseudo-Dionysus, 36
Punjab, 179

Redaction Criticism, 66, 69–70
Redemption, 12–13
Reductionism, 96–103, 111
Reeves, Clement, 220 (n. 7)

Relationality, 30–31, 47–54, 114–119, 122, 125–126, 150–151, 159–160, 162, 164–165, 170
Relativism, 53–54, 123, 138
Religion and State, 172–174
Religion, definition of, 3–8; goals of, 12–17
Religionswissenschaften, 55, 57, 73, 218 (n. 19)
Rhetorical Criticism, 66, 71
Ricoeur, Paul, 11, 68, 122, 140
Rig Veda, 61
Robertson, Roland L., 217 (n. 1), 218 (n. 1), 219 (n. 15)
Rosemont, Henry, 216 (n. 9)
Rousseau, Jean-Jacques, 17, 214 (n. 20)
Royce, Josiah, 46

Salvation, 15–16, 41, 43, 48, 56, 76–78, 104–106, 222 (n. 5)
Samartha, Stanley, 149, 224 (n. 3)
Sartre, Jean-Paul, 140
Scheler, Max, 49
Schleiermacher, Friedrich, 3, 58, 213 (n. 2)
Schmidt, Roger, 217 (n. 4), 222 (n. 1)
Schmidt, Wilhelm, 3, 136, 213 (n. 1)
Second Axial Period, 84–90, 218 (nn. 14, 15)
Second naivete, 11, 69, 79
Sengupta, Santosh Chandra, 29, 215 (n. 37)
Shari'a, 9, 34, 174
Shinto, 9, 55, 60
Sikhs, 56, 179, 196
Sivaraksa, Sulak, 169
Skinner, B. F., 220 (n. 6)
Skynner, Robin, 110, 113, 220 (n. 6)
Smart, Ninian, 220 (n. 4)
Smith, Jonathan Z., 223 (n. 8)
Smith, Wilfred Cantwell, 144, 223 (n. 16)
Sobrino, Jon, 222 (n. 5)
Sociological Criticism, 66, 70, 93
Sociology of knowledge, 47, 49
Sociology, 1, 47, 49, 55, 73, 78, 91–109, 128, 141, 154, 217 (n. 1), 218 (n. 1), 219 (nn. 10, 13, 15, 22, 28, 31), 220 (n. 36, 38)
Socrates, 14, 76
Söderblom, Nathan, 136
Sorokin, Pitirim, A., 82–83, 217 (n. 10)

Source Criticism, 66–67
Spencer, Herbert, 73
Spengler, Oswald, 82–83, 217 (n. 9)
Streng, Frederick J., 142, 223 (n. 11)
Sumer, 30
Sumner, William G., 92, 218 (n. 5)
Sunyata, 26–30, 39, 152, 155, 172
Swidler, Leonard, 186–187, 214 (n. 17), 216 (nn. 58, 63), 217 (n. 6), 218 (nn. 19, 20), 221 (n. 22)

Tang Yi, 215 (n. 38)
Tao Te Ching, 35
Tao(ism), 7, 9–10, 22, 25, 29, 31, 33–36, 75, 77, 95, 131, 153, 155, 168, 177, 215 (nn. 38, 54)
Teilhard de Chardin, Pierre, 36–37, 39, 86–88, 218 (n. 15)
Textual Criticism, 64–65
Theissen, Gerd, 219 (n. 12)
Thomas Aquinas, 15, 18, 23, 36, 51, 214 (n. 23, 24), 215 (n. 57), 216 (n. 8)
Tillich, Paul, 5, 25, 120, 213 (n. 9), 214 (n. 29)
Tobit, 183
Tremmel, William C., 6, 213 (n. 13), 223 (n. 3)
Trialogue, 186
Trinity, 25, 27, 95–96
Truth, de-absolutized, 47–54, 122, 146–147, 151, 195
Tu Wei-ming, 33, 215 (n. 51)
Tylor, Edward B., 92, 98, 218 (n. 6)

Ultimate Reality, 12, 15, 19, 21–42, 76, 95, 100, 153, 159, 166, 172, 196, 201
UNESCO, 197, 218 (n. 15)
United Nations, 83, 172, 183, 185–186, 189, 202
Upanishads, 29, 43, 82

van der Leeuw, Gerardus, 140–141, 143, 223 (n. 4)
Vatican, 11–12, 33, 131, 148, 150, 168, 176, 224 (nn. 1, 5)
Voegelin, Erich, 76

Wach, Joachim, 136–137, 140, 144, 223 (n. 5)

Way, 8–10
Weber, Max, 73, 101, 103, 130–131, 134, 219 (n. 30), 222 (nn. 2, 3)
Whitehead, Alfred North, 25, 46, 137
Wilson, Andrew, 224 (n. 2)
Wilson, John F., 6, 213 (n. 12), 222 (n. 1)
Wittgenstein, Ludwig, 49
Won Buddhism, 170, 184, 224 (n. 5)
World Conference on Religion and Peace, 180, 186
World Council of Churches, 149

World Parliament of Religions, see Parliament of the World's Religions
Worsley, P., 102, 220 (n. 36)

Yagi, Seiichi, 118, 221 (n. 22)
Yinger, Milton, 5, 106, 213 (n. 6), 220 (n. 39)
Yin-yang, 35
Yoruba, 224 (n. 2)
Young-Lee, Jung, 215 (n. 40)

Zoroaster, 75, 182